A Brush With Steam

A Brush With Steam

David Shepherd's Railway Story

David Shepherd OBE

~ David Shepherd ~

DAVID & CHARLES

Newton Abbot   London   North Pomfret (Vt)

British Library Cataloguing in Publication Data

Shepherd, David, 1931
  A brush with steam
  1. Shepherd, David 1931–   2. Painters—
England—Biography
I. Title
759.2   N497.S46

ISBN 0-7153-8157-1

Typeset by Typesetters (Birmingham) Limited, Smethwick, West Midlands
and printed in Great Britain by
Butler & Tanner Limited, Frome and London
and Redwood Burn Limited, Trowbridge, Wiltshire
For David & Charles (Publishers) Limited
Brunel House Newton Abbot Devon

Published in the United States of America
by David & Charles Inc
North Pomfret Vermont 05053 USA

Contents

Foreword

This is a very personal book. The various stories are the culmination of one man's dreams which became a reality in his lifetime.

When David Shepherd asked me if I would write the foreword to this book I said yes before I had even thought about it. After a while, however, the enormity of the request began to sink in.

How does one introduce David Shepherd? He is already a world-famous painter, a legend in his own right and the proud owner of steam locomotives.

I first met him on a cold grey April morning in 1968 on Crewe South Shed while I was busy preparing 92203, a Class 9 freight locomotive which later became known as *Black Prince*, and which David had just purchased from British Railways. I was privileged to be the driver of 92203 and, with David Shepherd on the footplate, we completed a memorable first stage of a journey, as far as Derby Midland Station. The ultimate destination was Longmoor in Hampshire.

The year 1968 heralded the end of steam locomotives on BR. The cutter's torch was destroying engines at an alarming rate. What a blessing that chaps like David Shepherd saved a number of locomotives so that we ordinary mortals could go on enjoying the wonderful world of steam locomotives.

The majority of people measure the passage of time in years, months, weeks, days, hours, minutes and seconds. David.Shepherd has added another dimension, heart beats—he never wastes one, such is the urgency of his way of life.

David is known from East Somerset to East Africa. He is just as at ease with royalty or presidents as he is with ordinary people, and it is this super trait in the man that makes him so endearing and so special.

His own brand of humour came to the forefront when he asked a sign writer friend if he would kindly 'line out' a locomotive in red. 'What size is it, 00 gauge or 0 gauge?' 'Well it's neither,' David said, and refused to commit himself any further: 'Perhaps you would care to see for yourself.' Duly they arrived at Longmoor, with the sign writer having no idea of what he was about to be confronted with—the outcome is related in the book.

In the following pages you will also read of the trials and tribulations in the world of locomotive preservation, riding on the crest of a wave one minute and sinking to the depths of desperation the next.

All these topics are now set down for the reader. David relates the story of the marathon journey with the two engines *Black Prince* and *The Green Knight* from Crewe South to Longmoor; the incidents that happened, some hilarious and others not so funny; the people he met and the different situations that confronted him; all is revealed and told with the gusto and animation one expects from a world-famous painter. I can hear again, as I read, the punctuation of the author's musical laughter, not to mention a few choice words of Anglo-Saxon origin!

You will read how *Black Prince* became a South African locomotive and Longmoor Military Railway was transformed into a point between South Africa and Mozambique. And how *Lord Fisher* steamed down the High Street in Godalming with a trail of traffic in her wake (talk about the Pied Piper of Hamelin!) Also read about the enthusiast trying to 'nick' some gas lamps and nearly blowing himself up in the process. And David painting quite happily at Crewe locomotive works under the travelling crane and frequently seeing a Duchess Pacific swinging over his head; phew! Not exactly the best of painting positions.

All these anecdotes make the reading of this book absolutely worth-while, and I can assure the reader that he will find David Shepherd, painter extraordinary, far from being shackled by adopting the literary medium.

The introduction of David's first book, *The Man Who Loves Giants*, was written by no less a person than James Stewart the film star. Although we both enjoy the same surname, regretfully I have to assure the reader that there the similarity ends. My world was the footplate and I can identify myself with the author's abiding affection for that wonderful feat of engineering, the steam locomotive. It is typical of David Shepherd that he should accord the honour and privilege of writing the introduction to this super book to an ordinary railwayman.

Bert Stewart

(*Pages 8 and 9*) I have a habit of collecting various bits and pieces of 'railwayana', some rather large. BR sold me this footbridge for £10, I got the gates for another fiver! See chapter 12 (*Photo Photographers International*)

7

To George Davies and all my other railway friends

Introduction

On the evening of 19 July 1971 I began to hate *Black Prince* and all that she stood for. My reader will discover why later. It is a love-hate relationship if ever there was one: when I manage to snatch a few brief moments on the footplate at Cranmore all the exhilaration and magic comes back; then all the way home in the car I worry myself sick about coal bills. So why on earth did I ever get involved in the first place? I have asked myself that question hundreds of times since 1967 when I picked up the telephone and bought two enormous locomotives from British Railways. I am still not completely sure that I know the answer.

Steam locomotives belong to a more leisurely and romantic age, but this fact surely justifies their preservation in full working order for the enlightenment and enjoyment of young people growing up in a modern and functional age in which built-in obsolescence and concrete seem to play so major a part. Progress seems to be the key word and we do not seem to care as much as we should about the great inventions of the past.

Some people think that we who indulge in this business of railway preservation are completely mad, but perhaps they do not understand what motivates us. There must be something which makes so many of us slave away in the most awful conditions of mid-winter, sweating our guts out and risking hernias, laying lengths of railway track on to a track bed from which British Rail has only just torn it up; or painstakingly restoring engines and coaches only to watch the weather undo the fruits of our hard labour; or, most important of all, worrying about where the money is coming from to pay for it all. All of this, when we could be at home in the warm watching television. But then watching television is nothing like as exciting or rewarding.

I have seen it all, since those euphoric days of the mid 1960s when there was so much to save of our rapidly disappearing steam-railway heritage and so little time in which to do it. Now we live in a different world, and most (but not all) of us have grown up a great deal since those early days, or I would like to think that we have. There have been times when I have asked myself why I have become chairman of a railway company with its difficulties and permanent financial worry, when I should be painting pictures in my studio. Then, when I go down to the East Somerset Railway, I know why. I see our marvellous team of

11

volunteers working like demons possessed because they believe in striving for something worthwhile, and I am proud. I am also a realist. The preserved steam railways of today have to be run as a business; otherwise they will die. It is as simple as that.

There are still dreamers among railway preservationists, but in the 1980s dreaming can be dangerous. It can so easily cloud the vision and remove one from the harsh reality of the materialistic age in which we live. The dream starts at a crumbling railway station and there are many of those still to find. Many of them have become dumping grounds for the products of a wasteful and affluent society. Where the little branch-line trains used to run on sleepy, sunny afternoons, now one finds gas cookers, soggy mattresses and wrecked cars. The dreamers stand on the rotting platform and gaze sadly at the little stone-built goods shed, ivy-clad and windowless, its emptiness reflecting a railway gone for ever. They look longingly into the distance along the track-bed now rapidly disappearing under a jungle of undergrowth. Perhaps they have just a little too much faith and not quite enough sense of reality. The railway has gone. It has returned to nature, inhabited by badgers and foxes, and it is best left like that. Nevertheless, dreamers dream that money will grow on the nearby trees and perhaps the trains will run again some day. I have been through all this myself, but that was many years ago, and it seems a lot longer than that.

75075 by the coal stage at Fratton .

So why has the steam engine stirred the hearts of so many people for over one and half centuries? What is it in the depths of the great iron monster that excites such emotion and nostalgia? Why do I get so excited whenever *Black Prince* is in steam? How do we account for this almost fanatical involvement with a machine that we are told no longer has a place in this progressive (but not always necessarily sensible) age? Why is it that so many people give up every free moment of their leisure to work on locomotive maintenance, laying track and a thousand other tasks on a preserved railway, to be rewarded by a few brief moments when life is restored to their charges and once again they can breathe fire, smoke and hot engine oil? I believe the secret is here. Ask any railway enthusiast or steam locomotive driver and he will say that the steam engine *lives.* This is the magic. This is why we do it. We want it to go on living, and we intend to see that it does.

Geoff is a friend of mine and he hates steam engines too, sometimes. His locomotive is about the same size as *Black Prince*. He was under his engine one day with his best suit on because it was an open day at the depot. His engine was playing up. He had to get out of the cab and underneath her. Lying on his back on the ashes, with hot engine oil and red-hot clinker dropping on top of him, cursing everything to do with steam railways, he heard voices. He looked out between the 6ft driving wheels and saw two pairs of feet walking down the side of the engine. They stopped opposite Geoff and turned inwards. He began to wonder with considerable misgiving what was going to happen.

One pair of feet said to the other pair of feet, 'These bloody preservationists haven't got a clue—it's the wrong shade of green.' And then came, 'He's got the lining half an inch too wide on the tender.' The two pairs of feet had no idea that Geoff was under his engine. For him it was just too much. To the consternation of one pair of feet Geoff's hand shot out and grabbed an ankle. 'Why the hell don't you bloody people stop criticising and do something constructive for once!'

Geoff knew their sort. They come to the various preserved railways. On one occasion he had seen a whole carload of them sitting in the car park. Because they were too mean each to pay their admission fee, they had given their cameras to one of their number who had then paid to go in and take photographs for all the rest of them. For every so-called railway enthusiast who behaves like that, happily there are many thousands who are very different. It is to some of these that I dedicate this book.

Since I purchased my two engines, numbers 92203 and 75029 all those years ago, I have made so many friends who share my determination to save just a little of our fast vanishing heritage. It is impossible to mention them all individually; there are too many and it's safer that way anyway. (I might leave someone out!) Some have stayed with me from the earliest days and they feel as much affection for *Black Prince* and *The Green Knight* as I do. I dare not mention some of them by name anyway, because I have to protect the guilty! Disclosure of some of their activities in print might terminate them prematurely and we all want things to go on falling off the backs of lorries.

During the heartache and disappointment of the Longmoor and Liss saga about which I write, we were given wonderful support by the military authorities. Then, when I found Cranmore, I was joined by so many new friends of all ages and backgrounds. It takes real dedication to work perhaps forty hours a week in your spare time for a preserved steam railway, usually doing paperwork in the office, or laying track in the dark in the winter months. (We have to look after the public during the summer.) Some members of the East Somerset Railway never see a steam engine. They are too busy cooking meals and washing up dishes in the restaurant car, selling prints of my elephant pictures in the Signal Box Art

14

Gallery to help pay the coal bills, or making fluffy animals at home to raise money. Some scarcely ever come to Cranmore at all. These friends support me in my talk shows which I put on during the winter months in theatres all over England for the benefit of the World Wildlife Fund and the East Somerset Railway. A vast amount of work is done behind the scenes that the public does not see. Lighting up engines in a cold shed in the early hours of the morning when the rest of the country is sleeping is not everyone's idea of enjoyment. The endless amount of work involved in locomotive and coach restoration can often be heart- as well as back-breaking. Huge amounts of legal and financial paperwork have to be attended to, as well as publicity and fund raising. The diversity of tasks, both clean and dirty, on a preserved steam railway is endless, but the enthusiasm amongst our team on the East Somerset Railway matches it.

We receive help from many walks of life. The Services have helped us so much over the years, very often unofficially. We staged an air-show at Cranmore and the Royal Naval Air Station Historic Flight from Yeovilton flew over the railway. The Royal Air Force Battle of Britain Memorial Flight Lancaster gave us a spectacular show over the roof of our shed, because I knew the pilot. The Army have loaned us helicopters and fighting vehicles for our vintage vehicle weekends and so much more.

I must mention British Rail. Without my involvement with them my life might have taken a very different turn. I have no intention of knocking BR in this book. Far too many people seem to do just that sometimes, it seems, just for the sake of it. I am utterly sick of the eternal jokes about BR sandwiches and dirty trains. It is not BR who makes the trains dirty, it is some of the people who use them. I do have a few digs at BR in this book from time to time. After all, it is my whole story and BR are an integral part of it. A few stupid and unnecessary things have happened over the years, but that is the way with any large organisation. For every man in BR who perhaps does not show as much sympathy as he might for what we are trying to do, there are many thousands who have steam in their blood as I do and who understand. I like to remember the moment when I rang BR at their vast office complex at Croydon, to buy a footbridge(!) When I said who I was, the gentleman on the other end of the line said, 'Ah, David Shepherd, the friend of British Rail. What can we do for you?' That's how I want to keep things because BR consists of super people. I fell asleep once on the last train at night from Waterloo to Godalming, and woke up suddenly to see Godalming disappearing in the distance. It was too late. Was I going to spend the night at Portsmouth Harbour? Fortunately the train stopped at the next station down the line from Godalming, Witley. I leapt out and went up to the signal box. 'Are there any more trains going back to Waterloo?' I asked the signalman. 'Yes, there is one more, but it doesn't stop at your place.' Somehow, he seemed to know who I was. Perhaps he had remembered my two steam engines

15

going past his box a few years before on their way to Longmoor. He went on, 'I tell you what, you stand on the end of the platform. I'll give the driver a red, and when he stops, you hop up into his cab. He's not supposed to stop at Godalming, but if you are nice to him I am sure that he will drop you off.'

All went according to plan. When I got out at Godalming, the porter on duty said, 'That will cost you a bloody painting, mate!' That is how I want to remember things.

I must thank Bert Stewart for writing the foreword to my book. I could not possibly think of anyone more appropriate. Bert was a top link driver on BR when I met him very early one morning in Crewe South locomotive shed. He was rostered to drive 92203 on the first stage of her journey away from Crewe to the South and the beginning of her new life with me. A few years ago I contrived a footplate ride with Bert on an Inter-City that he was driving from Crewe down to Euston and back again. The inspector with us let me take the controls and I seem to remember approaching 100mph going through Watford. Bert was chain smoking and he had never smoked a cigarette at all before that journey. The inspector remarked that if the 500 passengers behind could have seen what was going on, they would probably have baled out and he would have joined them! Bert now runs a splendid pub in Chorley, Lancs.

In 1975 my good friend Prince Bernhard came over from Holland to Cranmore. His Royal Highness opened the East Somerset Railway for us and it was a most generous gesture from a very busy man. Appropriately, we gave all the proceeds from our royal opening to the World Wildlife Fund to help save elephants!

I must never forget George Davies to whom I dedicate this book. He was a very dear friend, and also a generous bank manager!

Then there's my family. It must be hell sometimes to be married to a railway enthusiast like me and I think that all such wives deserve medals. It must be bad enough to put up with spare sets of connecting rods or great lumps of signalling equipment under the bed, but there are certainly very few wives who would stay with a husband who sinks so much money, which he does not have, into his hobby over such a long period. Never once did Avril suggest that I should play golf instead, and without her unending support over the years I would never have achieved anything. None of my four daughters have ever been particularly potty about steam engines. Why should they be just because their father is? Melanie, daughter number three, deserves a very special mention, however. She did a crash course in typing and one of her very first assignments was to type this book for me, aided by my long-suffering secretary.

Finally, I must never forget my four-legged friends in Africa for, without them, there would be no East Somerset Railway today.

16

1

*Model railways
and the beginning of it all*

If the people who live in a certain house in North London wonder why
their chimney always seems to be smoking, I can tell them. It is because
steam trains used to run around the best bedroom before the war.

My love affair with steam railways began in the bedroom of that house
in Totteridge, in the early thirties. My father was a typical model railway
enthusiast and, like so many others who pursue that hobby, he did the
most dreadful things to our house. Taking over the best bedroom wasn't
enough. He had located Watford just inside the door, and Carlisle was
over the other side of the room, in the dormer window. He couldn't make
the room any bigger, and so in order to achieve a more realistic curve in
the layout for the journey north, he bored a hole right through the
chimney, somewhere around Rugby! This structural alteration may to
this day cause dreadful problems when a fire is lit downstairs, but on the
other hand my father's magnificent layout played its part in the birth of
another railway, to a scale of 12in to the foot, in Somerset, very many
years later.

Even in those early days I was crazy about animals too, and it was this
that would eventually lead to the setting up of the East Somerset Railway,
but that comes much later. I remember having my very own Natural
History Museum in the cupboards below my father's railway. I found a
dead song thrush beside the road one day and this was the prize exhibit
amongst all the feathers and sea shells that I had collected from our
holidays by the seaside, until I suddenly learned to my dismay that things
gradually happen to dead bodies. I was not too popular when, early one
evening on his return from London, my father found 'Watford station' to
be unusually busy. The platform was crowded with maggots, wriggling all
over the place like drunken commuters! One had even managed to
squeeze into the miniature 'gents', but had got stuck because he was too
fat to get out again.

My father was London, Midland & Scottish Railway, totally and
uncompromisingly. As a small boy I was allowed to gaze in awe, and,
under strict control, to participate in the working of his railway when he
was operating it. He had a magnificent stud of some twenty Bassett-Lowke

17

locomotives, ranging from small Jinty tank engines, Fowler tanks, and 4Fs for goods trains, to Duchess Pacifics for main-line passenger work. Four of these beautiful models of Stanier's masterpiece were 'on shed'. Two were the models without streamlined casing and I remember even then much preferring these. The other two, one in red and the other in blue and silver, seemed to me to be rather ugly, but they were of course so typical of the age of Art Nouveau and 'Odeon Cinema' design. (That's no doubt put the cat among the pigeons already—railway enthusiasts never agree about anything!) To complement the locomotives, he had a superb collection of Exley coaches. I remember how beautifully sprung these precision-made coaches were. The dining cars had little people in them at the tables laid for dinner.

My eyes would almost pop out in wonderment as trains used to come and go from the main-line station which my father had built in the dormer window of the bedroom. He had meticulously constructed the huge curved roof from wood and cellophane—this was long before the age of plastics. I could look right into the station and see all the people waiting for their trains on the platforms. The whole place was a hive of activity. Railway porters were pushing barrows with suitcases on them, and people were buying magazines from a little book stall which had tiny magazines and newspapers on it. It was enough to send a small boy quite dizzy with excitement.

It was a great event when my father took me with him on the underground from Totteridge into London to buy another coach or locomotive from Bassett-Lowke. That company has long since left the shop in Holborn but, happily, the miniature railway signals on the shop front, which were so much a part of their image and which must be a memory cherished by many like myself, are still there. They were not removed when Bassett-Lowke moved out to give way to a shop selling the mass-produced toys of a plastic age.

I also had my very own model railway at this time and I could of course play with it to my heart's content. Although it did not claim to have the realism of my father's layout, my train set, like my father's, would command enormous value today as a collector's item. I refer, of course, to the old tin-plate Hornby trains on which so many of us must have cut our railway teeth. The 0-4-0 tank engine seemed to owe most of its parentage to Doncaster and the London & North Eastern. What these models lacked in realism was amply compensated for by their charm and unbelievably robust construction. No matter how often they were trod on, kicked or dropped, their clockwork interiors always responded to the enormous push-and-pull rod sticking from their cabs, providing one did not lose the key! The trains would run round and round forever, without complaining, through little tin-plate stations and over the level crossings. Of course every small boy had to have a tunnel on his railway, and I was given for a birthday present one of those grotesque lumps of scenery with a hole right through. They were always painted in an impossible shade of green, and would rise obligingly from wherever they were put on an otherwise flat landscape floor.

There was always a crane in the little siding alongside the country station, and hours were spent happily loading and unloading the wagons by winding a tiny handle on the side. At bedtime, if the layout was permitted to remain overnight on the floor, the engine would also go to bed—in a delightful tin-plate locomotive shed with painted brickwork, the sides of which were held together with little tabs which slipped into slots on the corners. Otherwise the whole layout would be dismantled and put into a box, but it never seemed to mind and it was always fun. Birthdays and Christmas during my childhood in the thirties were never any problem for my relations. Cows, chocolate-vending machines, porters' wheelbarrows, signals, milk churns—the possibilities were endless and I was fortunate in having plenty of aunts and uncles. Like all little boys, I would flatly refuse to go to sleep on Christmas Eve, or would wake up at an unbelievably early hour to gaze in agonised anticipation at my stocking at the foot of the bed. From the top there would always be sticking the shape of a big red box, and on the box would always be the magic word 'Hornby'.

In those days so long ago, when the sun always seemed to be shining, we nearly always spent our family summer holidays at Birchington, on the Kent coast. We went there for the donkeys, the good healthy air, and the sand castles. It was a marvellous place for children, with mile upon mile of wonderful sandy beaches. There was another reason why my father always chose Birchington. (I wonder now if my mother ever had

This must be one of the first steam trains that I ever saw—my dad took the photograph from the line-side at Birchington, Kent, in 1935

19

any choice in the matter.) Near Birchington were several marvellous line-side vantage points where we could watch the trains go by. My brother and I did not need any persuading to go along with my father, who probably soon became bored with building sand castles with us. It must have been there that I saw my very first steam train. Indeed, I remember particularly one level crossing where we used to climb onto the gates and watch hypnotised as, it seemed every few minutes, a lovely green locomotive with 'Southern Railway' written on its tender would race past us and the whole ground seemed to shake. I did not know, and would not have cared anyway, whether these engines were Maunsell or Urie. I knew nothing of such things. They were steam trains.

My father had a movie camera and used to take films of those marvellous trains storming by. The films were 9mm with the perforations down the middle, and the film came out of a little round black tin which fitted onto the spindle of the projector. We still have dozens of those little black tins today, in the attic. We put little labels on the side of each tin and wrote the title of the film: 'Hendon Air Display, 1938', 'Watching the trains go by at Birchington' etc. It is pretty historic stuff, and I wonder how many others have similar films in their attics!

When we lived in Totteridge my mother and father became great friends with a music-hall comedian who went on stage with the splendid

A small boy's dream come true—his first visit to a real engine shed. That's me on the right, with the shed master, the comedian 'Stainless Stephen' and my brother, at King's Cross top shed in 1938. It is interesting to note that the locomotive is *Sir Nigel Gresley*, then brand new. She was to be saved many years later by the preservationists

name of 'Stainless Stephen'—my older readers will no doubt remember him. 'Stainless' happened to be a railway enthusiast like my father, and he loved visiting the steam sheds around London. I must have been about seven years old when 'Stainless' took my brother and me to the great and legendary King's Cross top shed. I have a faded photograph in my collection of two small schoolboys standing beside one of the huge A4 streamlined Pacifics. The number of the engine, by happy coincidence, was 4498, *Sir Nigel Gresley.* She is of course still with us today, having been saved by the preservationists.

During the following years, when I was growing up, I no longer gave the real railways around me a second glance. After all, steam engines were everywhere, a part of the landscape. The war came. There was now no longer any time for playing O-gauge trains. My father was in the army and I had to go away to boarding school. The only railway memories I have of this period, in the mid forties, are those of the 'school special'. At the beginning of each term during my years at Stowe School in Buckingham, three or four coaches would be attached to the end of an ordinary service train for Bletchley. The great and smokey Euston station of old would ring to the clatter and excited chatter of a mob of schoolboys, all looking clean and scrubbed after the 'hols'. Some would be greeting their friends, exchanging stories of the past weeks away from school discipline; a few would be making weepy farewells to doting mothers. All of a sudden, a Stanier whistle would blow. We would all leap into the train and the carriage doors would clang shut. We had not even noticed the steam engines all around us.

I suppose boys of any era are much the same. We got up to all the usual pranks on the journey north. It must have been a last fling of the holidays before having to face the discipline of a new school term, and we took it out on the poor old train. The passengers waiting for their trains at Berkhamsted and other stations on the route north would be liberally showered with light bulbs and toilet rolls as we sped through the stations. By the time we reached Bletchley the entire station staff, forewarned, had beaten a hasty retreat. At Bletchley, our four coaches would be detached from the main-line train and dragged to Buckingham behind a time-worn Fowler tank of the London, Midland & Scottish. Would that I had taken more notice of it, but we were too busy destroying our train—times have not changed very much. It was only a few years afterwards that this sleepy little branch line was discovered by Dr Beeching, and no vestige remains of it today.

I left Stowe School in 1949 and began my art training in Chelsea in 1950. During the holiday periods, when I should have been painting, I was in fact busy making Micromodels. (This was long before the age of the plastic kit.) Micromodels were obtainable in little packets containing card printed in colour, which had to be cut out and carefully folded and stuck. The range of railway models was enormous. In what I suppose would be N gauge today, the wagons, steam engines and coaches looked very realistic indeed, if made with care.

My father owned a hotel in Camberley in those days. I had built up a huge collection of Micromodel trains, and these, together with the little houses that I had built out of card, seemed to justify a separate building for the layout that I was now determined to build. With some help from a friend who looked after my mother's pig farm, and without giving a thought to such things as planning permission, we erected a fine 15ft square brick building alongside the hotel. This splendid creation did not cost me a penny, except for the cement. The army had obligingly built a large military camp on Camberley Heath during the war, which, now being derelict, was open for all to pilfer. We used to drive up to Camberley Heath after dark and, judging by the number of cars we saw up there, it seemed that all Camberley was doing exactly the same thing. Cars were going away loaded with bricks, doors, timber, electric wiring, roofing materials and everything else that you could think of. So the Barchester Railway was born, in a fine new home especially built for it.

The layout was constructed almost entirely from materials found around the house. It consisted of a harbour with ships at the wharves, Barchester City with its narrow streets of half-timbered houses and shops, and the railway. The rails were made of very thin string and many hours were spent cutting countless sleepers from thin cardboard and sticking them down. The dominating feature of the whole system was Barchester cathedral. This was made entirely from Balsa wood, card and cellophane, and was over 3ft in length. The cathedral had stained-glass windows, was lit inside and had a small tape recorder underneath the base board, so that it even had a choir singing inside. The BBC heard about my Barchester Railway and they featured it on children's television in 1951. The railway also received some further publicity. I used huge quantities of Balsa cement in the manufacture of the layout. I took some photographs of the city with a gin bottle standing in the market place to illustrate the scale. I sent these photographs to the manufacturers of the cement, who then used them extensively in their advertising. A few weeks later, a large crate arrived full of their product. This lasted me for many months.

During my art training, between 1950 and 1953, I used to drive from Farnham, where we were then living, up to Chelsea, almost every day. During this period I have but one memory of Britain's steam railways. It remains in my mind only because of the sense of frustration and regret at yet another lost opportunity. On my way up to London I remember frequently seeing an old shunting engine wheezing, groaning and clanking up and down Farnham station goods yard. It seemed to be doing exactly the same thing when I drove by again on the way home in the evening. I took no notice. It would certainly never have occurred to me to take photographs of it—after all, it would be there tomorrow. It was probably a Wainwright C, but that classification would have meant nothing to me and certainly I never bothered to ask anyone. Now it has gone the way of all the other members of her large class, except one which has been preserved. The goods yard itself has almost gone too, to make way for the inevitable car park.

It was after I had finished my art training in London that my passion for steam railways was rekindled. I was suddenly to see them from a completely different viewpoint. As a small boy I had never stood on the end of draughty station platforms, and I never had quite been able to see the point of filling endless notebooks with engine numbers. It was just the actual steam engines that had excited me. Now, however, as an artist, I realised that steam railways were going to give me the most marvellous subjects—the great locomotives, and the sheds and round-houses, those magnificent monuments to the age of steam, built with such pride and feeling by the architects of the last century. I feel certain that if Rembrandt had lived in the age of steam locomotives he would have revelled as I did in the cathedral-like interiors of the great steam sheds. The beautiful sombre colours of his palette would have been well suited to the portrayal of these marvellous scenes, which have now all been bulldozed into history. The engines were grimy work-horses in the twilight of their years, neglected, forlorn, but still working. Here, in the gloomy depths of the sheds, there was an intense beauty of the most dramatic kind, if you looked for it through the dirt and grime.

Shafts of sunlight penetrated broken panes of soot-caked glass in the roof and, through the steam and the smoke, played on pools of green oil on the floor. On the connecting rods of the locomotives one caught the occasional flash of brilliant light where slowly dripping oil caught the sun. All would be almost quiet as the steam engines were at rest, ready to go out on the road. A whisp of steam would eddy up into the darkness of the roof, and there would be a gentle murmur as the engines simmered. Lovely harmonies could be found in the cool greys, browns and mauves of the dirty engines. (Clean engines have never excited me as much as dirty ones.) The locomotives were coming to the end of their working life, but in all this dirt could be found myriad subtleties of colour—this was to me the very essence of the great age of steam. It simply had to be recorded on canvas.

We can speculate that Rembrandt might, had he lived later, have gained artistic inspiration from the great scenes just described, but I am certain that the composer Dvořák actually did. He was a steam enthusiast and it is said that, when he was in London writing one of his symphonies, he used to dash off in every spare moment to the nearest steam locomotive depot. No wonder he wrote such gorgeous music!

In those days of the mid 1950s, I had neither the responsibilities of

23

marriage nor the demands on my time that I now have, and I was able to paint many more pictures solely for pleasure. I did not have to worry too much about selling them. Fortunately at this time there were still plenty of opportunities to paint steam railway subjects. I grasped those opportunities. In 1955 I painted two pictures in Willesden round-house, one in York round-house, one in the great engineering works at Crewe, one of King's Cross station by night and finally one in Swindon works. I gained tremendous experience from painting these pictures, which I did entirely from life—I have always believed that the hardest way to do something is usually the best way. Moreover I was painting the pictures for fun and I enjoyed every minute of the experience, although I can seldom have looked particularly happy to any of the railwaymen who were standing watching me.

The conditions were appalling. I would start painting early in the morning and go on until the light faded in the evening. By this time, I was usually frozen solid. Standing in pools of oil, I would be fortified by layers of sweaters and endless cups of tea donated from the nearest steam locomotive. It always seemed to be freezing cold in the old steam sheds, even in mid-summer, and there always seemed to be a biting wind howling around the shed. Certainly the physical environment was hardly conducive to producing great artistic work, but one fought the conditions and hoped to win. This alone was a sense of achievement.

I remember one day in particular, in Willesden sheds. It was mid-December, and it was snowing. I had never seen snow a dirty brown colour before. It came through the roof and, by the time most of it had landed on either my head or on my painting, it was black! Willesden sheds, together with so many other places of happy memories, have long since been demolished.

I made many friends among the railwaymen who offered me their advice and help. They had probably never before seen an artist who was mad enough to paint in such a place, and they would comment on the painting as I was working on it. I would take note of their knowledgeable criticism, for they expected every nut and bolt to be correct. I feel strongly on one point here, incidentally—if an artist is painting a machine designed by someone else, he has no right to take liberties and alter the actual shape of it. I believe the secret of painting a realistic picture of a machine in its working environment, and yet also capturing the atmosphere of the scene, is to know what to leave out, whilst actually creating the illusion you have put everything in! If the artist puts in every nut and bolt, he might just as well take a photograph. It is the atmosphere that counts. However, I could take few liberties, with half a dozen engine drivers and firemen looking over my shoulder as a I painted 'their' Black Five. 'Cor, it looks a real treat, it's just like the real thing'—hearing that, I knew that I had passed the test.

For the first painting of Willesden sheds, which I still have in my possession, I set up my easel on one of the pit roads from the turn-table in the middle of the round-house. The patient and co-operative staff did everything possible to help. For the whole time that I was there, they put a red flag at the end of the road I was using, so that no driver would leave his engine blocking out my view. I had a Baby Scot on my left; all the other engines were 8Fs and Black Fives. On the locomotive on my immediate right someone had chalked 'Not to be removed from Crewe', an instruction which had obviously been ignored. Others had played a game of noughts and crosses in chalk on the cylinder cover, and I put this into the picture to give an added touch of realism. Several years later when the picture was exhibited in a London gallery, the staff were most concerned—they thought that a member of the public had defaced my painting!

York was the next place on my list. Like so many other artists, I had already painted several pictures in the narrow streets of that lovely city. However there was now another scene just waiting to be painted—the engine sheds! In 1955 I set my easel up in that marvellous place, which is now, of course, the National Railway Museum. The building itself is little changed except that it is much cleaner. Some, including myself, feel that this is rather a shame—we miss the muck and the dirt. I was there a few years ago doing a television programme with the BBC and to my delight I discovered that most of the features in my painting were still recognisable. Only the locomotives themselves were different, and cleaner. I had painted my picture beside one of the inspection pits leading to the turn-table. Both the pit and the turn-table were still there, though the former was now boarded over. I could not help wondering whether, if I lifted the boards, I would find all the filthy painting rags that I had thrown away into the pit, after cleaning my brushes, all those years before.

I have wonderful memories of that magnificent train shed at York. Every brush stroke was done on the spot, on a 36 × 28in canvas. I spent five days painting *Straight Deal*, one of the A2/3 Pacifics. I was able to concentrate on the locomotive undisturbed, because she was lying 'dead' on a shed road where there was no danger of her being towed away halfway through her portrait. After capturing her there, I moved my easel and continued the painting as though she was in steam on the turn-table. Photographers can't do that! In the background, in the sunlit gloom, the A2 and A3 Pacifics, with those romantic racehorse names—*Hornet's Beauty, Ocean Swell, Sugar Plum, Blue Peter*—simmered gently, ready to

(*overleaf*) Black Five Country. Stanier Black Fives at the Stoke-on-Trent coaling tower and ash pits. Near the end the locomotives were in appalling external condition, matching the degradation of their surroundings (*by courtesy of Solomon & Whitehead (Guild Prints) Ltd*)

go out on the road. One day, a railwayman came to take a photograph of me. His picture won a regional BR photographic competition. When I look at that photograph today, it evokes everything that a great steam locomotive shed should be—shafts of sunlight, gently escaping steam, warm engines. In the centre, there I stand, muffled, as always, against the biting cold.

The original painting of York sheds was lost in a fire. I had a very large one-man exhibition of my work in Johannesburg in 1968. As most of the paintings originally to be included were, inevitably, of wildlife, the gallery suggested that in order to make it as retrospective as possible, they should pay for my own private collection of paintings, built up over the years, including all my railway pictures, to be flown out for the exhibition. Among them was the York sheds picture which my father had purchased to keep it in the family. At the close of the exhibition all but one of my private collection were boxed up in several large packing cases and dispatched to Durban for shipment back to England. One of the cases contained a portrait and five of the six railway paintings. One evening, the warehouse in which this box was stored went up in flames and all the pictures were lost. Apart from 'York sheds', these included the original of 'Last Hours at Nine Elms', from which the well known reproduction had been made, and a semi-completed painting of two Merchant Pacifics outside Nine Elms shed. The only railway painting that I did not lose was that of Germiston steam sheds, Johannesburg. This had been retained by the gallery, unknown to me, because of the considerable local interest that it was creating.

Fortunately, I did not really lose possession of 'York sheds' completely. A few years after I painted it, I was commissioned by a friend to execute a smaller copy of it. He had this in his possession until his death, when it came up for auction. Another friend bought it, on the condition that if he gave it to me I would repay him with a painting of a giraffe! So, at least I have the smaller painting to remind me of those happy days in York sheds; rather, I will have when I have painted the giraffe!

The great engineering workshops at Crewe came next. As I was going to be there for a week or more, I had to look for a convenient hotel. I chose the Crewe Arms. It was convenient all right—it was built more or less on top of the main-line station. One night there was enough. The hotel was apparently nearly always full, but I very quickly realised why the room I had been given was always available. How could I sleep with Duchess Pacifics on their journey to the North thundering by at regular intervals or, worse still, stopping in the station right under my bed! If I did manage a few minutes' sleep, I would be immediately and rudely awakened by the booming voice, vibrating around the walls of the bedroom, of the station announcer. (If I could have foretold the future and foreseen the steam-starved days so shortly to come, I would gladly have given up my night's

1955. Sunlit gloom in the magnificent round-house at York, now the National Railway Museum. I spent eight days in the wet and cold painting this picture, but it was worth it! Unfortunately the picture was later lost in a fire

sleep and spent the entire time on the platform below!) After that one night at Crewe, I packed my bags and went down the road to the peace and quiet of Nantwich.

The hard training that I had undergone with Robin Goodwin, during which we frequently used to go out together into the streets of London and set our easels up in Whitehall, Piccadilly and other busy parts of the city, was now to prove its worth. In those earlier days, Robin and I would frequently have 200 or 300 people watching us paint. At Crewe, my easel stood in the middle of the erecting shops, and screens had to be put up around me while I was painting—not for my benefit, but because the entire work-force, it seemed, stopped work to watch me! I was told that 6,000 railwaymen were employed there at that time. There were other distractions for me, apart from the audience. The noise was tremendous, the whole place a hive of activity. I was right underneath the overhead travelling crane, and I would frequently see this mammoth piece of engineering trundling towards me, to dangle a Duchess Pacific over my head. If one can paint in conditions like these, one can paint anywhere!

My painting of Crewe works shows a brand new Standard 9F in the erecting shops. I used a little artist's licence for this painting, as I had for the York one. Once again, I changed location halfway through. I painted the portrait of the 9F in the peace and quiet of the paint shops, where she

My painting here is of Standard 9F No 92201 in the final erecting shop at Crewe – I moved out of the paint shop where the engine actually was to finish the picture. Little did I know that I would one day own one of her sisters, 92203

was standing completed, awaiting her delivery to BR. I then moved into the erecting shops, to complete the rest of the painting as though she was on the production line. It seemed quite reasonable to do this—after all could anyone categorically state that a freshly painted 9F could never go from the paint shop back into the erecting shops for, perhaps, one final mechanical adjustment before delivery?

The number on the 9F I painted in Crewe works was 92201. I could never have guessed that not so many years later I was actually going to own one of her sisters. My 92203 had not even been built at that time!

While I was painting at Crewe, if the weather was fine I used to wander down into the marshalling yards before going back to Nantwich to get a good night's sleep. It was on one of these evenings that I had my very first footplate trip. The night was pitch dark, but huge gantry lights illuminated the whole area of the yards. A Jinty tank engine was doing nothing in particular, and when my eyes met those of the driver who was leaning out of the cab, we realised that we had something in common—a love of steam engines. I was invited to climb aboard and there I was, ten minutes later, driving his engine up and down.

It was during my training with Robin Goodwin that I had my first experience of showing my pictures in public. Every May, Robin and I used to go along to the Victoria Embankment Gardens, alongside the Thames, to show our paintings in the annual open-air art exhibition that was, and still is, organised by the LCC. It is a free-for-all exhibition, open to anyone willing to get there early to lay claim to one of the 6ft square portions of the chain-link fence, which is put up especially and stretches the whole length of the gardens. It is a marvellous shop window for an artist's work, and I continued to exhibit there for many years after I finished my training. The variety of pictures has always been quite amazing. There were cats in baskets, endless pictures of Tower Bridge (for the tourists), the inevitable vases of flowers (usually rather badly painted), and pictures of whatever subject happened to be fashionable that particular year. I decided, for fun, to show my picture of Crewe sheds. It certainly caused considerable comment—it was probably the first time that the exhibition had included a picture of a steam railway subject. Furthermore, it stood out clearly from the pictures hanging on the next-door pitch—they were the sort that looked as though a bicycle had been ridden all over them. It was during one lunch-time that a group of railwaymen from Waterloo walked through the gardens. They showed great interest, willingly giving their comments on the painting—mostly, I am happy to say, complimentary.

None of the paintings that I was painting at this time had been commissioned by anyone. Nevertheless, I took them around to the various regional offices of BR, as I thought that they might be interested. They were. They bought all except one of the two Willesden shed pictures. They paid me £60 for each, and that included the frame. I'm very glad that they didn't buy the remaining one—I've kept it.

The painting of King's Cross Station, 'Service by Night', which was purchased by the Eastern Region of BR, was also turned into a poster. I was very green in those days and I was so thrilled at the prospect of having my work seen by thousands of people (if they bothered to look when it was pasted up) that it never occurred to me to suggest to BR that they might give me a little extra for the copyright. They didn't suggest it, and so I had to assume that the £60 was to include that as well!

Painting 'Service by Night' certainly had its moments. It was a night scene, so the picture had to be painted in the studio, but it entailed sketching in the dark, with a torch, at King's Cross. The spot I chose was quite dangerous, as it was just outside the tunnel mouth where all the tracks come into the station. I had to be escorted out from the end of the platform and to have someone with me all the time while I was working, because they soon discovered that I was the sort of person who would get carried away by the excitement of it all and step over one of the rails, with disastrous results. In front of me was the most complicated jumble of coloured lights that I have ever seen. To my completely untrained eye, it seemed to be absolute chaos. Trains were coming in and out of that

31

station all the time, and every time there was a train movement, something went up, down or sideways, various lights changed from red to green and vice versa, and all sorts of figures flashed on or off. I was totally bewildered.

As I knew nothing about the technicalities, the painting was full of faults when it was first delivered. This was no good for BR. The poster had to be accurate in every detail. If it wasn't, from the moment the first copy was posted up on a station platform, the railway would be plagued with telephone calls from railway enthusiasts only too keen to catch me out. When I showed the painting to the Eastern Region publicity people, they hardly knew where to start. 'You can't possibly have a passenger train coming out of there—it's the milk yard.' (How was I to know? It was rather a nice train, and it had taken me hours to paint, but it had to come out.) 'You can't have that signal like that because there is no engine on the end of that train in the platform.' And so it went on.

After about six attempts, the painting was passed as accurate. It went to print, and many thousands of posters must have been run off before another major mistake was noticed. We had all been so intent on getting the signalling correct that a major fault in the points right in the foreground had been missed. I had created a potential major railway disaster! A junior employee at the printing firm had to change every single copy by hand. (It must have driven him completely potty, and I am very glad that I never met him!) I remember my feeling of enormous pride when I stood on various railway platforms and looked up at my painting—I even drove to several railway stations in the hope that it was there. (It usually wasn't!) In its original form, it is quite a collector's item now and, because of its nostalgic theme, it has been republished in a smaller size.

The days were coming to an end when I could indulge myself in the luxury of painting for fun. As the need to go out and earn a living like everyone else became more urgent, there was no longer the time or the justification for spending many hours in the great steam sheds on the chance that someone might buy the painting when it was finished. The bills had to be paid, and I needed the security of commissioned work. However, there was one more place which beckoned me, and that was Swindon.

I never have been one of those railway fanatics who believe that every engine has to have a copper-capped chimney and belong to God's Wonderful Railway, and who are unwilling to accept that good engines might have been built at Doncaster, Brighton or Crewe. To me it is the visual impact of a steam locomotive that is thrilling—where it was born is of no particular concern to me. Nevertheless, I was excited at the prospect of painting Great Western green engines in a paint shop, and British Railways willingly gave me the necessary permission. The challenge of

32

Discussing some technical points with the experts, at the LCC open-air exhibition on the Victoria Embankment in 1956. The painting receiving critical attention (and, fortunately, general approval) is the one on which I am shown working in the photograph on page 30—the brand-new No 92201 at Crewe works this particular subject was the complicated roof of the works. I must be a glutton for punishment, but it was very good training. I sweated it out and painted every girder that was in front of me, and I do not think that even the architect could find fault with it.

As always, everybody in the works gave me the most marvellous co-operation. They moved the traverser up and down for me, and even moved engines if they blocked my view. It was summer, and I didn't need my half a dozen sweaters. I made some marvellous friends among the workforce. One of the men in the paint shops used to bring in fresh strawberries from his garden every morning and put them on the easel for me. *The Earl of Berkeley* had been parted from her tender and was the centrepiece of the picture, standing alongside a tank engine, No 6622. In front of me was the usual orderly chaos of a huge and busy locomotive works, in apparent total disorder—that was all part of the atmosphere so important to me.

The Swindon picture was one of the ones bought by BR. When I later enquired about its whereabouts, they told me that they had 'lost' it. It was apparently last seen about ten years ago, hanging in the apprentices' cafeteria at Swindon works, no doubt rapidly disappearing under a liberal coating of fish and chip grease! (If any reader knows where this painting is, I would be very glad to know—the National Railway Museum at York want it for their collection.) British Railways have also 'lost' the original of 'Service by Night'. (York want that one too!)

After I had finished my training with Robin Goodwin in 1954, one of my first clients was Sharpes' Classic Christmas Cards, of Bradford. For reasons that I could never quite understand, the scenes I painted always had to be set in the 1890s, with people in crinolines. They always wanted a dog somewhere, though I protested that I couldn't paint them, and of course they had to have snow. They asked me to do a railway subject, and so I decided to paint St Pancras station. At least I wouldn't have to paint snow this time! It was easy enough to get the roof of the station right because it hadn't changed much in sixty years. The other details were more difficult and I had to do a great deal of research into the period, for the costumes and, more especially, for the trains themselves. It was a highly successful Christmas card. By the time I had reached the stage in my career when I neither needed nor wanted to do Christmas cards commercially, Sharpes' owned over thirty of my paintings, and I still couldn't paint dogs!

A final memory of this period is of the great, late lamented Euston station. I was commissioned to paint a picture for the Cheshire Regiment, which meant a train journey to their home city. I was at Euston, looking for my platform and not really noticing the steam engines around me, when I caught sight of a once-proud, but now very dirty Duchess standing alone and simmering gently at one of the buffer stops. Shafts of sunlight were filtering through the smoke and gloom—it would have made a wonderful painting. Her formerly magnificent maroon finery had long since vanished under layers of grime and filth. The great locomotive was shorn of her name-plates and the complete obliteration of even her cab-side numbers completed her sad anonymity. It is strange that the memory of a then everyday scene seems to become stronger with the passage of time. I even know the date—it was 23 September 1963. Maybe a railway enthusiast somewhere has the Euston train movements for that day and my Duchess may emerge for me once again from the total obscurity which engulfed her and her sisters so prematurely. There isn't even any gloom left now in the new, antiseptic and concrete Euston station of today. Such is progress.

35

2
Elephants all day, steam in the evening

I have been keeping a diary for over twenty-five years. Living within a few miles of Guildford for most of this time, I must have driven over the railway near the station on many occasions. The smoke drifting upwards from the locomotive shed below the bridge was once all part of the daily scene, so I never bothered to notice it. In the mid 1960s, however, like countless railway enthusiasts all over the country, I suddenly realised that the whole steam scene was going, and it was going very fast.

Over the previous years I had begun to get various commissions for paintings but none of them had anything to do with railways. In any case, what was the panic—steam railways were all around us? In 1960 my career had 'taken off' almost overnight in the specialist field of painting wildlife, but that is another story. By 1966 the pressure was mounting—I had a family and a great many responsibilities, and everyone seemed to want pictures of elephants. I was beginning to work seven days a week. The exhibitions of my wildlife work had been highly successful, and during 1966–7 I was working for my first exhibition in New York.

It was in July 1966 that I drove to Guildford, parked the car, walked up over the bridge and looked over the parapet. Down below me was a very strange looking engine that didn't look at all English, but as I had never been a loco spotter or engine-number collector, and as I hardly knew one engine from another, it meant nothing to me. Steam engines had always been merely very exciting things to look at and to paint. I was soon, however, to get to know this strange engine. She was No 30072, one of a class of USA tanks shipped over to this country during World War II and later taken into Southern Railway stock. The lads in Guildford shed called her 'Little Jim'. (Everyone assumed at that time that she would end up as scrap metal—she is now on the Keithley & Worth Valley Railway.)

In spite of the pressure of my painting commitments, the 'pull' of Guildford shed finally became too strong to resist. Time was running out and something of the age of steam simply had to be put down onto canvas in those final months before it was too late. No matter how rough the sketches, it was now or never. A few weeks later, on the evening of 9 September 1966, I wandered into Guildford shed for the very first time. It

36

was one of those beautiful English late-summer evenings, when most people would have wanted to go out into the country for some fresh air. But not me—my fresh air was Guildford shed, loaded with coal dust and lovely steam-engine smoke! The shed master had gone home. No one seemed to be about. Half a dozen locomotives were simmering away gently, unattended. Some of the engines were the new Standards. These, like the Ns and the Us which were also on shed, were filthy and looked forlorn and neglected. Their condition was not the fault of the shed staff—what was the point of cleaning an engine for the benefit of the scrap merchants? Those that were in steam were waiting to go out on ballast trains to Woking and Aldershot. Few of them had more exciting or glamorous work than that.

To my delight, there was one big main-line locomotive in the shed that evening. She had obviously strayed from Waterloo. She was *Bere Alston*, one of the West Country class. She was obviously in for a temporary service, which would almost certainly be her last. She was shorn of her name-plates, her rods were on the shed floor, her lovely green finery had long since disappeared under layers of grime, but she was still proud and magnificent, and a subject for a lightning thumb-nail sketch. Some of the locomotives were cold and lifeless, passively awaiting their fate. Nevertheless, there was the same old atmosphere of gently escaping steam through which shafts of light played on the pools of oil on the floor, of dripping water and the warm smell of engines. All the memories of the Willesden shed and distant days came flooding back to me.

At the end of Guildford shed, in the gloom, I could discern a wooden hut standing at the foot of the sheer chalk cliff that surrounded the shed and which was such a feature of the place. With mounting excitement and anticipation I walked through the shed between the locomotives to the hut. I opened the door. A couple of railwaymen were drinking tea and reading the *Daily Mirror*. The place could hardly be described as a hive of activity. I intended to stay only a few minutes to introduce myself, but steam railwaymen are the same the world over—as soon as they realise that you are one of them, you are 'in'. I stayed three hours, and my New York exhibition was temporarily forgotten. 'A permit to sketch in the shed? Oh, you don't want to bother about things like that, mate. Come in and have a word with Norman Coe tomorrow—he's the shed master and he'll fix you up.' So it was arranged, over a 'cuppa', which is surely the way it should be.

So began my all-too-brief acquaintance with Guildford shed. I made many happy visits on those summer evenings of 1966, after painting elephants all day in my studio. It was pure relaxation. I very quickly got to know the men, those great men, some of whom have since died and most of whom left 'the railway' with the locomotives they loved. I was always assured of a warm welcome whenever I went to the shed, and my brief

Guildford shed on 9 July 1967, the last day of steam working on the Southern. The three locomotives are West Country Pacific No 34018, USA tank No 30072 and a BR Standard Class 4 *(Photo K. P. Lawrence)*

friendship with them was only cut short by the premature end of steam in the South of England a few months later.

Some of my visits to Guildford shed were so short that I barely had time to do the briefest of sketches. It was a question of catching on canvas anything that would remind me—later, when steam was gone and we were in the colourless and functional age of the diesel—of the glorious days of steam.

Guildford was not the only place to cast its spell over me. I had seen Nine Elms shed on brief occasions when going up to Waterloo by train. Looking down the slope from the main line, I could see the massive coaling-stage thrusting skywards through the clouds of smoke from seemingly countless filthy steam locomotives. I could hardly believe that such place was real, and I just had to get there before it was too late.

Steam locomotive sheds always seemed to be impossible to find. After getting lost half a dozen times in the jungle of Wandsworth's back streets, I finally found the place. Nine Elms never had quite the intimacy of Guildford shed, because it was so much bigger. Here, nevertheless, I found the same friendly co-operation from everybody. We talked the same language. Believe it or not, I actually took the trouble to obtain a permit. I remember the BR people being quite surprised at someone asking for one.

Certainly no one seemed particularly interested in it when I offered to present it at Nine Elms shed. Nobody cared about such things in the last months of steam. British Railways were marvellously tolerant. In fact it would have been virtually impossible to give a permit to everybody if they had all asked for one because of the sheer numbers of enthusiasts who descended on Nine Elms and other such places in the last months. You just wandered into the shed like everybody else. Indeed, at times it seemed that there were more members of the public in the shed than there were railwaymen! How British Railways ever managed to run a railway in the last months of steam, I cannot imagine.

Every corner of Nine Elms shed seemed to be a potential oil painting. Merchant Navy Pacifics, West Countries and all the other engines that anyone could ever want were everywhere. Almost without exception, they were all very dirty and stripped of their name-plates. It seemed that engines were coming and going every few minutes from the great train shed of Waterloo up the line, which all contributed to the excitement and atmosphere. And there was the inevitable scrap line, with its long and forlorn row of once-shining, green locomotives, awaiting their fate. They were now rusting and silent. Connecting rods and other bits and pieces were lying all over the place amongst the piles of ashes, twisted firing irons, old buckets and all the other rubbish that marked the end of our great steam age. Growing everywhere, by a minor miracle, was that marvellous plant the willow herb, proving with quite dramatic effect that nature has the most amazing ability to clothe in a fleeting but nevertheless great beauty the most squalid and decrepit areas of industrial wasteland.

The coaling-stage reared its great concrete bulk into the smoky sky—what a sight that was, what a memory that must be for so many railway enthusiasts! The line under the stage, and on which, over the years, so many great locomotives must have paused to have their tenders replenished, had by now sunk several inches into the ground through heavy use and lack of maintenance. Now, at the end of it all, we witnessed the sight (and sound!) of several tons of coal crashing down into the bunkers of Merchant Navy Pacifics, so that they became so heavy that they were unable to get out of the coaling-stage the other side! Wagner himself would have been inspired by the amazing scene. Giant locomotives were trapped, often for many minutes at a time, as they struggled in torment to be released from this smoky hell. Clouds of smoke and sparks were hurled into the sky as the thunderous sound reverberated around the blocks of high-rise flats and houses that surrounded Nine Elms shed. (The wife of one railway enthusiast I knew who lived in those flats complained with great feeling that the Bulleid Pacifics interfered with her sex life. Every time a locomotive was being coaled and was trying to get out of the coaling-stage, her husband would leap out of bed and rush out with his camera to record the scene. She was longing for the day when

Agony at Nine Elms - a Bulleid Pacific struggles
to climb out of the coaling stage

steam would finish!) Unless one was a steam enthusiast, living near Nine Elms cannot have been much fun, as wheels spun and tortured rods thrashed in vain to try and get a grip on the rails. No steam locomotive was meant to be treated like this, but it was an inspiring sight never to be forgotten by those who witnessed it and photographed it.

As I stood amid this excitement, I wondered how many other artists had ever set up their easels in the shed? It was paradise for a painter. Every minute was valuable and had to be made the most of. There was only time for quick thumb-nail sketches, and those that I managed to do in Nine Elms and Guildford are now irreplaceable. There is no better way to work than 'on location', in the heat of the moment, fast. Sometimes there might be less than half an hour before the daylight would fade or an engine that I was sketching would move away. There was no time to bother about technical accuracy—the camera would give me all that. All that I could hope to achieve was to record onto canvas something of the subtle nuances of light and shade, the colours to be found in the dirty locomotives either in the sun or in the smoky gloom of the sheds. It was simply a question of getting colour and atmosphere down onto the canvas before it all passed into history.

It was one day in 1967 that I met Paul Barnes for the first time. He wandered into Nine Elms shed as I was painting, surrounded by steam locomotives. 'What a marvellous subject for a movie that would make', Paul said. At that moment a beautiful little film was born. There were only a few weeks to go before the end. Both of us were busy people, but in some eight sessions together at Nine Elms, we made a half-hour documentary recording the last days of steam at Nine Elms shed, as seen through the eyes of a painter. It was an abstract portrayal of a great steam shed, and Paul had a marvellous eye for seeing detail and beauty through the lens of a camera. He even managed to find the most evocative music that perfectly fitted the sequence showing me standing among the dirty and simmering locomotives in the depths of the shed as the smoke eddied up into the roof above. I remember one sequence in the film with particular pleasure. Being of an inquisitive nature, I was rubbing the thick, oily grime on the side of a West Country tender to see what the paint-work was like underneath. (My wife had given up hope of my ever having a clean handkerchief.) Suddenly an area of shining Brunswick green and orange and black lining appeared. Clearly this paint had not seen the light of day for many a month, but the oily layer of muck had protected it from the elements, and it was as good as new. Paul saw me doing this and filmed it. The sudden emergence of such a beautiful splash of colour in brilliant contrast to the dark and sombre tones of the shed interior made, I think, one of the highlights of the film. Paul was entirely responsible for the shape of the film—the cutting, editing and narration—and we paid for it between us. *The Painter and the Engines*

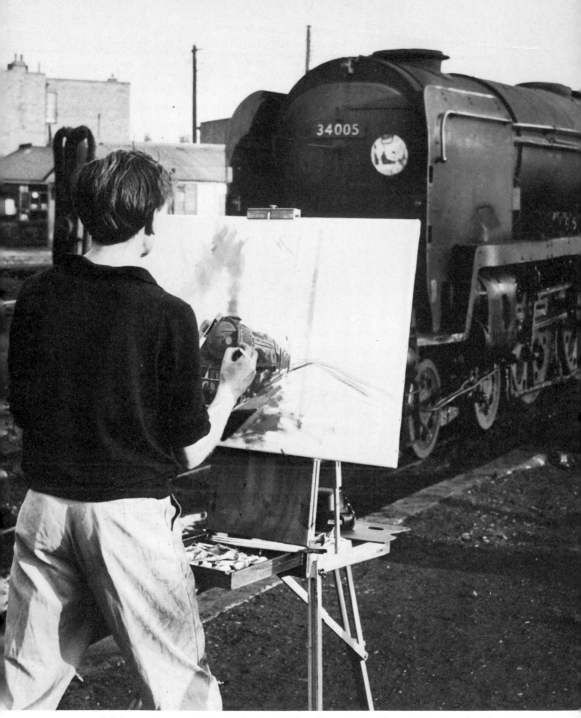

I did sometimes work in the fresh air! Here I'm at Nine Elms, with only a few days to go before the end of steam in the South, so I had to work fast—besides, they kept moving the engines! (*Photo P. Leaviens*)

was premiered at the National Film Theatre and achieved much acclaim from railway enthusiasts. A copy is now in the archives of the British Film Institute—thanks to Paul, we have recorded on film a fascinating glimpse of railway history that is already valuable as a record of days gone forever.

During the time when Paul and I were filming *The Painter and the Engines* at Nine Elms, I was caught, for the first (and only) time, unashamedly stealing from British Railways. I was always dressed like a tramp in my messy old painting clothes. As we were walking out of the shed one evening, we passed an enormous pile of grimy railway lamps. 'I really must have one of those', said Paul. 'Go on, get me one.' Without giving it a second thought, I picked one up for him. After all, I usually left Nine Elms carrying something, like everyone else! The place was like a junk yard, with all manner of things lying around, including loco lamps, which had been thrown away. No one took any notice—usually. A voice boomed out in the background: ''Ere, put that bleedin' thing down where it came from!' It is bad enough being caught stealing for oneself, but far worse when you are stealing for somebody else. We went back the next day and Paul got his lamp.

It was inevitable that while I was painting in Guildford and Nine Elms sheds I would draw the attention of the Press. The *Evening News* came into Nine Elms shed one day when I was painting a picture of the coaling-stage. On the centre page that evening was a photograph of a very young David Shepherd covered in coal dust, under the title 'Shepherd's Sheds'!

I have never believed in giving up a night's sleep for my art. However, I did just that, in Guildford shed, just once, and it was worth every minute of the effort. With only a few months to go, it was now or never. I had to paint a night scene. At 10.30pm on 17 September 1966, after I had been painting a wildlife picture all day in my studio, I walked into Guildford shed with my easel. Engines 31619 and 31408 were dead, waiting to be towed away for scrap. I knew that they were not going to be moved for a few hours at least, so I set myself up in front of them, and began painting a 30 × 20in canvas.

Fortified throughout the night by cups of tea and plenty of encouragement from the few members of the shed staff who were around, I had finished by 5am. The conditions were atrocious. I had to paint by the dim light cast by a single bulb in an enamel shade hanging from the dirt-encrusted roof above me. It was almost impossible to determine what colour I was putting onto the canvas. I didn't worry about the shapes of the engines—it was simply a question of trying to get some of the atmosphere down on canvas. I believe that I have a reasonable colour 'note' of a shed full of steam engines in the dark, with just a few dim lights hanging from the roof. One day I hope to have the time to paint a large canvas of such a scene and I couldn't do it without that sketch.

Euston Station
London NW1
Euston 1234

Extn. 2082

H C Johnson Chairman & General Manager

D. Shepherd, Esq.,
The Studio,
Winkworth Farm,
Hascombe,
Godalming.
SURREY.

27.9.66.

Public Relations
Mr. K W Ashberry

y/r
o/r

Date 19th September, 1966

10 weeks from today

I have received your letter of 15th September and am pleased to say that having regard to your close interest in rail transport it has been agreed that you be granted the facility of visiting the steam depots on this Region enumerated below for the purpose of preparing your sketch material for future paintings.

Those depots outside this Region are also indicated * and it will be necessary for you to approach the General Managers of these Regions for their permission.

This letter will serve as your authority for entering London Midland sheds but you should see the Shed Master at each place before proceeding with your works.

London Midland Region

✓ 8 Lostock Hall, Preston
Tyseley. (Birmingham)   -   closes on 7th November, 1966
6 ~~The Mills, Liverpool~~
✓ Wolverhampton (Oxley).
✓ Crewe South
✓ Derby   ✓ STOKE
✓ Birkenhead ✗   ✓ WIGAN
✓ Carnforth
~~Lancaster (now closed)~~
✓ Carlisle Kingmoor
~~"   Canal   (closed)~~

*   Eastern Region

~~Canklow~~
~~Grantham~~
~~Doncaster~~

North Eastern Region
✓ Leeds Holbeck
~~Sunderland~~
✓ York · LEEMAN ROAD
~~Newcastle.~~
✓✓ BLYTHE 1 & 2

Scottish Region

~~Inverness~~
~~Dundee~~
✓ POLMADIE

BRITISH RAILWAYS BOARD   B.R. 19141/1
BRITISH RAILWAYS

Your Reference

Our Reference P/VS   14TH SEPTEMBER   19 66

Dear Sir,

If permit is not used, kindly return for cancellation.

In accordance with your request, I have been pleased to arrange for your visit(s) to Motive Power Depot(s) as shewn below, and I hope you have an instructive and enjoyable visit.

On arrival at the Depot, this letter should be presented immediately at the Depot office and a responsible member of the staff will conduct you round.

In the interests of safety, no person under 16 years of age will be allowed to visit a Motive Power Depot unless accompanied by an adult, and the visit must finish before dark. The only luggage allowed in the Motive Power Depot will be cameras, and photographs may be taken for private collection only.

Yours faithfully,

FOR T. R. B. T...
...MANAGER

'SPECIAL'

Motive Power Depot to be visited	Date	Time	No. of Persons
Nine Elms	Available during week-commencing 19th September.	09 00 17 00 hrs.	1

To :— Mr. D. Shepherd.

Today on the site of the great steam shed of Nine Elms stands the new Covent Garden Market with its concrete and glass. Surely no steam-locomotive enthusiast, as his train approaches Waterloo, can fail to look longingly to the right-hand side of the line to a place of so many haunting memories.

There were other places that I simply had to visit before the engines were sent for scrap and the bulldozers brought the steam sheds crashing down to make way for housing estates and multi-storey car-parks. In my scrapbook I have an extremely dog-eared letter from the chairman and general manager of BR London Midland Region, dated 19 September 1966. The letter states that, 'having regard for your close interest in railway transport, it has been agreed that you be granted the facility of visiting the steam depots on this region as numerated below, for the purpose of sketching for future paintings.' There was no problem, therefore, except that, having lived in the South all my life, I had never even heard of most of the places in the letter!

The list was a formidable one. The letter not only served as an authority for entering any London Midland shed that I had wished to go to, but it was also the introduction to sheds on other regions. I allowed myself ten days. Lostock Hall, Preston, Tyseley in Birmingham, Wolverhampton, Crewe South, Derby, Birkenhead, Stoke-on-Trent,

Wigan, Carnforth and Carlisle Kingmoor were the London Midland sheds that I chose. On the North Eastern Region I decided to go to Leeds Holbeck, York and the two Blythe sheds. If I had time I would manage Polmadie on the Scottish Region. The Southern was not on my schedule—living in the South, I would squeeze it in somehow in odd moments. There would be no time for sketching with paints and canvas—this work had to be with camera only. Armed with my letter, off I went. I was to learn a great deal more about the geography of Great Britain by the end of the ten days. I was also to learn quite a bit about photography. I had borrowed a camera from a friend and it seemed to be covered in knobs. I have never been technically minded, so I had no idea what most of them were for. Astoundingly, I got some quite good pictures. I suppose it was because I took so many. I was pouring film through the camera in every shed that I visited. As I never had any intention of publishing any of my photographs, I did not really bother about composition. It was simply 'sketching with a camera'. I was photographing every little detail that I thought might go into a future painting and which would not be seen again after a few more months: shafts of sunlight coming through shed roofs and glinting on coupling rods or bits of valve gear; wheel barrows; water dripping from taps; railwaymen shovelling wet slime and coal out of inspection pits; whisps of

Chester shed

steam; the shapes of shadows on engines; details of shed architecture; old
fire buckets; and anything else that caught my eye. (I also photographed
the locomotives!) I ended up with over 600 transparencies, and all are
impossible to replace. It was time well spent.

In those ten days I also saw a great many back streets of a great many
towns. Always the doors of the sheds were open wide to me and there was
the same warm welcome. They provided me with a feast of material for
future paintings. I sometimes visited two or three depots in one day.
Always I found the long lines of rusting engines awaiting their fate beside
the sheds. In one depot alone, I remember counting over thirty
locomotives waiting to be towed away to the scrapyard.

I went to Blythe, in Northumberland. I had never been near this part of
the country. The people were wonderfully friendly, as of course I knew
they would be. I stayed in a most delightful bed and breakfast place, where
everything was shining like a new pin. It was in contrast to the shed that I
was going to the next morning. There were two sheds at Blythe—Numbers
1 and 2—and they were probably the muckiest places that I have ever
seen. Almost all the engines were very old J27s ending their days
amongst the piles of coal and ashes, and they were very dirty. The whole
place was a veritable museum, dating from the last century. There was
even an old blacksmith's forge in the ancient workshop. If only BR could
have left the whole place completely as it was at the end of steam, it would
surely now be one of the greatest tourist attractions in the North East!

I remember Birkenhead, in Cheshire, for very special reasons. First of
all, it was probably the most spectacular, from the point of view of painting, of all the sheds that I visited. Moreover it is quite possible that I was
seeing for the first time that evening one particular locomotive that I
would get to know very well in just a few months' time. Once again, I had
a frustrating time trying to find the place, driving around the maze of poor
back streets of industrial Birkenhead, with the depot enticingly near—I
saw great clouds of smoke drifting up into the evening sky over the
Victorian roof-tops. I shall never forget the sight that confronted me when
I finally found the great shed. Well over ninety engines were in steam.
The evening sun was sinking towards the horizon, behind the gas works.
Beams of warm orange light were shafting through the smoke, which was
so thick that you could almost have cut through it with a knife. I stood on
top of a small rise in the middle of the shed yard looking at the vast mass
of steam engines in the orange glow in front of me. There were a few
Crabs, the occasional Jinty and the inevitable Black Fives and 8Fs, but the
vast majority of the locomotives were Standard 9s. All were absolutely
filthy. This gave them a marvellous warm brown and orange colour, and
the whole place looked like an old oil painting. I am sure that Turner
would have gone mad with excitement!

There is a very good chance that down there in the smoky gloom, with

'Grab' at Birkenhead

her many sisters, was a standard 9F, my own No 92203. I will never know, but I do know that she ended her British Railways days in Birkenhead shed.

As time was running out, I was determined to have some more foot-plate trips. There was never too much of a problem. I had made so many friends in Guildford shed and other places that it seemed to be a waste of time to fill in any forms. I simply jumped up onto the foot-plate of the nearest steam engine. It seemed that everybody else was doing exactly the same thing—whenever one saw a passing steam locomotive, there was invariably at least one extra passenger on board.

In June 1967, there were only a few weeks to go before the end of steam. Things were now so urgent that I gave railways absolute priority in my life. I actually neglected elephants for a whole week and I spent all that time riding on ballast trains from Woking to Guildford, Aldershot and Farnham. By coincidence, I always seemed to be riding on the footplate of either 73115 or 77014. I became very fond of these two locomotives. The latter belonged, so I was told, to a very small class of Standard locomotives which were generally allocated to the Scottish Region. However, this particular engine had somehow found her way down to the South where she ended her days. She was not exactly a pretty locomotive, but she had plenty of character. Many happy hours were spent sitting in

48

the sidings of what used to be the old London & South Western terminal station in Godalming. I never discovered what this engine and her motley collection of wagons were supposed to be doing!

No 73115 did not over-exert herself in her last weeks either. It seemed that she, like 77014, never had anything very important to do or anywhere very important to go. However, we did spend many cheerful hours together at Shalford and other places around Guildford, sitting in the sidings, in full steam, waiting for other trains to go by. I stood on the foot-plate for hours on end, talking steam engines and drinking cups of tea with the crew. It was all very leisurely, I was always in wonderful company and the sun always seemed to be shining. Such was my affection for 73115, after getting to know her so well, that she featured in my painting 'Last Hours at Nine Elms'. I have her 'temporary' smoke-box number-plate, which someone had 'botched up' with wood and tin numbers to replace the real one which had, of course, been stolen.

I did some crazy things on some of those foot-plate trips. I always had my movie camera with me. I must have yards of Super 8 movies of wheels and connecting rods pounding around on the various journeys to and from Guildford and Woking. I would lean out precariously from the cab, holding on with one hand and filming with the other. I remember one particular occasion when I was going through Woking station on the main line, with a train coming in the opposite direction. I was filming it coming straight towards me—I knew that I was being stupid, but I have some quite interesting and now historic film!

I was not content just with ballast trains. I wanted a main-line footplate trip from Waterloo. I thought that I had better be a bit more official about this and ask British Railways for a pass. I never thought that I would get one, as BR became tighter about these things at the very end. So many people were asking for passes that they had to clamp down. I was lucky—they said yes. On Tuesday 4 July 1967, with just four days left of steam on the Southern Region, I arrived at Nine Elms shed to sign on. They told me that I could go from Waterloo to Basingstoke and back again. It was a happy coincidence that the engine for the first part of the journey was No 35028, *Clan Line*—this must have been one of her very last main-line trips. She had already been earmarked for preservation. I left *Clan Line* at Basingstoke, and returned to Waterloo on the footplate of a very sad and forlorn 219 Squadron.

During those very last days of steam, the difficulty of obtaining a footplate pass didn't seem to deter some enthusiasts who were determined to have a ride by whatever means. One only had to walk to the end of a platform at Waterloo and look over the footplate door of any express locomotive, about to leave for Bournemouth or Weymouth, to see several small boys, and some not so small, crouching down out of sight until the train left. The fact that they were there illegally no doubt added a spice to the once-in-a-lifetime adventure for them. During these last days, many regulations seemed to be being ignored. I gathered that scant attention was being paid at times to even the speed restrictions on certain sections of the main line. We heard several stories of Merchants and West Countries doing well over the 'ton' through Fleet, in Hampshire. That very fast straight stretch of main line was a magnificent vantage point for photographers and there were many of them filming the magnificent spectacle. The strange thing was that all the locomotives had seen better days. They were suffering neglect through lack of maintenance, but they, and their drivers, were going to have one last fling and to hell with the consequences! In one respect at least, steam was going to go out in a blaze of glory.

Last days at Nine Elms shed

3

The great buying spree
and the start of a dream

The mid 1960s were the peak scrapping years for this country's steam engines. We had all the coal we needed and in those days we had to import every drop of oil from abroad, but the bureaucrats had decided in their infinite wisdom that 'King Diesel' would take over the railway system of Great Britain and this process was happening with an indecent haste. Our great and proud steam railway heritage was dying, and it was dying in ignominy. At the expense of the poor old taxpayer who footed the bill, dozens of locomotives were making their last sad journey to the scrapyards every month. Every steam shed throughout the land had its own scrap line. Row upon row of rust-red steam locomotives waited to be towed away by diesels which were quite possibly not much newer than the engines that they were towing. Their journeys ended in the yards of Cashmore's of Newport, Draper's of Hull, and other scrap merchants, whose premises rang ceaselessly to the scream of the cutter's torch. The queues of locomotives awaiting their fate grew ever longer.

Enthusiasts looked each month in *Railway Magazine* and *Railway World* at the lists of withdrawn locomotives. They would look for, and perhaps find, their favourite engine. Such was the degree of emotion that it was not perhaps entirely inappropriate to compare this to the casualty lists of a great disaster or battle. Some of the engines going for scrap were almost new. Many of the Standards, in particular, were scarcely ten years old. They had many years of life left in them. To a great many people the whole situation seemed completely crazy, and a monstrous waste of money. Many engines bore names, and their name-plates were stripped off and sold to anyone who wanted one. In those days you could pick up a famous name-plate for just a few pounds, while the engine itself went for scrap. Some of the locomotives carried famous names and would surely be cherished now by the preservationists, who instead, have ended up, in some desperation, by purchasing wrecks from Barry scrapyard. It seems scarcely conceivable that *Sir William Stanier, Eton, King Henry VIII, Silver Jubilee, Fighter Command, Papyrus* and *Coronation* were cut up for just so much scrap metal. Most of the locomotives going to scrapyards were time-worn old stagers which had soldiered on faithfully, ending their

51

days under layers of grime and filth gathered over the years from the environment in which they had worked—the mines and slag heaps of the industrial Midlands and North East.

In just one issue of *Railway World*, for November 1967, we read of the withdrawal of no less than thirty-eight Stanier 8Fs. In the same magazine for September 1967 and *Railway Magazine* for the following month, we read similarly that eighteen of the 75XXX Standards were withdrawn in just the space of a few weeks. (Only seventy-nine of these Standards had been built, just a few years previously.) On one day in January 1967, one diesel-hauled freight train was seen hauling no less than nine Jinty tank engines to Kettering for scrapping.

Stoke-on-Trent;
the coaling tower and gantry for
removing the buckets from the ash-pit

Some very strange things happened in those days. The single Class 8P, No 71000, *The Duke of Gloucester*, was apparently sent to Cashmore's of Newport in error. If she had stayed there she would not have lasted very long. Cashmore's always cut up every locomotive very quickly. In fact, she was sent on to Barry, where her rusting hulk stayed for several years before eventual purchase for preservation.

Many of the locomotives which were running their last revenue-earning miles for BR were tended, towards the end, with loving care by people who had nothing at all to do with British Railways. The legions of enthusiasts up and down Great Britain were not going to see all the engines going on their way to the scrapyards in the disgusting condition

53

which seemed to represent the official attitude at the end of steam. If 'they' never bothered to clean the locos, then 'we' would, and a blind eye was turned to the activities of the private bands of cleaners who descended on many a shed in those last weeks. Many locomotives went for scrap not only cleaned, but carrying corny but sincere slogans of affection chalked onto them by well-wishers. I noticed many such messages when I was at Nine Elms shed sketching for my painting, 'Last Hours at Nine Elms'. On the cylinder covers of 73115 someone had chalked, 'For sale, 7/6 and 3,000 green stamps'. Other engines had similar messages: 'Goodbye, old friend', 'Steam forever', and many and varied references to Dr Beeching, most of which were so impolite as to bear no repetition here. I remember one particularly humorous message which I saw chalked on the tender of a Black Five awaiting scrap at Stoke-on-Trent: 'This locomotive will be melted down to provide watches for retired railwaymen.' (A nice thought!) Emotions were running high indeed and there is no doubt that these last few weeks proved conclusively the unique place that the steam engine holds in the hearts of many people, arguably a more important place than any other machine.

A number of steam engines were actually put aside at this time for possible preservation and were held in store at various different places on BR. Vandalism was always a problem, particularly at Stratford, in East London. Among the engines stored there was *Britannia*, the name engine of her class. According to a report from an enthusiast, she had been 'more or less destroyed'. Because of the damage done to *Britannia*, it was suggested that *Oliver Cromwell*, another member of the class, should masquerade as the same engine. *Oliver Cromwell* subsequently became the last steam locomotive in BR's service to have a heavy overhaul in Crewe works, and she was preserved officially instead of the name engine of the class. However, *Britannia* herself was eventually purchased for preservation as well. As for the other locomotives stored at Stratford, which included *Lord Nelson, Sir Lamiel* and *Cheltenham*, apparently 'nothing that was removable or breakable was intact'. Happily the locomotives survived this treatment and, after languishing for many years in various different places, were finally restored in running order as part of the national collection.

Some of the main-line locomotives still in revenue-earning service with BR right at the end of steam were in such a run-down condition that it is a wonder that they ran at all. In one of the railway journals early in 1967, we read of the Merchant Navy Pacific, *United States Lines*, which was failed at Weymouth on 6 January, after working the 8.35am train from Waterloo with a cracked driving wheel! The mind boggles at the prospect of a locomotive of this size hurtling down the main line with fifteen coaches behind her, in this condition. It was amazing that the crack was detected at all under the layers of grime and filth which no doubt covered the engine in her last weeks of life. It is all the more incredible to imagine engines running in that condition when one considers the extraordinarily high standards of safety and maintenance now demanded from those who own steam locomotives on preserved railway lines.

History was, in a sense, repeating itself. All through the last century, there was a mania for building railways. The map of England was liberally criss-crossed with branch lines, all fighting for a market which was not always there. Several went to the same small towns in competition with each other and quickly went bankrupt. Many years later the country's network was to endure the Beeching axe, which seemed to many, as railway after railway was closed, to be an orgy of destruction. Now the locomotives were being discarded with equal haste and, realising that the steam engines were going from them almost overnight and that the flow of scrapping had become a flood, railway enthusiasts all over the country decided that they had to do something about it. In 1966 another sort of railway mania was upon us. Those were the days of starry-eyed, and, it seemed, reckless enthusiasm. There was little or no thought for the future. Locomotives weighing over 100 tons were the prize, and the fund-raising to save them consisted of selling biros and calendars. The engines just had to be saved, somehow.

To try to establish some sort of order in the chaos that seemed to be looming, the Association of Railway Preservation Societies stepped in to act as an umbrella organisation for all the enthusiasts. Capt Peter Manisty, recently retired from the Royal Navy, had now become the driving force behind the movement and was master-minding the whole gigantic exercise like a military operation. No doubt his background gave him the expertise so desperately needed to deal with a crowd of head-strong individuals, many of whom needed their heads banging together. He certainly banged plenty of heads together in those early days and a lot of us began to grow up.

It was essential to bring some credibility and sense of responsibility into the situation and to co-ordinate this great buying spree. BR bore the brunt of it, and they showed quite remarkable tolerance and patience with us all—after all, they were trying to run a railway. At the same time, however, they were receiving hundreds of letters from all sorts of people of all ages from all over the country: 'How much would it cost me to buy a Britannia Pacific?'; 'I've only managed to raise £48 15s, but is this enough for a deposit on a Duchess?' No wonder there were certain people in BR who longed for the end of steam—to them, it all seemed completely crazy, like a lot of children running wild in a toy shop.

In some cases the situation verged on anarchy. One particular locomotive, A2/3 Pacific *Blue Peter*, which was the last of her class to be withdrawn, was the cause of a minor battle between the preservationists. While the locomotive awaited her fate on a scrap line in Scotland, BR, to their very great credit, watched patiently from the side-lines, as two societies, both trying to raise funds to save the engine, refused to speak to each other. Both societies were appealing for funds, sometimes by methods which were only just on the right side of the law. Advertisements were being taken out in *Railway Magazine* and *Railway World* which could not always be paid for, and many well-meaning people were giving money to one or other of the two groups. I had tentatively offered some small financial assistance to one of the societies but, even after writing five times, had no form of acknowledgement whatever to my letters. On threatening once and for all to withdraw my offer, I was telephoned at 1.30am by the so-called secretary of this particular group, who didn't seem to realise that some people like to go to sleep between the hours of midnight and six o'clock in the morning. Eventually, after a great deal of bad feeling had been generated, the ARPS persuaded the two groups to see sense and join forces. The money was pooled and the locomotive was eventually saved. That kind of thing was the worst side of locomotive preservation.

The faith of some people was phenomenal. Few, I believe, had any idea of the full implications of what they were trying to do. At the worst, some of the engines we were trying to save were worn out; at the best, some were almost brand new. Looking back to those momentous days the question must be asked: if we had known the full implications of what we were doing, would we still have acted as we did? I believe that we would have, because I also believe that one of the great national characteristics of the British is a determination to fight for what they believe in. There are many people in this country (I am happy to be regarded as one of them) who are labelled as eccentric, or just plain crazy, just because they believe in fighting bureaucracy or apathy, or both, to save something of our historic past, whatever the odds against it.

It was now the beginning of 1967 and nearly the end for steam in the South. I was still making visits to Guildford and Nine Elms sheds whenever the opportunity arose. In those last weeks I was becoming even more closely involved with the groups and individuals who were each trying to save particular locomotives. At Nine Elms I met people who had decided to try to raise funds to save a Merchant Navy Pacific. The amount required, £2,100, seemed to be an impossible target to reach—it represented a very large number of biros and calendars! They had chosen 35028, *Clan Line*, and, although on the withdrawal list, she was still in service at Nine Elms. The inevitable happened. I have an impulsive nature and I began to dream. Things moved very fast after that. I simply had to have my very own steam engine. I had stars in my eyes. If problems occurred to me, I pushed them to the back of my mind. I hardly gave a thought to where I would put the locomotive when I bought it, how I would look after it when I got it there, or the money.

75029 — driving wheel

Having made this rather momentous decision, I had to think about which engine I would buy. There were not many classes left by then. I didn't mind what region the engine belonged to, or whether it was built at Swindon, Crewe or Brighton. The problem now was that I wanted to buy every engine I looked at. It only made matters worse when I thumbed through my many railway books full of photographs of locomotives. There was one particular engine—I saw her at Crewe South shed when I was doing my mad whirl around the country taking photographs. She was the Stanier Black Five with a double chimney, No 44767, with the Stephenson Link Motion. She was in steam when I saw her. BR in their infinite wisdom had even decided to give her a re-tube, though they must have known that she only had a few months of service to go before withdrawal. But then I finally came to a decision—I would buy a 75XXX. There were still a number of the class left in service, and I now had to decide which one was the best.

The problem was made more difficult by a footplate trip I now had. I was sketching in Guildford shed one morning when one of my driver chums came up to me and told me that he was taking a train, in the early hours of the following morning, from Guildford down to Portsmouth Harbour, steam-hauled. He asked me if I would like to come. 'It'll be bloody early—you'll have to be on Guildford station at 4.30.' I think it shook him rigid when I turned up—I had never got up at that hour before, even for steam engines. At about 5am, the train arrived in Guildford station. It was diesel-hauled, and had come overnight from Hull. It was a holiday special and, for some strange reason, steam was to take it on to Portsmouth Harbour. An Eastleigh engine, 75074, was the loco. Although, like so many other members of her class, she only had a few weeks to go before withdrawal, she had actually been cleaned and was in excellent external condition. We had a marvellous ride down to Portsmouth Harbour, through Godalming station. Indeed, that train was the last steam-hauled special on that line before the end of steam. Should I buy 75074? I went down to Eastleigh and talked to the shed staff who knew '74. They advised me against her—she was in poor mechanical order. She would have to go to scrap unless I or somebody else bought her. She went for scrap.

One of my chums in Guildford shed said: 'Why don't you go for 75029? She's a fine loco—thin tyres but a bloody good boiler. I knew her well at one time, although I don't know where she is now.' I soon found out. She was at Wrexham, which had been on the list of sheds that I intended to visit with my camera, but I had never managed to get there. Now I had an extra reason for going. I arrived at the shed and, once again, found the usual mixture of Standards, Black Fives and 8Fs, and an

No 75029 seen here in 1955 in BR service and as originally built (in 1954) with her single chimney. She is running between Worcester and Evesham *(Photo R. J. Blenkinsop)*

assortment of tank engines. Standing on her own in front of the shed was an engine even dirtier than all the others, but unmistakably a Standard Class 4. Her smoke-box door number was missing. It had probably been stolen. The number, which I could just discern on her cab side, was 75029.

I drove home from Wrexham deep in thought. I was about to buy 112 tons 3 cwt of engine. Was I completely crazy? By the time I arrived home I had already begun seriously to doubt the sanity of it all. I knew absolutely nothing about things mechanical and now I was about to purchase over 100 tons of machinery. As I reflected on the enormous bulk of the steam engine that I was about to buy, I wondered how that absurd 3 cwt had crept into the statistics I had been given. Fill up a locomotive with water and coal and put the whole thing on a weighbridge, of course, but how do you tell precisely how much coal to heap into the tender? These were frivolous thoughts, perhaps a bit of escapism from the gravity of what I was undertaking. Having decided on 75029, the occasional mention of my plans began to appear in the railway press. As a result of this, I immediately started receiving verbal or written comments from apparent railway enthusiasts who disapproved of how I was going to spend my own money. A few of these obviously believed that unless an engine was built at Swindon for the Great Western Railway before 1948, it didn't exist. One person wrote and asked me why I was not going to buy a 'proper' engine, whatever that meant. One letter was even stronger: 'What on earth do you want to buy one of those ghastly modern things for?'

I liked the sturdy and workmanlike appearance of the Standard Class 4s. A few of the class were built with double chimneys and this, I think, improved their appearance. (I was not particularly interested whether it made them more efficient.) All the Standard classes were designed to be as simple as possible to maintain, and also to facilitate the interchange of parts and fittings between the various classes. However, things never really worked out like that, and many of the engines seemed to be anything but standard. I knew that, some time after 75029 was built in 1954, she was given the locally designed Western Region double chimney, which I thought hideous, though I liked the Southern Region one. For reasons best known to British Railways, the Western Region version was 4in taller.

After I had actually paid for 75029 and she was mine, she was up at Crewe in the old locomotive shed, and I asked the local staff if they would possibly change the chimney. I don't think that they had very much to do at the end of steam, and they did the job, willingly and free of charge. I found out afterwards to my embarrassment that she had already had a Southern chimney fitted earlier in her life and they were simply changing one for another that was identical! However, no one seemed to mind too

No 75029 in 1957, now seen with her hideous Swindon-designed double chimney, which was later replaced with one 4in shorter, designed at Eastleigh (and they called them Standard locomotives!) (*Photo C. Wheeler*)

much. The odd thing was that I had not spotted when I first saw the locomotive that the change had already been made—I can only suppose that I was too excited to notice.

I was by now in the final stages of painting for my New York exhibition of wildlife pictures, but once I had decided to buy my own steam engine, there was an even greater incentive to keep going back to Guildford shed—spare parts! Back in the familiar surroundings of the shed, any doubts about what I was doing were immediately dispelled. I was lucky, for I was in at the beginning. The British Railways stores were full, as there were still plenty of Standard locomotives left on the various sheds in the South. Norman Coe, the shed master, and his staff, could not possibly have helped me more. They drew up a list of spares which they considered were most needed and I put in my official application to the Southern Region 'scrap sales' people at Waterloo. The list was a long one, but the whole lot only cost £34. I was certainly getting good value for money, particularly as quite a few extra bits and pieces were thrown in for good measure. I seem to remember that, in those days, there was one splendid regulation that stated that no single item of equipment or material could be purchased from BR for less than sixpence. I virtually cleared Guildford shed of all the shed furniture, which was almost certainly going to be burned when the shed finally closed. Since 1967 all the Shepherd family have sat at their breakfast table on renovated benches out of the drivers' mess room at Guildford shed. I bought ten, and the whole lot cost me 5s. We cleaned all the locomotive oil off them and gave them a repaint, and my wife has added padded seats—they now make very attractive and sturdy items of furniture with years of life ahead of them (and would probably cost a small fortune if purchased in Selfridges!)

I also raided Salisbury shed. I borrowed a large, covered furniture van, but could not get near enough to the shed itself; so, for a whole afternoon, the shed steam crane was lowering trestles, benches, tables, wheelbarrows, and just about everything else that we could find, over the shed wall into the van below. Most of that cost me nothing at all. (The lovely old Salisbury shed steam crane was bought for preservation by someone else!)

I suppose that, with the passage of time, one's memory does tend to become slightly clouded. In any case, it is all past history now, and most of the story of what went on behind the scenes in those days when we were dealing with our friends in BR can surely be told now. I do remember that we were terribly good at 'cadging' and generally acquiring. I cannot speak for others, but my feeling was that we were all in this crazy thing together, to desperately try to save something of our steam-railway heritage. We had to grab what we could when we could. We all know about things 'falling off the backs of lorries'—the local people in BR were marvellous, and many lorries were tipped up for us. Who were we to say no?

There were plenty of 'gift horses' in Guildford shed, certainly. In those final days when I used to dash over to the shed to do some sketching, my departure was more often than not delayed by members of the shed staff who, having the future of 75029 at heart as much as her new owner, would run after me with various bits and pieces: 'Wait a minute, you haven't got one of these', and another lovely piece of brass would be loaded into the back of my car (and I had not even actually purchased the engine yet).

I remember being telephoned from Guildford shed on the very last day of steam operations in the South. It was the evening of Sunday 8 July. This was the moment, perhaps more than any other, when I was tempted to step outside the law altogether. The voice on the other end of the phone said: 'The shed's closing tonight. There will be no one on night duty except me. BR is coming to start the inventory on Tuesday. Do you want to come?' I drove over at about 10.30pm. All was by now like the grave. The engines were dead and cold, awaiting their fate. There was no longer that lovely warm smell of oil and steam. The place was full of ghosts.

There was only a glimmer of light from the stores. I went in. There, in front of me, were enough spares for fifty locomotives, a glittering fortune in brass and spare parts. I sat with Fred drinking tea. My empty Land Rover was outside. No, I resisted the temptation to take anything and of course I was right. We did all sorts of small fiddles in those days—tit-for-tat favours with railwaymen achieved miracles—but there was always a very thin dividing line between outright theft and acquiring things the way that we were doing it. I think that most of us in those days who were trying to save steam engines knew that dividing line, and I would like to feel that none of us stepped over it. It would have only taken one wrong move, conviction in a court of law, and the whole movement would have been discredited. I left empty-handed, but I enjoyed my cup of tea and the early-morning natter about steam engines.

Sunlight and shadow - Guildford shed

4

Two telephone calls and our first home

My elephant paintings enabled me to buy my steam engines and Christ found them their first home. I mean that with no irreverence.

It was in 1964 that I undertook probably the most challenging painting commission of my career. The army chaplains asked me if I would paint a picture to be a memorial to all the regiments that had been stationed at Bordon Camp, a large REME depot between Petersfield and Farnham, in Surrey. I vaguely remember reading somewhere that the army had some sort of railway at a place called Longmoor, which was nearby. Whilst I was researching this immensely exciting and rewarding commission, an 8ft × 15ft portrait of Christ to hang behind the altar of St George's Church, Bordon, I became friends with an army officer who happened to be a railway enthusiast and was based at Longmoor Camp. We inevitably talked steam locomotives and, in the course of conversation, I mentioned that I was proposing to purchase a Standard Class 4 and that I had nowhere to put it.

'Do you think that there is a chance that I could bring my locomotive to Longmoor?' I asked. There's nothing like jumping in with both feet! The reaction was as favourable as it was unexpected: 'Well, I suppose it might be OK, although she is a bit big, isn't she? However, I imagine we could possibly hide her away somewhere as the system is fairly extensive.' I seem to remember the conversation going something like that anyway.

I am the sort of person who acts on impulse and then worries afterwards. Now that it seemed that I had a home for my engine, I would act. I picked up the telephone and spoke to Bob McMurdie who, at that time, was the BR Divisional Motive Power Superintendent at Stoke-on-Trent. 'Bob, I want to buy an engine.' There was a silence that seemed to last for several minutes. 'Good God, you must be bloody mad; where on earth are you going to put it?' 'Oh, that's no problem,' I answered, 'the army have said that they will give me a home at Longmoor.'

I was 'jumping the gun' a bit here. The army, first of all, had said no such thing, not officially anyway. Then there were little matters like how much it was going to cost me to buy the engine, and how I was going to get it down to Longmoor, assuming that the army gave me official permission. As my departure for the New York exhibition was imminent, I decided to shelve the whole thing until I returned; rather, I more or less shelved it, for I now began to get other ideas as well.

During the last months of steam, when I had been dashing around sketching and photographing every engine that I saw that excited me, I had fallen in love completely with the Standard 9s (there were still plenty of those around). In fact, I had come to the conclusion that the 9Fs with double chimneys were the most imposing of all the locomotives remaining on BR. But I had to be sensible—I couldn't possibly buy one of them, they were too big.

All the paintings in my New York exhibition sold out in the first half-hour. I came home and, before I realised what I was doing, I had picked up the telephone: 'Bob, I want a Standard 9F as well!' The silence on the other end of the 'phone was even longer this time. Quite clearly Bob had by now decided that I was living in a fantasy world, but he was much too nice to say so. He also realised that I had determination. 'How on earth are you going to cope with two?' That was a reasonable question to ask, but the problem was not really his. It was mine. It did not seem to have occurred to me that it might be harder to hide nearly 120ft of locomotive on army property than just 60ft.

Meanwhile, at Nine Elms, the situation was getting more complicated by the minute. Somehow the feeling had got around that I was establishing rather a good rapport with the army. I was sketching in the shed one day when I met the lads who had decided to buy *Clan Line*. (They must have sold a tremendous number of biros and calendars.) They had nowhere to put her. One of their team had heard on the railway grapevine that I was going to purchase 75029 and that I had apparently found a home for her on the army railway. 'Do you think that you could ask that army friend of yours if we could hide *Clan Line* down on the military railway as well?' he asked. I went back to see my colonel friend. Surely we could hide her somewhere on the system with 75029? (I really was a bit naïve in those days.) Furthermore, I did not mention that I was thinking of buying another massive locomotive myself. Amazingly, he more or less said 'yes' to *Clan Line*.

A week or so later I was back at Nine Elms sketching, and the same thing happened all over again. A number of the shed staff at Nine Elms had decided to buy their own locomotive, No 34023, the Bulleid Pacific, *Blackmore Vale*. 'How about asking the army if they could find a home for *Blackmore Vale* too?' On the same day, the two people who had purchased the Ivatt tank engine, No 41298, asked me the same question. So it was back to the Colonel, who responded: 'You know, this really is getting rather out of hand. The War Office are bound to find out if we end up with more privately owned ex-BR engines on the Longmoor Military Railway than the army has themselves. There really won't be any more, will there?' I realised that I would have to come clean. 'Well, actually, I have just bought another locomotive myself, a Standard 9F.'

I don't know exactly what went on behind the scenes after that, but I do know that we achieved something that had never happened before. We were a group of private individuals dumping our enormous steam locomotives on military property, and it seemed that the red tape simply did not exist. We never filled up a single form, and the whole situation seemed a bit unreal, but how wonderfully British!

I have mentioned before that I know nothing about the mechanical workings of a steam locomotive and am not particularly interested in this side of things. However, it made sense even to me to get locomotives which were in good running order. I did not want to be palmed off with junk fit for the scrapyard. I knew 75029 was a good engine because I had been told so by my friends in BR. When I telephoned Bob and asked for a Standard 9 as well, I asked him for a 'good one'; after all, there were still dozens to choose from which would otherwise be thrown away. 'Well, David, you're in luck. We have got a good one—92203 is in marvellous mechanical order. She's just had an overhaul and been painted especially for a special run. She's just hauled the last steam-hauled iron-ore train from Liverpool docks to the Shotton iron and steel works. We've got plenty of 9Fs, so I suppose you can have her. We'll take her out of service especially for you.' Bob was true to his word—she was withdrawn a few days later.

The average life of a steam locomotive, if properly maintained, is probably at least forty years. 92203 was just eight years old when I bought her. She cost just under £40,000 to build, at Swindon, in 1959. Now, just eight years later, I was getting her for £3,000. 75029 was only a few years older, having been built at Swindon in 1954. Two almost new steam engines in full working order were mine for £5,200. Then, and for several months afterwards, BR threw in quite an amount of spares for good measure; so, all in all, it didn't seem a bad deal!

The time now arrived actually to buy the engines. Bob would do anything that he possibly could to help me, but he was not in a position to negotiate the sale. This had to be done through the scrap sales controller of British Railways, at Derby. The ARPS (Association of Railway Preservation Societies) was now to prove its worth. By this time, BR were being deluged with letters from people trying to buy steam engines with money that they didn't have. Not unreasonably, therefore, BR insisted on dealing with all potential purchasers through the ARPS, and this organisation was now to do several big package deals with Derby. One involved a total sum of £21,125, which came from a large number of societies and private individuals. The list of locomotives purchased in this deal included my own two, as well as *Clan Line*, *Blackmore Vale*, 41298, a USA tank engine, a Jinty, a J27, and several other engines and coaches.

65

In retrospect, we were getting a great deal of hardware for what now seems to be an absurdly low price. *Clan Line* cost just £2,100, and *Blackmore Vale* substantially less.

There were at this time a few people in BR who seemed to think that private individuals who were going to buy steam engines and save them for posterity should pay more than the scrap value. I could never understand this attitude—if we hadn't bought the engines, the scrap merchants would have done so. The scrap sales controller at Derby, however, was in sympathy with what we were trying to do. Because the ARPS had brought some sort of order out of the potential chaos and had established a very good reputation with BR, most of us did in fact get a fair deal. In any case, Bob and my other senior friends in BR assured me that there was nothing to worry about: 'Never mind, David, if you do have to pay over the odds, we will get you at least that value, and more, in spares out of the stores.' (Lots of people in BR certainly did just that, for me and many other enthusiasts who were buying steam engines.) If there were a few people in BR who regarded us with not only some amazement but also some suspicion, it is hard to blame them. Up until this time, Alan Pegler was almost the only person who had bought a steam engine—he had blazed the trail for all of us when, in 1963, he purchased 4472, *Flying Scotsman*. Now it must have seemed to BR that everybody was going mad.

Both locomotives were now my property. Bob told me that 75029 would be hauled over to Crewe South locomotive depot for me to 'collect', whatever that meant. He told me that 92203 would join her as soon as possible. However, I could wait no longer to see my own engine; so, in the most eager anticipation, I drove up to Crewe. It was a miserable, damp, cold evening and nearly dark as I walked into the almost derelict steam shed. The only other privately owned steam locomotive there was the A4 Pacific, *Sir Nigel Gresley*, also awaiting collection by her new owners.

When I saw 75029 in the gloom of the shed she looked twice as big as when I had first seen her at Wrexham a few weeks earlier. I broke out into a cold sweat. What on earth was I doing playing around with these things? And what I saw in front of me was only half the problem! I had no money left, only a slightly uncertain offer of a home a very long way away and a note from BR which stated, in effect, that I must move my engine as soon as possible. Furthermore, the eviction order told me that they were not prepared to tow either of my locomotives anywhere on the system.

Early in November Bob telephoned me to tell me that 92203 had joined 75029 at Crewe. I returned to the now familiar steam shed. Steam locomotives seemed to be lying around everywhere. Many were in the dump, looking forlorn and neglected. A number were in steam and a few had been cleaned. These stood out like diamonds in a pile of ashes. In those final months a number of the locomotives were kept in surprisingly good external condition by a few of the more dedicated BR staff in the various depots. Right at the end of steam, there was still a deep sense of pride among the fitters. I say this, because there was very little encouragement from above—I heard one young fitter being told not to bother to do a decent job as the engine was going for scrap in a matter of weeks anyway. However, pride dies hard amongst true railwaymen and many of them were determined that the locomotives in their care would go to the scrapyards with at least some dignity.

I walked down the line of locomotives alongside the shed. Here was a Black Five shining in a new coat of paint with a gleaming red buffer beam. She had just had an overhaul. It would certainly be her last. Nearby was a Stanier 8F in absolutely appalling external condition. She was totally anonymous. Her smoke-box number-plate had been removed, probably stolen, and her cabside numbers had long since disappeared under layers of muck. On her smoke-box door someone had painted two large eyes weeping tears at her impending doom. With my heart beating ever faster in anticipation, tempered by not a little anxiety, I walked to the end of the shed. Suddenly, there she was, standing all alone, gleaming in a new coat of black paint. She looked enormous, and I could hardly believe that she was mine. She had been 'titivated up'. It was the practice in those days to enhance the appearance of some of the steam engines by picking out in white paint such fittings as smoke-box door hinges, lamp brackets and other attachments on the side of the locomotive. She had received this treatment for her run from Liverpool docks, and although it did not really improve her in my eyes, I suppose it did smarten her up a bit. Imagine my feelings when I saw one more thing—she was in steam, especially for me!

There was another surprise for me. BR evidently knew that I was coming to view my purchase for the first time, so they decided to lay on a small handing-over ceremony. George Dow of the London Midland Region was there, with the senior BR staff from Crewe, as well as Sir Richard Summers of the Shotton iron and steel works. A photograph of the handing-over ceremony appeared in many of the local newspapers the following morning, with David Shepherd looking a great deal younger than he does today. (I later discovered, quite by chance, that my good friend Terence Cuneo had painted a portrait of 'my' engine. The painting, commissioned by the iron and steel company, portrayed Sir Richard in the driving seat on the last ceremonial run. I have a fine reproduction of it.)

News of anything interesting spreads like a bush fire within the railway fraternity, and within days of my purchasing 75029 and 92203 everyone seemed to know about it. In those early days of railway preservation, before everybody seemed to be buying an engine, I suppose it was quite an event for one man to buy two engines. I was immediately delighted and surprised by the fact that people now began to send me photographs that

November 1968. I walked round the corner of Crewe shed, quaking at the knees at the thought of what I had just bought, and came face to face with my very own 140 ton steam locomotive for the first time—and BR had 'lit her up' specially for me!

News spread fast within the railway fraternity that I had bought 75029 and 92203. A particularly pleasant consequence of this was that I began to receive photographs of my two engines earlier in their lives. This one of 92203 was taken in April 1959 when she was brand new out of Swindon works (*Photo C. P. R. Shaw*)

(*opposite*) A very happy David Shepherd formally takes possession of 92203 in a small handing-over ceremony, with George Dow of the London Midland Region (centre), and Sir Richard Summers of Shotton iron and steel works

they had taken of my two engines during their short working lives with BR. It's quite remarkable that so many pictures were taken of these two locomotives, bearing in mind, of course, that when the photographs were taken, there was no hint that the engines might be saved. One photograph is extra special. Someone quite unknown to me sent me a small slightly blurred photo of Swindon engineering works. He had spotted two brand new locomotives which had just been outshopped from the works and which were waiting to be accepted for service. Gleaming in their shining new paintwork, one of the engines was a Standard 9F. The photograph clearly shows the number on the cabside of the 9F. It is 92203.

Although the Standard 9s were designed primarily as freight locomotives, they did excellent service hauling express passenger trains in many different parts of the country. Particularly appropriately, 92203 spent some considerable time working, very successfully, on the Somerset & Dorset Joint Railway, which crossed the East Somerset Railway just 3 miles from Cranmore. I have been sent several photographs of 92203 during this period of her life, when she was hauling heavy passenger trains up and down the severe gradients of that much loved and late lamented railway.

A particularly interesting photograph of 92203 shows her at Swindon shed. She is standing next to *Cookham Manor*, which was also purchased, in the early days, for private preservation. It is a happy coincidence that

92203 had spent some time hauling express passenger trains on the Somerset & Dorset Joint Railway, passing—by a strange coincidence—very close to Cranmore (*Photo Ivo Peters*)

Still in service with BR, this picture shows 92203 at Swindon shed, with alongside, by happy coincidence, another engine that would later be saved from the scrap merchant, *Cookham Manor* (*Photo Mike Pope*)

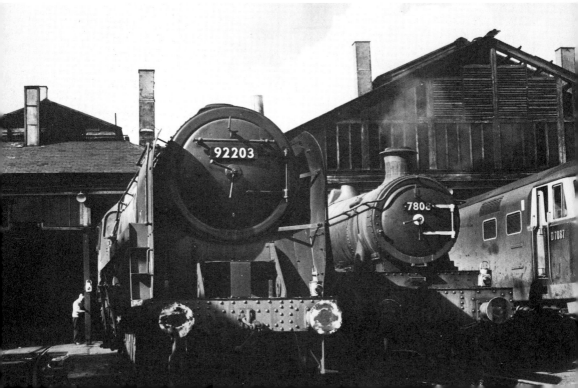

these locomotives happened to be photographed alongside each other during their working lives with BR. Another picture shows 92203 in a very sorry state at Tyseley in Birmingham, and still another in a still worse state at Banbury, with her front bogie wheels removed altogether. 75029 worked on the Cambrian Coast in North Wales for some time and I have a number of superb photographs of her in that beautiful part of the world. Another picture shows her with her experimental and not very attractive Western-designed double chimney. These photographs of my two locomotives before I purchased them form a valuable and interesting collection for my archives, and I am happy to say that people are still sending me pictures.

So it seemed that a collection of privately owned steam engines was now to find a home on the army railway at Longmoor, provided that we could get them there. As I mentioned earlier, BR had told me that they were not prepared to tow my engines anywhere on their system. This seemed to me to be totally illogical—if one owns a steam engine, then surely the best way to move it from one point to another is on a railway line. Furthermore, I would have been a paying customer, and my locomotives would presumably have been treated as normal freight; I was not asking for favours. It seemed that BR did not want the job. Was I seriously to put my two purchases on low-loaders and go down the M1, clogging up every town and village between Crewe and Longmoor with traffic jams? It seemed so.

Happily I have had only a few battles with bureaucracy over the years; one of them was about to begin. It was a long one, lasting nine months, and it was a stupid one, fatuous and unnecessary; but I was determined that my two steam engines would steam down on their own through the Midlands to London, and then on to the Southern Region to Longmoor. I have some interesting newspaper headlines about the fight which, at times, became quite acrimonious: 'Artist fights for the dignity of number 92203' and 'Mr Shepherd gets steam up over British Rail'. (Such puns make me wonder whether the standards of journalism will ever improve on some local newspapers!) After six months, the Midland Region at last relented, just a little. They informed me that my two locomotives would not have to go down the M1 motorway. BR was prepared to tow them down to London, by diesel. I suppose that I could have accepted this, but it seemed to be quite ridiculous. My locomotives were in perfect mechanical order and quite capable of steaming their way down. After all, there was still a great deal of steam around in the Midlands anyway. And it would surely be a marvellous public relations exercise for BR to allow my two

(*overleaf*) No 75029 in 1967, in her last weeks of BR ownership (and this time with her proper chimney), working the Cambrian Coast line in North Wales (*Photo Tim Stephens*)

engines to make the journey to London on their own. Everyone would love BR!

After more gentle persuasion on my part, I was told that my two engines could be in steam, but that they would still have to have a diesel engine in front of them. I wrote again to the London Midland Region. This time I pointed out that the interest from the media, both national and local, and also among the very large railway fraternity throughout the country, was mounting. I suggested that the sight of two almost new steam locomotives, in steam, apparently 'pushing' a BR diesel all the way down through the Midlands to London would not show up BR in a particularly good light in the eyes of many hundreds, if not thousands, of railway enthusiasts, not to mention the media! This suggestion seemed to do the trick. The Midland Region relented. I had won—or had I? The Southern Region said that in no way were they going to have steam engines in steam on their metals, however short the mileage!

Finally, as a last resort, I wrote to the chairman of BR himself, and that appeared to work. I was told that 75029 and 92203 would not have to have a diesel in front of them on their journey south. I was, furthermore, told that I could ride on the footplate of whichever engine I chose. (I chose them both!) Common sense had won the day.

The rest of the arrangements went relatively smoothly. The date was fixed—the great journey was to take place on the weekend of 6 April 1968. All the preparations were made at Crewe shed, where the staff gave

Another glimpse of 92203's life before she met me. Here she is, in a very sorry state, at the back of Banbury shed in 1965

6 April 1968, and the exciting journey down from Crewe to Longmoor. We stopped at
Derby for our first change of BR crews, to water the locos and to have a 'brew up'. Bob
McMurdie, then the Divisional Motive Power Superintendent at Stoke-on-Trent, had
taken his white collar off and appropriately come along for the ride as inspector. He is on
my right, and on my left is Bert Stewart. Sitting between my other BR chums is Neil
Cadman, Bert's fireman. Great men, all of them!

me every possible support. I drove up the day before and, walking through
the shed, saw my very own two steam engines. They were both in steam,
fully prepared for the journey. The coal was piled high in the two tenders,
and I was sensible enough not to ask where it came from. That Friday
night, into the early hours of the Sunday morning, was one of the most
entertaining that I have ever spent. We spent it digging holes in the coal
in both tenders and burying brass spare parts and fittings. All the staff at
Crewe understood what I was trying to do. The stores were full and who
was I to refuse the offers of material help that would keep my locomotives
running into the future?

The following morning I was up at the crack of dawn. The BR crews for
both engines were rostered and, after a short ceremony, we were off. I
was especially delighted when Bob McMurdie said that he would like to
come with me on the footplate as far as Derby. Despite the fact that a
considerable amount of steam was still found on the London Midland

Region, it was a rare, if not unprecedented, thing for one person to buy two steam engines, and there was very great interest. People were waving all the way down the lineside. We stopped at Derby to change crews. It was only a short stop, but a lot of my friends who live in the area were there to meet me on the platform and we had drinks to celebrate. With the engines now coupled together, 92203 leading, we continued our journey through to Wellingborough, where the crews changed again and the engines were watered. Paul Barnes, who had filmed me in Nine Elms shed and made the movie *The Painter and the Engines*, had accepted my invitation to ride on the footplate of 75029. We now have some fascinating and historic film of the whole event. I also have a considerable number of photographs that were sent to me by people along the lineside.

In the late afternoon of the Saturday we steamed into Cricklewood shed, where we were to be stabled overnight in preparation for the journey on the Southern Region to Liss, in Hampshire, and the rail connection with the Longmoor Military Railway. The media were there to welcome the two engines, and included BBC Television News who were covering our arrival for transmission that evening. Our reception at Cricklewood was ecstatic. The shed master was there to greet us. He had obviously been there a good many years and had witnessed with sadness the rapid decline of steam all around him in the London area. His shed was now full of diesels. He was almost as excited as I was. He leapt up onto the footplate of 92203, explaining how marvellous it was to have steam back in his depot once again, even if it was only for one night. He then turned around

<table>
<tr><td colspan="2">BRITISH RAILWAYS BOARD 24042</td></tr>
<tr><td colspan="2">British ~~Railways~~ LONDON MIDLAND Region................. 2 APR 1968</td></tr>
<tr><td colspan="2">FOOTPLATE & DRIVING COMPARTMENT PASS</td></tr>
<tr><td colspan="2">The Bearer .... *Mr D SHEPHERD*..............</td></tr>
<tr><td colspan="2" align="center">Non, B.R.B. Personnel is authorised to Ride</td></tr>
<tr><td align="center">Upon</td><td>In the driving compartment of</td></tr>
<tr><td>Main Line ⎰ Locomotives
~~Shunting~~ ⎱ *92203 & 75029*
(~~Rear cab only~~)</td><td>~~Diesel~~ ⎰ ~~Trains~~
~~Electric~~ ⎱
~~train from~~</td></tr>
<tr><td colspan="2">Between .... *CRICKLEWOOD*.............</td></tr>
<tr><td colspan="2">and .... *LISS (S.R.)*.............</td></tr>
<tr><td colspan="2">~~until~~/on .... 7 APR 1968.............</td></tr>
<tr><td colspan="2" align="center">(Delete as necessary)</td></tr>
<tr><td colspan="2">Issued for the B.R.B. by.............</td></tr>
<tr><td colspan="2" align="center">PASSENGER CLAIMS & IS OFFICER</td></tr>
<tr><td colspan="2" align="center">This pass to be shown when required and is issued subject to
the conditions printed on the other side.   B.R. 87102</td></tr>
</table>

75029 running on the main line *en route* for Longmoor (*Photo H. D. Ramsey*)

and looked back into the tender. We had come a long way. We had burned most of the coal, and many bits and pieces of brass were now fully visible. 'My godfathers, what on earth is all that?' he asked. 'You know jolly well what it is,' was the response. 'Oh, we must see what we've got,' he then said. Half an hour later, various members of the shed staff were engaged in adding more fittings to the collection.

Then the locomotive had to be coaled and, just by happy coincidence, a fully loaded coal wagon had been placed alongside my two locomotives. I did not ask questions. Within half an hour several tons of coal had been transferred into the two locomotives' tenders by many willing hands.

I have another delightful memory of those few brief hours spent at Cricklewood. When 92203 arrived, one of the fitters from Cricklewood depot climbed up onto the footplate. I was sitting in the fireman's seat in my BR overalls and engine driver's cap; my face was covered in coal dust and sweat. I obviously looked completely at home, and like a railwayman. 'Cor, this is —— exciting mate, to have bloody steam locomotives back in the old place again!' 'Yes, it is rather super isn't it. I own both of them.' His face lit up in utter astonishment: 'Blimey mate, you're a bleedin' gentleman!' That must have been one of the nicest remarks that has ever been made to me. I suppose that he expected the owner of two locomotives to be wearing a suit. Far more important to me than trying to dress up was the fact that I was among my true friends, the railwaymen, and it is to my great delight that I have kept in touch with so many.

Off we went the following morning on to the Southern Region, steaming through Hounslow, Staines, Virginia Water, and on to the Portsmouth line to Liss. There were more people than ever alongside the line, and in many places cars lined the road beside it. It seemed that half of the South of England was *en fête*. Unlike on the Midland Region, here steam had passed into history the previous July. Now it was back again, if only for a few hours. The public certainly made the most of it. We only had a few minutes in Hounslow station but the crowds clamoured around the engines. Shortly afterwards I was sent an article written for his local magazine by a schoolboy who had savoured those few exciting moments on the platform. Further down the line the railway passed a graveyard, and I remember seeing a lady laying flowers on a very fresh grave. When she heard the whistle of 75029 her flowers were abandoned and she ran excitedly to the fence to give us a wave. That is probably the greatest compliment that 75029 is ever likely to be paid.

Immediately after my two locomotives arrived at Longmoor, the army allowed 92203 to run some impromptu specials from Liss to Longmoor. Here she is, running over the bridge spanning the yard—'our' Nissen hut is just round the corner on the left (*Photo Soldier Magazine*)

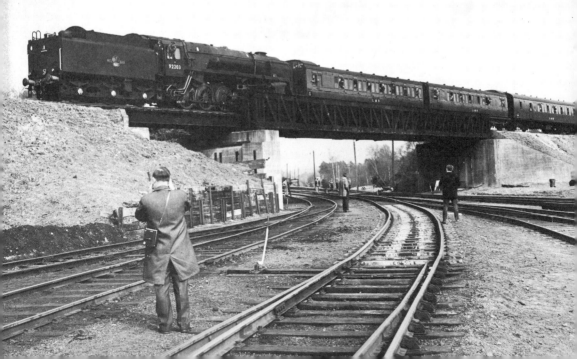

Arrival at Longmoor Downs station—my two locomotives reach their new home at last (Sunday 7 April 1968). With me in the photograph are my four daughters, my mother (I shudder to see her leopard skin handbag, given my more recent association with wildlife conservation!), my wife and Gen Errol Lonsdale. This must have been the first time that a privately owned ex-BR steam locomotive had ever carried a general's two-star plate! (*Photo Edward Griffith*)

My two locomotives were now steaming 10 minutes apart from each other. There were some moments when my hair stood on end. We were held at several signal checks and I saw camera-laden enthusiasts clambering through fences on to BR property, and squatting down between the live rails to photograph! The locomotives passed through Guildford station, which can seldom have been so crowded on a Sunday. A few minutes later it was particularly pleasant for me to have them steam through my own home town of Godalming, in Surrey. All my family and a huge number of my friends crowded on to the platform as we stopped for a brief unofficial moment of celebration. We were not supposed to stop, but I knew the signalman in the nearest box!

With the crowds along the lineside increasing in number as we approached our destination, the locomotives finally arrived at Liss on the

Southern Region to start their new life on the Longmoor Military Railway. They were given a warm welcome by both the military authorities and the public. The press were once again out in force. Some of the more sensible headlines read: 'A royal welcome to steam locos' and 'Locomotives steam to new Liphook home'. There were also the usual awful clichés in the local newspapers, including 'David Shepherd gets chuffed'—that really was the worst one!

The gates which divided the Southern Region of BR from the Longmoor Military Railway were opened up and 75029 and 92203 steamed slowly through. Their arrival had been organised like a military operation, with typical army efficiency and precision. However, it was much more than just a rather unusual military exercise—the interest from the general public in the surrounding area was enormous and over 200 cars were accommodated on the barrack square at Longmoor Camp itself. It was estimated that nearly 500 people witnessed the journey up the line into Longmoor Downs station on that Sunday afternoon. When we arrived at the station, the fire in 75029, which was now past its best, was dropped. There was still plenty of energy left in 92203. Gen Errol Lonsdale, who was then Transport Officer in Chief at the War Office, and who was there to see us arrive, suggested that four army coaches be put behind the locomotive, and we made two return trips down to Liss for all the people who had come to witness the great event. The military authorities did everything they possibly could to make sure that everybody enjoyed themselves.

In Longmoor Downs station, 92203 posed for photographers and one of the happiest shots in my collection is of my four daughters, my mother, my wife and Gen Lonsdale standing in front of 92203. There is a particularly interesting point about that photograph. Gen Lonsdale asked his driver to take the two-star 'plate' off the front of his staff car, and it was put on one of the lamp brackets of 92203's smoke-box door. This was surely the first (and probably only!) time that a privately owned, ex-BR, steam engine had had a general's two-star plate on the front. It was a gesture typical of Gen Lonsdale, and it was the beginning of a very long and happy association with a man who was to do much to help our cause at Longmoor over the next months.

5

Longmoor

The Longmoor Military Railway, in 1968, was a mere shadow of its former self, and was slowly being run down. Nevertheless, the army still had two of their own steam locomotives in working order. These were the 2-10-0 No 600, *Gordon*, and an Austerity saddle tank, No 196. In the scrap line, when we arrived, there were five more Austerities and the magnificent oil-fired No 601, *Kitchener*. All these were cut up for scrap shortly after we arrived. We had seen it all before, on BR. Now we were seeing it all over again.

A few months after my own two steam engines arrived at Longmoor, *Clan Line, Blackmore Vale* and 41298 were towed by diesel down the main line from Nine Elms to Liss, and into the military railway. There could have been problems from the moment of arrival of the rescued locomotives. The Merchant Navy Society, which owned *Clan Line*, and the group who had purchased *Blackmore Vale* consisted of a considerable number of individual, and individualistic, railway enthusiasts. Nevertheless, everything went marvellously smoothly, and we in turn had the fullest possible co-operation from the military people on the camp. We were told where we could go and where we could not. The line from Longmoor down to Liss crossed a bridge beside a road, just after leaving Longmoor Downs station. On one side of the bridge was the military complex of the camp itself, with its various railway workshops and sheds. On the other side, was an area surplus to army requirements. This was to be the engines' new home.

Steam locomotive enthusiasts make use of the most meagre resources, having an amazing ability to make the best of what they have. Just below the bridge was a crumbling and rusty old Nissen hut. This had a railway line running into it, although the line had obviously not been used for years and was only just visible in places above the sand. We were told that we could use it if it was of any value to us. Whilst it had clearly never been designed to take an engine the size of *Clan Line*, we decided, after some investigation, that we might just squeeze her in. After pacing out the length of the building we persuaded ourselves that there might even be a chance of getting 41298 in there as well.

We worked wonders with that hut. The tin doors were straightened out and rehung, the rubbish of years of neglect was cleared out, the worst holes in the roof were patched up and, inch by inch, 41298 and *Clan Line* were carefully shunted towards the shed. First 41298 was tucked up at the back against the back wall. Then it was *Clan Line*'s turn. With only inches to spare above her chimney, and with various bits of fir tree clinging to her sides after her passage through the forest of vegetation which was rapidly claiming the site, she was inside.

In what seemed to be no time at all, the Merchant Navy Society had turned the old hut into a most sophisticated workshop, a miniature Swindon works. The most astonishing collection of equipment, tools, work benches and all the other paraphernalia which was so badly needed was installed inside. The Merchant Navy people had acquired all this from BR just as I had, either for nothing, or for a knock-down price. For a few weeks *Blackmore Vale* languished outside the Nissen hut under tarpaulins. However, before long she was on the other side of the bridge, in the area which the army still used for their own purposes, and where we were told we mustn't go. She was inside the army's own steam shed, together with 196 and *Gordon*! The army were certainly being wonderful to us—we could hardly believe our luck.

Our involvement at Longmoor grew apace. Electricity over our side of the bridge had long since been cut off, but we bought a generator, and light and power were soon restored to the Nissen-hut workshop. Over the other side of the bridge, the owners of *Blackmore Vale* were lucky. They had electricity, inspection pits and all the other facilities of a steam running shed. The only problem was that occasionally, after heavy

Our old Nissen hut at Longmoor — never designed for Merchant Navy Pacifics, 'Clan Line' just squeezes in with inches to spare! ———-.

rainfall, the inspection pit filled with flood water; but who were they to complain?

After the arrival of our assorted collection of steam engines, the army authorities finally told us, in the nicest possible way, that it was now a question of 'full up—absolutely no more'. But they (and I) had not reckoned with Barry. Barry had met me in the very early days and had supported me in all my activities. He had just bought a lovely little Andrew Barclay saddle tank, *Lord Fisher*, from somewhere near Southampton. The inevitable happened: 'Do you think that there is a chance that they could take one more loco?' Back I went once more to the Colonel. I suggested that, surely, the best rules were meant to be bent sometimes. Furthermore, *Lord Fisher* was only a tiny engine, and could be hidden under *Clan Line*, so that nobody would find out. This frivolous approach seemed to work. She was given a home. Nevertheless, I was told very firmly that she really had to be the final locomotive to join our collection. The doors were now closed.

Relations with the army became so good that within a matter of months several army personnel were helping us in our various tasks of restoration and giving up their weekends to do so. We were allowed the most amazing amount of freedom bearing in mind that it was a secure area with guard dogs patrolling at all times. This certainly helped us, in fact, for it protected us from theft and vandalism. During the summer, the army at Longmoor had open days, when they put the whole place on show to the public. Now that there was a collection of privately owned steam locomotives on the site, they saw that these would be an extra attraction. They co-operated in every way possible, and indeed allowed us to have our engines in steam for our own special occasions as well. The first of these was in June 1968. The Bulleid Pacific Preservation Society, who owned *Blackmore Vale*, asked if they could have a special open day for their members, with their locomotive in steam. The army readily agreed, and the society arranged for a special train to run down from Waterloo to Liss, and then up to Longmoor Downs station. Although *Blackmore Vale* and the army Austerity, 196, would be in steam for the day, it was not possible for the former to haul the fourteen-coach BR train from Liss to Longmoor Downs, so 92203 deputised for her. My locomotive made a magnificent spectacle as she stormed up the bank, to the delight of the crowds.

I decided to take this opportunity to have 92203 officially named. A few people disagreed with my decision. Some even wrote rude letters to me! It seems that there will always be a small minority of dyed-in-the-wool railway purists who believe that no privately owned steam locomotive should ever be changed in any detail from its original form. However, many steam locomotives were rebuilt and changed out of all recognition during their lives in normal service anyway; one has only to

85

SERVICE BY NIGHT

BRITISH RAILWAYS   BRITISH RAILWAYS

think of the Bulleid Pacifics. Moreover, I maintained that by being named, 92203 would have an extra glamour which would undoubtedly add to her intrinsic value over the years; there is absolutely no question that this has been proved to be true. It is now surely difficult to consider 92203 as anything but *Black Prince.* A number of people asked me why I chose the name. The answer is a simple one: I like it, and it suits the engine. One of the Britannia-class Pacifics was called *Black Prince*, and I very soon received a letter from an enthusiast in Romford. He had purchased one of the name-plates off the Britannia when she had been withdrawn. He had probably only paid a few pounds for it. From the price he was quoting me, it was obvious that he was in the business purely for profit. I decided to get two new ones made.

I chose Swindon for the job, because I was sure that I would get a good job done. When the name-plates were completed I went down to collect them. I was appalled. One plate was crooked in two different directions and the letters on the other one were not even in line. It was one of the shoddiest pieces of work that I have ever seen. Unfortunately there was no time to get a new set made. I took them to Longmoor and we put them on to 92203, hoping that no one would notice when the time came for the naming ceremony. My wife made a pair of brown velvet curtains to put over the name-plates and, appropriately, we asked Gen Lonsdale to unveil the plates in front of the large crowd that had gathered at Longmoor Downs station.

I am delighted to say that the whole event went off happily and no one appeared to notice from a distance how bad the name-plates were. If they did notice, they were too polite to say so. As soon as the ceremony was over, we removed the curtains. I put them down on the ground and, almost before my back was turned, saw a railway enthusiast pick them up and run off with them. I shouted after him: 'Would you mind telling me what you are doing?' 'You've finished with them, haven't you? You don't want them.' (Some railway enthusiasts will apparently stop at nothing to acquire anything that has been on a steam locomotive.) Looking rather sheepish, our friend returned the curtains.

The invoice for my two name-plates duly arrived from Swindon. I refused to pay. Unfortunately a lot of ill feeling was generated. Eventually I had a very blunt letter from someone fairly high up in British Railways threatening that if I did not pay, further action would be taken. I told them that I had no intention of paying until I got a decent pair of name-plates. Then, and only then, would I be happy to settle the account. The whole matter dragged on for several weeks but another set was finally made.

(opposite above) Guildford shed, painted from life, 1967; *(below)* Service by Night. Painted in 1955 the original was purchased by British Railways for £60. They turned it into a poster and then lost it!

They were perfect and that was the end of the matter; but it was a pity that it had happened in the first place.

For the rest of that year we all co-existed most happily at Longmoor, and the army were always helpful with all our diverse, and sometimes devious, activities. Restoration work on *Clan Line* forged ahead in the Nissen hut. Under the bridge on the other side of the railway, *Blackmore Vale* was being rapidly but methodically dismembered.

When I took delivery of 75029 from BR, her paint scheme was decidedly well worn and disreputable, so I decided to have her repainted. As it happened, the army had some surplus labour at Longmoor, and some of the army people, who were only too delighted to earn a bit of pin money, combined with our own volunteers. 75029 emerged after a few months, gleaming in her brand new BR Brunswick green paint scheme. She was towed out of the paint shop by *Black Prince*, in steam especially for the occasion. I filmed the event, but forgot to put some film in the camera!

In one of my more unfortunate moments when *Black Prince* was stabled at Longmoor, I decided to see what she would look like 'lined out' in red. I knew a sign writer, who in his spare time lined out model locomotives for people. I rang him up: 'Would you like to line out a locomotive for me in red?' 'What size is it? Is it 00 or 0 gauge?' 'Well, actually it's neither. I don't have the engine with me, but if you don't mind coming with me to see it, I'll take you over to where she lives.'

We drove to Liphook and turned right, on to the road to Longmoor. He still had absolutely no idea of the task that awaited him. He thought that I was taking him to a friend who had a model railway.

We reached Longmoor and got out of the car. By now, he was beginning to wonder. We went around the corner and there was *Black Prince*. To say the least, he was quite surprised. However, he agreed it made a change from model locomotives, and he lined out *Black Prince*, but she looked so terrible that she very soon turned back to her original unlined black.

Sadly, during the second half of 1968, things began to change for the worse and we realised that the euphoric days which we had known at the beginning of our time at Longmoor might well be over. There was talk in high places of all future railway training for servicemen being moved to West Germany. Indeed when it was announced that a final open day would be held in July 1969, it seemed that the days of army railway training at Longmoor were definitely numbered. I decided that this would be a most appropriate occasion to have 75029 named *The Green Knight*. This seemed a good name to go with *Black Prince* and there had been a BR Standard locomotive which had carried the same name. I had the name-plates made privately. Barry also decided to take this opportunity to have *Lord Fisher* renamed. It was a glorious summer day and, because of the

The open day at Longmoor

sad significance of the occasion, a huge crowd attended. The naming ceremony of the two locomotives was a most happy event, again performed by Gen Lonsdale, and the champagne and the beer flowed generously.

Shortly after the open day, there was a change in command at the camp and an immediate and total steam ban was imposed on any privately owned locomotives. Furthermore, questions were beginning to be asked at high levels, and for a time there was even a complete halt on all our activities and working parties. It was at this time that we first began to realise that there might be a chance to step in and take over the whole system and turn it into a major transport preservation centre, the potential for which we had all seen from the moment we arrived. We had by this time gathered the support of many well-placed people in industry and commerce who were as keen to save the Longmoor Military Railway as we were. A detailed and very carefully thought out feasibility study was drawn up. We set up our own organisation, the Longmoor Trust, and invited Gen Lonsdale to become the first chairman. The centre would be called the Longmoor Steam Railway & Southern Transport Centre. Represented were members of each society owning items of rolling stock, including myself, and the Transport Trust, whose chairman was Sir Peter Allen. Sir Peter was the chairman of ICI. He gave us his support right from the earliest days, for he, like us, saw Longmoor's unique potential. It was useful and very pleasant to be allowed sometimes to hold our meetings in his chairman's suite at the ICI headquarters on Millbank; it seemed peculiarly British to talk about steam engines in those sumptuous surroundings, where far-reaching business decisions are made. We sent the feasibility study to Denis Healey, who was the Minister of Defence at that time, and then we sat back and waited.

I am glad to say that while we were waiting for a decision on our future, I had become friends with the brigadier who had taken over command of Longmoor Camp. The steam ban was lifted, at least temporarily. For some reason that now escapes me, we decided to light up *Black Prince* and *Lord Fisher* in the middle of one of the coldest spells of that entire winter, in February. It was a miracle that none of us got frost-bite, but it was fun in a masochistic way. I got up at 4am to drive to Longmoor. We cooked bacon and eggs over a primus stove in a filthy old concrete hut in the middle of the camp. (I was never a boy scout and I wonder how I survived the ordeal!) How we managed to get the water into the locomotives is beyond me—the temperatures were so low that the cast-iron water column split wide open from top to bottom. But I suppose it was worth it: because of the cold, frosty air, we got some magnificent photographs of *Black Prince* with the diminutive *Lord Fisher* in steam beside her; and the bacon and eggs tasted good!

At the end of the year, the water and electricity in the shed were cut off. It was heartbreaking that all the effort we had put in, particularly on the ancient Nissen hut, was for nothing—everything would now have to be dismantled. That was bad enough, but we also feared eviction, with nowhere to go. A few months later, in October 1969, the army railway closed altogether. Shortly afterwards we heard from the Ministry of Defence that they were not prepared to approve our proposals for a Historic Transport Centre. They pointed out that they still needed large areas of the surrounding countryside for firing ranges and other military training purposes, and they were concerned that this would conflict with our activities and those of the public who came to see us. We naturally felt bitter disappointment as we looked at all the facilities that the Longmoor Railway had to offer us and which we knew would now be redundant. We had started out with such high hopes for the future, but we now shared a deep feeling of disillusionment and disappointment. We had grown from just a few individuals, when we first arrived at Longmoor, into a very happy and close-knit group of societies, all with the same aim. Now, it seemed, it was all going to collapse around us.

Early in 1970, there was a ray of hope. The Ministry of Defence had decided that the southern section of the Longmoor Military Railway at Liss was surplus to their needs, and they offered us a six-month lease on the area. We decided that this might be better than moving away altogether.

9 February 1969, and we must have been completely mad! This was the occasion when we decided to 'light up' in the depths of winter —we all froze solid, including the water column! *Black Prince*, which had by now been named by Gen Lonsdale, is seen alongside Barry's saddle tank, *Lord Fisher*—the locomotive I had managed to persuade the army was sufficiently small to fit under *Clan Line* and not be noticed (*Photo Mike Pope*)

After carefully considering the situation, we had realised that even if we had an alternative home to go to, the cost of removal from the area would be considerable and would involve highly complicated and costly train movements, and that was on the assumption that BR would be willing to co-operate. The area around Liss forest was quite attractive and very rural, and there did seem to be a fair amount of space around Liss itself. We were told that if we could obtain planning permission to develop the area on a permanent basis we could have an option to purchase. It would obviously be a very much watered-down version of what we might have been able to set up at Longmoor itself, but here at least was a 1⅓ miles of track and a considerable area of sidings. Furthermore, we would have a link with British Railways at Liss, on to the Waterloo to Portsmouth Harbour main line. This would obviously be of great value if we expanded our operations in the future. There was space on the sidings for a locomotive and carriage shed, if and when funds permitted one. At Liss itself, alongside the British Railways station, there was a run-round loop and a single platform on which stood a small and typically austere corrugated-iron hut. This latter had served the military authorities as a station since the 1920s, when the

Longmoor Military Railway opened. There was also a water tower in working order.

After a lot of heart searching, we decided to make the best of what was offered and to go for the six-month lease at Liss, commencing on 1 April of that year. Following this decision, the military authorities gave us notice to leave Longmoor at the end of March. All the army rolling stock and equipment which was of further use. was now to be dispersed from Longmoor to other military camps throughout the country. At the same time, a number of coaches and wagons were declared redundant by the military authorities and put up for sale. In spite of our uncertain future, we obviously saw potential in these coaches and wagons, especially as we were actually at Longmoor with the rolling stock and so were in a good position to secure the items at reasonable prices. I made a number of worthwhile purchases, the prize item, as far as I was concerned, being an LMS 1928 first/second class composite coach with a fascinating history. It had been requisitioned by the army in 1939 and turned into an ambulance coach. It had then been shipped out to France, only to be captured by the Germans. They used it throughout the war, but it was then recaptured, when hostilities ceased, and brought back to England. The army used it at Longmoor until it was declared redundant. I don't think that £110 was a bad price to pay for it! I also purchased two ex-BR surburban coaches at knock-down prices, as well as a number of very ancient wagons, some of LSWR ancestry, which dated back to just after World War I. All were in running order, and one wagon cost me just £4 10s.

The move to our new home might seem very simple to the uninitiated, but in fact we were faced with little short of a major military operation. We had already learned plenty from our friends in the army, and the few military personnel who were left on the army railway were now an unending source of expertise and willing help. We certainly needed it. Between us we now owned a lot of rolling stock, some of it in extremely doubtful condition. Some of the military wagons we had purchased were almost falling apart, and we had to embark on an emergency repair programme to see that they were in reasonable operating condition for the move. In some cases complete floors had to be manufactured and installed in the wagons. Doors almost falling off had to be removed, rebuilt and replaced, and we had to make sure that the brake gear on the wagons was in working order. Moreover, because of the enormous amount of equipment that we had now collected, all of which now had to be dismantled, we had to make sure that there was storage space available in our coaches and wagons. The last days of the military railway at Longmoor were therefore a period of activity such as had probably not been seen there since the end of World War II. Because of the sheer complexity of the task, the army generously gave us a reprieve, to allow us more time to prepare. Military personnel from other camps in the country were specially drafted into Longmoor to assist us. The army Austerity tank loco, No 196, was now the only suitable army steam locomotive left in working order. It had by now been named *Erol Lonsdale*. I doubt whether this locomotive had ever worked as hard as she was to do now, in rendering absolutely invaluable assistance in the move down to Liss.

In the middle of all this activity, I decided to give *Black Prince* a repaint which, in retrospect, may not have been particularly sensible, in view of the urgency of all the other tasks to be done. However, she was allowed to go into one of the covered sheds at Longmoor, and we made the most of an opportunity which would probably not come again for months, or even years. The work was completed in record time by me and a dedicated band of enthusiasts.

We were now holding frequent urgent meetings in an office which had been allotted to us at Waterloo station. Some of these gatherings were more than lively. Put into one room a crowd of railway enthusiasts, all with different ideas about urgent matters, and there are bound to be sparks. Some of us felt more confident about the future at Liss than others. The owners of the tank engine 41298 decided to pull out altogether and take their engine away. Another group, however, joined us at this late stage with a USA tank, No 30064. We formed ourselves into a new working committee which we called the Longmoor Group, and decided to name our proposed new transport centre at Liss the Longmoor Steam Railway. At least we would keep the name alive.

One of the important things that we had to decide before moving down to Liss was the direction in which the bigger main-line locomotives should face. We had to consider any future operations that we might be able to develop at Liss—once we arrived, it would be too late to turn any locomotives facing the wrong way. The army had a triangle at Whitehill at the northern end of the Longmoor Military Railway. This end of the line had scarcely seen any railway operations to speak of since the end of the war. Nature had rapidly taken over and much of the line was a jungle: trees were growing up between the rails; and beyond the triangle, on what was known as the Hollywater Loop, the railway line disappeared altogether at frequent intervals. There was little evidence of any ballast under the railway lines anywhere in the area. The whole system had been deliberately run down, and we all agreed that the triangle now looked hopelessly inadequate for turning two massive ex-BR.steam locomotives. However, after the track had been inspected, it was decided that we would have a go and *Errol Lonsdale* was steamed up and made ready.

It was at this time, in 1971, that the BBC decided to film my life story for their television series, 'The World About Us'. The 50 minute colour documentary would be called *The Man Who Loves Giants*, and would take me all over England, and abroad, and involve my association with wildlife, as well as my interest in aviation and steam railways. The idea was to bring in as many aspects of my diverse and enjoyably hectic life as possible, and the BBC decided to film the turning of my locomotives on the triangle. They asked if it might be possible to get some air shots, which might turn out to be fairly spectacular. I had painted many pictures over the years for the Army Air Corps at Middle Wallop, in Hampshire. Knowing the commandant, I rang up and asked if a helicopter might be used by the BBC for filming, strictly, of course, as a military exercise! As I expected, the authority was willingly given.

The Green Knight was taken up to the triangle first, with the BBC cameraman duly installed at the open door of a Scout helicopter hovering overhead. The whole exercise was a nail-biting experience. The rail on the army railway at Longmoor was only 90lb in weight, and that end of the system had seen almost no use for years. Slowly, and at less than walking pace, *The Green Knight* was towed by *Errol Lonsdale* around the triangle, through the bushes and undergrowth, to the accompaniment of creaking and groaning rails. The radius of the curve was really far too tight for a locomotive of her size and wheel arrangement, and we were amazed when the giant emerged at the end of the triangle almost unscathed, and facing the right way round and the right way up! Next came the turn of *Black Prince*, and taking her massive bulk around the triangle was just as hair-raising. Inch by inch, we edged our way along the track as the bushes bowed underneath her at one end and sprung up again at the other. Fortunately the whole operation went without mishap and the BBC got some splendid film. The army helicopter landed astride the railway lines, the BBC cameraman hopped out and the machine returned to Middle Wallop. It was of course all jolly good Army Air Corps pilot training! (They enjoyed it too!)

Down at Liss, the matter of security was of paramount importance. There was at that time no fencing around the area in which we were to put our rolling stock. Bearing in mind the considerable value of the locomotives and coaches, we had immediately to purchase a large length of very expensive chain-link fence. The money was subscribed by the various individuals and member societies according to the length of stock they owned. The fence was erected in record time.

Black Prince was the first engine to be towed down to Liss. She was hauled down to her new home by *Errol Lonsdale* without mishap, to the accompaniment, once again, of the helicopter flying overhead with the BBC filming from the open door. Having left 92203 inside the new chain-link fence at Liss, No 196 returned to Longmoor Downs to collect 75029. On all these journeys to and fro she had a brake van attached, in order that some of us could travel with the rolling stock to ensure that all went well and to put out any fires that we might start *en route* amongst the heather and bracken alongside the railway line.

Blackmore Vale had to be quite literally tied together with ropes as most of her streamlined casing had been removed and parts were hanging off all over the place. *Clan Line* was the heaviest locomotive of all and we were genuinely concerned for her safe passage down to Liss over such light rails, bearing in mind particularly that the track had received almost no maintenance over the previous years, and had certainly never been prepared for carrying a locomotive of her weight. However, all went well, although several of the pins holding the rail down to the sleepers actually popped out as she passed over them! No 196, resplendent with her new name-plates, performed all the tasks which were given to her without complaint. The army's last remaining diesel locomotive also assisted in the work. All our various items of rolling stock, including our £4 10s wagons, creaked and groaned as they were marshalled into position into the various trains which had to be made up for the journey to Liss. The five coaches which we owned were made into one train, and all the wagons into another. This latter train gave us all considerable cause for concern due to the amount of stores and equipment that we had crammed into the ancient and protesting vehicles.

We were in the middle of the most hectic period of our withdrawal from the area when we blotted our copy books for the only time, and it was not really our fault. The army had decided to allow the Transport Trust to become permanent custodians of their WD 2-10-0 locomotive, *Gordon*, and the three historic Blue Saloons. In true military tradition, they decided to have a formal handing over ceremony, on Longmoor Downs station. The event was a happy one, carried out with typical military precision and ceremonial, complete with a military band. Right in the middle of the ceremony, 196 decided to derail herself, with one of our brake vans, just outside the station. I don't know whether anyone noticed, but the ceremony carried on as though nothing had happened.

All the remaining engines were subsequently taken down to Liss and positioned inside the compound in the correct order. Possibly the most spectacular task that *Errol Lonsdale* had to perform was the final positioning of *Clan Line*, *Blackmore Vale*, *Gordon*, *Black Prince* and *The Green Knight*. They were all coupled together and hauled into position in one go by the Austerity tank engine and, to the delight of official army photographers, the sound was spectacular and the sight remarkable. The hard-working tank engine once again returned to Longmoor camp to collect the five coaches and, finally, the train of ancient and decrepit wagons. In a blaze of glory, and a trail of sparks, with clouds of black smoke, this train was almost the final movement away from Longmoor Downs station. It was followed by the army diesel, just in case the wagons fell apart *en route*. After this move was completed, 196 finally returned to Longmoor and her fire was dropped. She was subsequently purchased by the Kent & East Sussex Railway.

6

Barry scrapyard
and other adventures

A very great deal has been written about Barry in South Wales. To many people, it's a place to go to for sun, sea and sand. To many others, it's much more than that—Barry has become a mecca for steam-locomotive enthusiasts from far and wide. Much has also been written about the now famous Woodham Brothers' scrapyard, which has quite possibly put the place more on the map than the sun, sea and sand.

Woodham's are, first and foremost, scrap merchants. As such, like the rest of their profession, they are businessmen. Nevertheless, they have been fair to the railway fraternity over the years and, on many occasions, more than tolerant. (The yard became something of a tourist attraction and, at one point, there were organised coach trips to visit this private yard. Woodham's turned a blind eye to it all.) I have come to know and respect Dai Woodham. I am sure that, like many of us who have occasionally featured in the press, he has had many a quiet chuckle over the rubbish that has been written about him. In one article, a railway preservationist even called Dai 'the God of the preservation movement'! I'm sure Dai was most flattered! In fact (and I am sure that he would agree), it is most certainly not through sentiment and a deep love of steam engines that so many engines have remained for so long in his yard, gently rotting away. It is simply that cutting up railway wagons brings in a quicker financial return than cutting up locomotives; and Woodham's have certainly cut up vast numbers of wagons over the years. I wonder that there are any left in BR. I don't know whether it is true, but I have been told that the scrap from the chopped-up wagons is packaged up, loaded aboard ships at Barry docks and sent to Japan, where, after being turned into Datsuns and Toyotas, most of it comes back to Britain again. So if one is unpatriotic enough to buy a Japanese car, at least one can console oneself with the knowledge that it may well be built from ex-BR wagons! We live in a crazy world!

In 1968 there were well over 200 locomotives in Woodham's yard. It was a gold mine for spare parts. I wrote to Woodham's asking them if I could come down with a truck and purchase what I could for the two engines that I had just bought from BR. I received a very helpful and co-operative reply. The yard was open to me.

At Longmoor I had struck up a firm friendship with an irrepressible Geordie, Steve Pattison. He was the regular boilersmith for the army's engines, and was never happier than when covered in grease from head to toc. There was almost nothing he did not know about what makes an engine tick. At this same time I met a colleague and friend of Steve's who was also in the army. His name was Corp Bin Abdullah. He married a Malayan girl whilst in the army and, according to custom, had taken her name. Otherwise he was Maurice Lawson. To everyone who knows him, he's simply 'Bin'. We found a weekend when we would all be available and hired a Bedford 3 ton truck from a garage in Aldershot. We set off for Barry with a few other helpers in attendance. I was driving separately in my own car as I would be going on elsewhere after my visit to the scrapyard. Barry scrapyard in those early days was very different from today. There was hardly any need for security, and everything was very free and easy. This was long before the hordes of railway enthusiasts descended like vultures, and the appalling thieving, which would later spoil things for everybody, started. These offences were committed by only a tiny unscrupulous minority, but in later years they reached such a pitch that the yard had virtually to be closed, even to the vast majority of honest and well-meaning enthusiasts who have always regarded Barry as a marvellous source of spare parts for their locomotives.

At the time of our first visit, Woodham's were buying their last steam engines from BR. At Barry Docks station, we saw a row of engines, including a Standard 9F. She was complete with all her fittings. We could have steamed her away. We reached Barry in the late afternoon, just in time to get to Woodham's head office. In those days this was in the yard in a dingy back street of the town. We found a man dressed in oil-soaked overalls stoking up a burning pile of old rags in the yard. We asked him if any of the Woodham Brothers were around. 'I'm Billy Woodham, can I help you?' was the reply. We explained who we were, and he was clearly expecting us. I asked him whether we could take some bits off the 9F we'd just seen in the station. 'Yes, but you'll have to hurry up. We're going to strip the engine on Monday morning. If we don't, then someone else will. You'd better use our oxy-acetylene and take what you want while you have the chance, and the best of British!' We bedded down for the night in the yard in a couple of old brake-van bodies. It could hardly be said to be the most comfortable accommodation, but at least we were on the site.

The following morning we set to with a vengeance, using the Woodham's equipment. There was nothing sophisticated about our methods. It was a matter of chop, chop, chop. No 92212 was our target. She was complete and we were allowed to take whatever we wanted. There was certainly no hint in those days that any of these engines were

97

likely to be purchased for preservation. Indeed at that time every scrap merchant who purchased steam engines from BR had to sign an agreement that no locomotives would be passed on to other parties for preservation. We left 92212 with several large holes in her. Little did we know that her remains would indeed be bought for preservation many years later, when the whole scene would be so different.

I had a friend with me with a movie camera, and I now have some very funny movie of our activities over that weekend. I have always believed in 'mucking in with the lads' and getting my hands dirty. However, I believe my physical exertion, and in particular what I was doing with my hands, did give my friends some cause for concern. With fingers missing, there would be no elephant paintings to pay for it all. They became particularly alarmed when they saw me lowering the connecting rods from inside the tender of 92212 over the side and on to the ground. They were no small weight. A health and safety inspector would have had a fit. Dragging the rods to the lorry at the far end of the yard provided some wonderfully funny film material which, on viewing afterwards, seems to have all the makings of an early Harold Lloyd silent comedy film.

Most of the Standard locomotives in the yard in those days still retained their lubricators, placed high up on the footplate of the engines. We could guess even then how much it would cost in later years to manufacture such items. They were there and they were available for the taking. It was

At Woodham's yard in Barry, we plundered 92212 for spares for 92203, leaving several large holes in her. Little did we know that years later she too would be purchased for preservation

late on the Saturday afternoon that we decided to concentrate on the removal of one of these, as a spare for 75029. It was by now pouring with rain. We had not bargained for the weather and this was perhaps my first experience of the really filthy side of steam-locomotive preservation. The locomotive that we had chosen was up at the far end of the yard. Her lubricator seemed to have long since almost disappeared under inches of thick oily muck and dirt. After very many minutes of struggling in the rain, we managed to disconnect all the copper piping, so that the lubricator was free. Soaked to the skin and beginning to wonder whether all the misery was worth it, we managed to lower the great soggy lump slowly down a plank with ropes on to the ground. We then put it in the back of my estate car, which I had parked as near as I could to the engine, on the other side of the fence. I then had to drive around from that end of the yard, through Barry town, back to the main entrance to inform Billy Woodham of my purchase. As I was going on elsewhere to a very different location, I had my best suit (my only suit) on a coat hanger lying in the back of my car. I was driving through Barry when I had to brake suddenly half-way down the main street. With a series of enormous dull thuds, a very large and oily lump of machinery slowly rolled from the back to the front of the car, right over my suit. It didn't do the lubricator any harm.

Although it was Saturday, Billy was still in the yard. He was sheltering from the pouring rain in his yard 'office'. This was an old GWR brake-van body, standing in a desolate wasteland of rusting locomotives, half-demolished railway wagons, mountains of axles and wheels and rotting old van bodies. Parked alongside this centre of administration was his Rolls-Royce.

I sloshed my way through the puddles into the office and told Billy about the lubricator in the back of my car. The weather conditions obviously had very much dampened Billy's enthusiasm for leaving shelter, for whatever reason. However, being an honest sort of a chap and thinking ahead to future visits for more spares, I insisted that he should inspect what I was going to drive away with. 'How much does the bloody thing weigh?' Billy asked. 'I haven't the foggiest idea.' Under some protest, Billy put an old sack over his head and ran over to my car. I opened the tail-gate and Billy looked inside at the large, oil-covered 'lump'. He pushed it with one hand, and it moved a few inches. '12s 6d—is that OK?' I gave him £1, and, in the pouring rain, he solemnly gave me 7s 6d change. Those were the days!

By lunch-time on Sunday our truck was fully loaded with all sorts of goodies. Happy with our purchases, we started the long haul in convoy home to Longmoor. We decided to stop for an evening meal at the Severn Bridge Service Area on the M4. This place had only just been opened and everything was new. We had of course taken off our filthy oil-covered overalls. However, after exertions in a place like Barry scrapyard, with no proper washing facilities, it is impossible to clean up completely. The oil somehow soaks right through everything. After we had selected our meals from the self-service counter, I was leading our team up to the cash desk. 'Are you transport?' asked the cashier, rather abruptly, I thought. I suppose I was tired. I was annoyed. 'No, most certainly not,' I answered, indignantly. 'I only asked because, if you were, you could have had your dinners at truck drivers' prices.' (That'll teach me to get on my high horse!) We selected a couple of tables, put them together and sat down to eat our eggs, bangers and chips. I regret to say that on getting up to go, that little part of the M4 service area looked exactly like the canteen of an old BR steam shed. The cruets, the plates and the edges of the table were covered with oily, black finger marks. We hadn't done it on purpose, but we beat a hasty retreat!

Our truck, by this time, was running on only half its cylinders and only just made it back to Longmoor, sounding very sick. When we arrived it finally died altogether. It had not only been a hilarious and enjoyable couple of days, but it had also been well worthwhile. We had a 3 ton truck-load of connecting rods, clack valves, lubricators and, in vast quantities, brass fittings and bits and pieces, all of which would be of great use for 75029 and 92203. At the request of Billy Woodham, I sent them a list of what we had taken. A few days later I received a bill: £110 for the whole lot. Accompanying the bill was a note saying that it had been a pleasure doing business with us.

I was in the yard on another occasion, with several of my friends, looking for spares for *Black Prince*. Our friends from the Keithley & Worth Valley Railway were also there, looking at several 9Fs in the yard with a view possibly to purchasing one for preservation. They hadn't noticed us in the yard and we heard one of their team say to another: 'That booger Shepherd's 'ad all the bloody bits off this bloody loco.' I went back again several months later and someone had written in big white letters all along the rusty boiler of one of the 9Fs in the yard: 'Hands off, Shep'. It was all meant in good fun. One played fair. If locomotives were not reserved (and they were not in those early days) you had to get what you could, when you could.

We were to have another great adventure. As long as there was still steam around in the North, great numbers of depots still had stores full of spare parts, and we had to seize the opportunity to acquire anything we could while the chance was still there. At that time, my mother bred Welsh ponies and cattle, and had a horse-box, 1948 vintage. It had seen better days, but it seemed an ideal form of transport for stores 'raids', particularly to places like Chester and Crewe, where we had good friends in BR whom we knew would help us. The only weekend that we could all manage was in the depths of a freezing cold spell. The others drove the horse-box while I followed in the car. Everything was going fine, and we were full of confidence, when the first problem hit us on the M6 near Preston. Two of the rear tyres on the horse-box blew. I had not even bothered to check whether there was a spare, and in any case I hadn't the least idea how to change a wheel on such a vehicle. We waited six hours before we were rescued by a breakdown vehicle which, at enormous cost, got us once again on our way.

Our first port of call was Chester. It was already late in the day when the battered horse-box arrived, to the consternation and amusement of all the steam-shed staff. Perhaps horsepower was returning to BR shunting yards . . .

One of the problems about many steam depots was that there was inadequate road access and, to add to our difficulties, all the stores and spares that we wanted always seemed to be in the wrong place. That visit to Chester involved a punishing few hours humping great lumps of steam locomotive on sack barrows across several sets of railway lines to the horse-box. It was certainly lucky that few BR trains seemed to be running that afternoon; otherwise there might have been a railway disaster, because I kept getting my sack barrow stuck on the railway lines.

'odds and ends' – Chester M.P.D.

With more faith in the strength of a Bedford horse-box than wisdom, we loaded brake blocks, springs for both Standard locomotives, further connecting rods, fire bars and a huge pile of fire bricks into the groaning and protesting vehicle, and off we went to Carnforth to collect still more. In those early days I had met Dr Peter Beet up at Carnforth and we became good friends. Peter was instrumental in saving the place when BR declared the steam depot redundant at the end of steam in 1968. He was known, to me anyway, as 'the steaming doctor'. He once told me (and I'm sure that he won't mind my repeating it here) that he sometimes managed to get contributions for his steam engines by telling his better-off elderly lady patients that their 'tubes needed cleaning'—this made them laugh and they gladly made a donation.

Peter had known we were coming, and over many months had been acquiring by devious methods various bits and pieces for my two locos. What he could not hide behind sacks in dark corners, he was actually burying. These spares included some massive and extremely heavy fittings for the fire-grate of the Standard 9F and, to hide these, Peter had to dig several large holes around the depot. It now took quite a time to find some of these items, as they had sunk well and truly out of sight. However, most were found in the end, and were loaded into a, by now, rather unhappy horse-box. There is still a centre bar for the fire-grate of a Standard 9 up at Carnforth; we left it buried. We had done enough excavating, and in any case it was obvious that we were stretching the horse-box to its physical limits, and even beyond.

After such a long day, it would have made sense to stay the night and depart the next morning for the south, but we decided to press on home that evening. After a cup of tea with Peter, we departed. Steve and Bin were driving the horse-box direct to Longmoor and I was to follow by car. After parting company somewhere on the M6, I would go straight home to Surrey. The sky was full of threatening black clouds, and it was getting dark, when I saw the horse-box leave. I delayed an hour or so but still expected to catch them up. I didn't, so I assumed that all was well, and that they were making good progress. I drove straight home during what was rapidly becoming one of the coldest nights of the winter, and went straight to bed.

My wife and I have two separate telephone numbers at our home, with a telephone on either side of the bed. One is my business telephone and the other is for the family. It does happen sometimes that my business 'phone rings on my side of the bed at some unearthly hour in the middle of the night. It might be an American who had forgotten about the time

(opposite above) A cosmetic overhaul for West Country class *Bere Alston* in Guildford shed. Just a few months later the engine was scrapped and the shed was bulldozed flat; *(below)* Evening at Birkenhead shed—92203 is probably in there somewhere!

difference between England and America, but in those early days of railway preservation, it was more often, sadly, a railway enthusiast who seemed to have no idea that people do occasionally sleep at night. It was never much fun to be asked whether it was true that I was buying, say, 'three Britannia Pacifics and a couple of Merchant Navys', at 1 o'clock in the morning! On this particular night, the telephone rang on my wife's side of the bed at 4.20 in the morning, on the family telephone number. It was Steve. He was ringing from a telephone box in a remote lay-by somewhere in the frozen depths of Berkshire. His voice sounded quite weird, and there was obviously something dreadfully wrong. Apparently,. after a perfectly horrendous journey, the horse-box had finally died on them.

What followed had the makings of a tragicomedy. While I was talking to Steve and trying to decide what to do, my business telephone rang. It was an American client (who had indeed forgotten about the time difference) asking about an elephant painting. With a disbelieving and very sleepy wife lying beside me, I was sitting up in bed with a telephone in each hand, talking on the one about elephants, and on the other about broken-down horse-boxes. The hardest part was to talk to each while convincing the other that it was not some huge joke. My American client got the message quickly; he knew about my mania for steam locomotives. Full of apologies, and asking why I didn't get myself a new horse-box, he promised to ring back at a more sensible hour. This left me to continue my conversation with a very frozen and incredulous Steve. I told him that they should stay where they were (they hadn't much choice), and I would come to rescue them in the car.

It was 5.30 in the morning when I arrived in the lay-by. The whole landscape was frozen into a deep frost, as white as snow in the light of a very cold moon. The horse-box was frost covered like everything else. I banged on the door, but there was absolutely no sign of life inside. I could not see anything through the windows as they were completely frozen up. My immediate reaction was one of admiration, that two of my friends had actually given their lives for steam preservation. It certainly looked like it! I hammered louder, but there was still no reaction. I very slowly and carefully opened the creaking door on the driver's side, and a frozen body started to fall out of the box; I caught Steve just in time before he hit the ground. After considerable pummelling and shaking on my part, some sort of life was restored to him and he woke up. Both of us then had to concentrate on Bin, who was in an even worse state. It reminded me of those awful pictures of the Russian front in World War II. If this was Reading, then what was the South Pole like?

When they had both revived, they took my car and drove to my home, to a hot bath and bed. I valiantly sat out a long and frosty vigil until the world around me began to come to life. At one minute past eight, I telephoned the nearest garage in Reading. Two hours later, a heavy lift breakdown truck arrived in the lay-by. The front of the grossly overloaded horse-box was lifted up into the air and, with the front edge swinging precariously, the poor old vehicle was towed unceremoniously on its back wheels into Reading, where it took up residence in the forecourt of the garage. It stayed there for many weeks, and we had to drive a hire truck to Reading, to off-load all the stores and take them down to Longmoor. I am glad to say that the horse-box finally recovered, after a lengthy period in intensive care. Steve and Bin didn't need such treatment; like rubber balls, they bounced back to rude health within a matter of days.

While the BBC were making *The Man Who Loves Giants* they told me that they would like to film my team and myself engaged in the restoration of 75029, *The Green Knight*. She had of course already had her repaint in the Longmoor paintshop and was in full working order. For the purposes of the film, therefore, we had to go down to Barry scrapyard and find a sister engine to 'stand in' for 75029. I was asked if I would act as the 'make-up man' and change the cabside number of any 75XXX that might prove suitable. I had never attempted anything like this before. I went down to the yard with oil paints and pallette. No 75069 seemed a suitable candidate. The locomotive was in typical scrapyard condition and I would only have to change the '6'. The painted numbers on her cabside

While Harlech Television (who were making a programme called *Elephants and Engines*) went off for lunch, I took the opportunity to do some sketching of one of the wrecks

were pitted with rust marks and the paint was peeling off in several places. However, with my oil paints, I managed to turn the '6' into a '2' quite convincingly, and even to match the faded and stained BR colours. I painted in some rust marks as a bonus. I was quite proud of myself—I might even get a job with a film company!

I packed up my equipment and decided to take a stroll around the yard. It was then that I noticed a railway enthusiast going down the long lines of locomotives with his spotter's notebook. He was taking down all the engine numbers. When he came to 75029, he paused. He looked quizzically at the number, and then into his book. 'Funny', he must have thought to himself; he had a feeling that he had read somewhere about 75029 being preserved, but obviously he was wrong. He recorded the number in his book and walked on down the long line of engines, round the end, and then back along the other side. Following him, I saw him then record the true number, 75029. The extraordinary thing was that he never noticed that he was recording two numbers for one engine. He would no doubt get quite a surprise when he reached home to find that the numbers he had collected did not tally with the number of steam engines in the yard.

We spent a whole day in the yard filming with the BBC camera team. The camera angles were selected, with different sections of the locomotive to feature in the various sequences. First Steve, a couple of others and myself were filmed in close-up scraping the muck off her connecting rods. This was supposed to portray the beginning of restoration work on 75029. Then, after a change of clothes to suggest a time lapse, I was filmed putting undercoat on to a part of her boiler. Moving towards her smoke box, we then did a close-up of me applying the final paint scheme of Brunswick Green. No 75069 ended up looking like a patchwork quilt, but the illusion was successfully created.

The next sequence caused us all to collapse with laughter. Steve was asked to climb right inside the frames of the locomotive, underneath her boiler. Everything was covered in layers of oily filth. I was then told to ask Steve, in front of the camera, about the condition of the engine. His head was to appear from above the frames inside the black hole, and give me his answer. This is where the problems started. The whole film was unscripted. Chris Parsons believed that it would sound far more 'natural' if we ad libbed. He had not bargained for just how 'natural' Steve could sound. The instructions were given to roll the camera. 'What's it like in there, Steve?', I asked. 'It's a . . . . ing load of c . . p.' Chris held his hands up in horror and at once stopped the filming. 'This, Steve, is a family film for Sunday-night viewing; let's try again.' Once again the cameras rolled. 'What's it like in there, Steve?', I dutifully asked again. 'Jesus, the s . . t is about five inches thick!' came the reply.

It was only after a supreme effort on Steve's part, and four or five

For BBC television, 75069 becomes 75029, with the aid of my oil paints!

further 'takes', that he was able to use language sufficiently mild for the film to be deemed suitable for showing on television. Steve had certainly never expressed himself in such a restrained manner before, and when the film was shown, the general comment from those who knew him was that it couldn't possibly be him. No one recognised him because of his language!

One thing that has always made me extremely angry is the waste of materials of just about every description—by commercial undertakings, large and small, nationalised and otherwise, and by private individuals. BR is no exception. I have seen a brand new box of typing paper thrown away because the top sheet was just a little grubby. I have seen a large and nearly full carton of soap thrown away because the stores were automatically due for a new allocation. I have seen discarded, for the same reason, office furniture from desks to doormats, biro pens, paper and envelopes, filing cabinets, and shovels and other items of track maintenance equipment. Small wonder then, given my strong feelings on this issue, that I welcome things 'falling off the backs of lorries'. In 1967, a certain gentleman who drives for BR joined me. We had better call him Smiff, which is not his real name, but I have to protect the guilty. (Apparently he is known as Smiff to his friends in BR.) Ever since I have known him Smiff has been willing to get up to any prank for the sake of steam. He's actually an honest man (I think!), but he has a great gift for persuading people that they are better off without their property if he thinks that it will help the cause!

Smiff came up to me one day, a very worried man. 'David, I am getting bloody worried, because I have had nothing but greens lately.' I knew he was not a vegetarian, so I asked him what on earth he was talking about. 'Well, I have been doing my regular run with my Brush 47 down from the Midlands to London and, over the last month, I have been putting aside little heaps of goodies in the bushes by various signals along the line. When I get a 'red', I stop and load it all up into my cab. Having nothing but bloody greens, I can't stop and nip out and pick it all up, and I am getting bloody worried that someone is going to nick it.'

I was most concerned on another occasion when I saw Smiff; he had singed off most of his eyebrows. Apparently, BR had torn up the track many years ago in the sidings where Smiff worked, but they had left the old gas lamps with their lantern tops. These were collector's items even in those days, and Smiff had decided to do some investigating as to the possibility of their removal. One dark night he climbed up the ladder and started fiddling around with the connecting screws. He was smoking at the time, and had nearly blown himself up—the gas had been left on!

When we were at Longmoor, I had my own Bedford 3 ton truck. I received a telephone call from Smiff one day. He was ringing from his depot, and he invited me to come up to see him, but it must be with the truck. He had apparently made very good friends with the new depot manager and, after some investigation, had discovered that a great deal of equipment in the depot was due for renewal. He thought that a journey there and back with my lorry would be well worth while. I drove to the depot and Smiff introduced me to the depot manager who, I am quite sure, knew what was going on. I entered his office, wiping my feet on the bare boards; Smiff had already had the doormat. Whilst I sat chatting at his desk, I heard my truck start up outside the window. It came back in half an hour, fully loaded up with heaven know's what, and with a tarpaulin neatly tied down with ropes. If my readers take offence at these actions, then so be it. All I can say, once again, is that having seen perfectly good office furniture, good for years of further use, being burnt on a bonfire simply because it was too much trouble to take it away, I do not regard it as dishonest if one puts such things to further use, especially in a good cause.

It was shortly after the end of steam in the south that I decided to visit Cashmore's yard at Newport, in South Wales. This would not primarily be a visit for spares. As they were one of the biggest scrap merchants buying redundant steam locomotives and coaches from BR, I felt sure that there would be some marvellous material for paintings. People have often asked me why I don't paint clean locomotives and happy subjects. As an artist, I have never been particularly attracted by gleaming locomotives storming through a sunlit landscape. It may seem strange but I can see very little satisfaction in this sort of thing, which can, and indeed has been, well covered by the camera. To me, there is a far greater depth to the whole locomotive scene than this. When I visited Nine Elms, or any of the other derelict steam sheds, amongst all the squalor that marked the end of steam, I could feel the locomotives talking to me. They were telling me of their years of proud and faithful service. Here was all the emotion and nostalgia of the steam age, under the layers of grime and filth.

Cashmore's yard was certainly no disappointment. Outside the yard was a line of some twenty locomotives, all complete with fixtures and fittings and mainly from BR Southern Region, awaiting their final journey through the gates of the yard to the cutter's torch. Inside the yard, I was aghast at what I saw; I had never been to a place like this before. There was wreckage wherever I looked. In the middle of the yard was a mountain of cut up locomotives, mostly in very large sections; one could quite clearly recognise large parts of many and varied historic locomotive types. There must have been dozens of complete smoke boxes and other large items, all piled in total confusion. At the centre of this Wagnerian scene was a Black Five actually in the process of being cut up. It was just like a body being dismembered, piece by piece. She was complete except that, where the boiler should have been, just a few remaining boiler tubes above her frames remained. Smoke and flames were coming from the floor

109

underneath her cab, where the product of years of neglect by BR, the layers of muck and oil, had been deliberately set alight. From her smoke-box end sparks flew—a man was cutting, just below her smoke-box door, at her weakest point, with the oxy-acetylene. After just a few minutes there was a massive thud, as the entire front end of the Black Five fell to the ground. The cab of the locomotive had been cut around at the base, and I watched fascinated as a crane, with a large hook on the end of the jib, was swung towards her. A cable was passed through the broken windows of the cab and up over the roof in a loop and, with a great rending sound, the cab suddenly went flying into the air on the end of the crane. It was unceremoniously dumped in the yard amongst the rest of the debris. I was told that it took eight days to reduce a Black Five to nothing. It was a tragic and ignominious end to a machine which had given years of service to the community.

While I was in the yard, one of the management showed me round. Two coaches had just come in from the Southern Region for scrapping. All the compartments were complete, with cushions, curtains, light bulbs and mirrors. I asked the manager if I could have a couple of seat cushions from the first-class compartments for our two dogs, as they made splendid dog beds. 'They're ten bob each.' I protested politely: 'But you are going to burn the coach anyway, so why can't I have the seat cushions first, if I take them out myself? I am not asking anybody else to do it for me.' 'That's how we make our money' was the answer.

He then showed me around the rest of the yard. Along one side ran a canal, and, berthed alongside the remains of a naval destroyer which had been stripped almost down to the water-line, was a beautiful little Bristol Harbour Board steam tug. Even the wheelhouse, with its polished woodwork and ship's wheel intact, was still there. I could hardly contain myself. 'You are surely not going to cut that up?' 'Of course. There's a few hundred quid in her hull, but we will burn all the woodwork first. If you preservationists had your way, the whole country would be littered with junk!'

Cashmores yard at Newport;
the death of a Stanier 'Black Five' – No. 44835

His last few words seemed particularly ironic given the surroundings in which they were spoken. I suppose it was a point of view, but it was certainly not mine.

As I was about to depart in the evening, I watched, fascinated, the fate of the two BR coaches. Their bodies had been cut away from the frames. One of the men in the yard had climbed on to the roof of the carriage, and with his boot had smashed a window on each side. He then passed a chain right through the compartment and over the roof. The cable was attached via a winch to an 'anchor' in the yard. (The 'anchor' was a collector's item—it was a World War II Sherman tank!) The entire coach body was then slowly pulled over, so that it separated from the frames. With a gigantic crash and a thud, accompanied by the sound of smashing glass and interior fittings, and a huge cloud of dust, the coach body hit the ground roof first, rolled over several times and came to rest. A bucket of petrol was then thrown over one end of the coach and a match was put to the hulk. Within minutes the whole body of the coach was a raging inferno. The yard was then closed down for the evening. I came back the next morning and nothing remained of the coach except a few twisted pieces of still-smouldering framework. Apparently only the frames were of commercial use.

During that day, two more coaches came in for scrapping. When no one was looking, I got my seat cushions! If Cashmore's read this book and consider that I owe them £1, I would be delighted to send them it.

7

Liss and some very unhappy times

Liss would never be another Longmoor. Nevertheless the group had stayed together through some very tough times and we were friends. At least we had a home and were secure in our compound. We were determined to succeed and make the best of what the place had to offer. The area soon became another hive of activity. *Lord Fisher*, our diminutive but brave saddle tank was, as always, indispensable. Some amazing things were achieved with this remarkable engine, as she hauled impossibly heavy loads of coaches, wagons and locomotives around the place in the shunting operations needed to sort ourselves out.

We were stabled alongside the platform with its little tin hut. The public were allowed in free of charge, but we did our best to take their money off them whenever the opportunity presented itself, for we had considerable expenses to meet—coal, rent, restoration and many others.

We had not been at Liss for very long when the first murmurs of opposition were heard. It was the calm before the storm broke in all its vicious intensity. Perhaps it is as well that I didn't know right at the beginning what a miserable period I was personally going to go through in the next twelve months; inevitably perhaps, I bore the brunt of it. It soon became clear that Liss and Liss Forest were two quite different types of residential area. In Liss village itself, at the exchange sidings with BR, the people, some of whom lived very close to the railway, were, almost without exception, sympathetic to our views and aims. There was only one murmur of discontent, on the first occasion we were in steam, doing some urgent shunting which was taking longer than we had anticipated. Someone gently pointed out that they would rather not be kept awake after 9 o'clock by steam engines going up and down past their houses. We assured them that we would not make a habit of it.

Up at the other end of the line, at Liss Forest, things were very soon to prove quite different. Here, in the very much larger and more opulent houses, all of which were well out of sight and sound of the railway, screened by a thick belt of trees, lived a few people who were to show their true colours in the months ahead. These people were to go to almost any lengths, however vicious, to blacken our names and characters, and to see

113

that we failed in all our aspirations and our dreams came to nothing.

The first example of this hostility showed itself in a most dramatic way. One lovely sunny afternoon *Lord Fisher* was towing *The Green Knight* up to the exchange sidings. I was on the footplate of 75029, quite relaxed, without a care in the world. All of a sudden there were shrieks from a footpath leading from one of the big houses up the railway line. We all looked in astonishment in the direction whence the sound came, wondering what on earth was happening. I was then the target of a torrent of violent abuse, the like of which I had never heard before, certainly not from a woman. I was for once totally and completely lost for words. Perhaps it was just as well because, within a few minutes of this outburst, the woman went away. I never did discover what it was all about, and it would not be long before we found that there were half a dozen other people like her in the area.

Meanwhile we carried on as best we could in our new home. The various individuals and groups, which were still growing, somehow managed to keep and develop the comradeship and unity built up at Longmoor. We delegated tasks to those qualified to carry them out. Track was overhauled and refurbished; a quite sophisticated and professional signalling system was installed in an amazingly short time; and various miracles were being achieved that would, it was hoped, result in an efficient and professionally run, albeit small, steam centre.

Shortly after we had got ourselves sorted out at Liss, we formed an Association of Liss Enginemen. This would co-ordinate the engine drivers and firemen already qualified to run our engines, as well as taking on and training new personnel. We had various opportunities to steam the locomotives. Nos 75029 and 92203 were both in working order and on some occasions we steamed both for steam tests, or when we were visited by people who we hoped might help financially. One wealthy Greek shipping friend of mine (the only such person I knew, unfortunately) expressed a great deal of interest and arrived in his own helicopter, landing beside the line. We steamed *Black Prince* especially for him and he was most impressed with everything he saw. At least he gave us a few tons of coal! We even managed to steam *Clan Line* on two occasions, and it was marvellous to see her active once more, although it was rather like seeing a racehorse shackled in a very small back yard. On the other hand it was especially sad for those who had done so much work towards her restoration at Longmoor that *Blackmore Vale* was under wraps and in store, together with *Gordon*, for all the period of our stay at Liss.

Shortly after our arrival at Liss, we applied for planning permission to put up a locomotive and carriage shed on the exchange sidings, when and if we had the money. When the moment came for our plans to be announced in the local press, we began to realise the strength with which the opposition at Liss Forest would voice its views. We also realised that

114

There were times when we had to do some night shunting, although we didn't make a habit of it—the indispensable *Lord Fisher* and *Brussels*, the Austerity 0-6-0 saddle tank (*Photo Dick Weisham*)

we had created what seemed to be a social conflict between the two ends of the railway. Up at Liss Forest lived the shifting population of the commuters in the big houses. Down in the village of Liss itself were the 'real' people who lived with the railway on their doorstep. The chairman of the parish council at Liss supported our application wholeheartedly because he felt that the community would 'benefit from the recreational and the educational points of view from what [we] were trying to achieve'. This incensed the residents of Liss Forest to such an extent that war almost broke out between the two places. Letters started flying to the local papers and the hate campaign began in earnest. As the conflict gathered momentum, and the news spread further afield, the circulation of the *Hampshire Telegraph* and the *Petersfield Post* must have gone up by leaps and bounds. People love to read about controversy. The letter pages seemed to be filled every week with a forest of abuse, of me and everything that I stood for.

Three of the Liss Forest residents set up a Liss Forest Residents' Association, and it seemed that they now set out to destroy everything that we were trying to achieve. There were utterly absurd letters being written to the local papers by these people and their friends. They complained that the peace and quiet of the entire area would be shattered

115

Safely inside our chain-link compound—*The Green Knight, Lord Fisher* and *Black Prince*. My two engines carry on their tenders the horrible crest that someone designed for the short-lived Shepherd Railway Preservation Trust—we all make mistakes! (*Photo Ivo Peters*)

Although we had a water column and tank inside our compound, other facilities were non-existent. Nevertheless, we managed to carry out quite heavy restoration tasks (*Photo Dick Weisham*)

We even cut up a surplus coach (*Photo Dick Weisham*)

by thousands of visitors daily dropping litter all over the place and thousands of cars blocking their driveways, and that their children would be in danger of being struck down by 'hissing, clanking, smoke-belching monsters' (quoted precisely from one letter to the *Petersfield Post*) as they ran 'unchecked through level crossings setting the countryside ablaze'. One letter was particularly colourful. It suggested that the lives of the 'kiddies' (a deliberately and well chosen emotive word) would be endangered on their way to school in the mornings in the winter. The thought of steaming 92203 backwards and forwards across footpaths in the cold winter mornings, during the week, hadn't occurred to us!

The hate campaign was now quite clearly reaching such a pitch that we had to try to do something about it. I suggested to the opposition that we should have a meeting in the village hall at Liss Forest. I hoped that at that meeting we could allay all the fears and misgivings that some of the local people seemed to have. We would listen to each other's point of view and, I hoped, clarify the matter through calm discussion. It immediately became evident that I was being optimistic about the vociferous minority who had been blinded by prejudice right from the outset. The meeting was anything but democratic. There was no one at all at the meeting to support me. I was totally on my own. I felt very lonely. Some 200 people crammed into the village hall. It had probably never been so full. Most of them probably only came to see the fun, and because there was nothing much on television that night.

I felt that the 'chairman' of the meeting, who was in fact the self-appointed spokesman for the opposition's case, was unnecessarily

117

offensive and rude to me. I stood no chance of a fair hearing. He spent ten minutes giving an extremely colourful and highly inaccurate account of what we were proposing to do, assassinating my character in the process. Inevitably, he completely 'won over' the assembled gathering with his rhetoric. The whole evening was a complete fiasco and I left the hall totally and utterly disillusioned and miserable.

Driving home, I stopped in a lay-by and wept. I was actually crying tears over *Black Prince*, a steam engine! It was perhaps an over-reaction, but it does show how the dashing of one's hopes and aspirations can bring one to utter despair. It also shows how emotional the business of steam-locomotive preservation can be if one is an emotional person, which I am. Why on earth was I involved in it? I had thought that the preservation of steam locomotives was supposed to be an enjoyable hobby. It was now unmitigated hell and I would gladly have got out of the whole business. What had I and my friends done to deserve this sort of treatment from a handful of vicious people?

I let the dust settle for a week or two and then I telephoned one of the leaders of the association and asked him if I could calmly and quietly come over to his house one evening to tell him and his wife what we were proposing to do. He agreed. I arrived and was shown into the sitting room. His wife was sitting on the sofa. She looked at me with a totally unsmiling expression and gave me a cold and unfeeling handshake. 'Why don't you go back to that studio of yours and carry on that painting, for which you have some talent, and drop that dirty and destructive hobby of yours?' Those were her precise words. I remember them. I always shall. It wasn't a very good start.

Even after this strange treatment, I still hoped that this couple might try to understand. Knowing that they had two teenage sons, I suggested that they might like to come down as our guests to Liss and have a ride on *Black Prince* to see for themselves. Yes, I tried to explain, it could be a dirty hobby to a certain extent, but that was to many of us part of the excitement of living and working with steam locomotives. In no way, however, was it destructive. We hadn't killed anybody so far, and didn't intend to. The invitation was bluntly declined. The sons themselves were not there and so had no chance to express an opinion. It was perfectly obvious that it was a complete waste of time talking to such people; but there was more to come. The wife continued: 'We will never be able to play tennis again in our garden. It will be just like Crewe Junction.' She pretended to choke on clouds of black smoke descending on her tennis court. She apparently believed that she was impressing me with her knowledge of railway junctions. I was not impressed. Her house was over a ¼ mile from the Longmoor Military Railway and there were thick woods in between. I tried to point out that the army at one time had possibly run five or six trains every day of the working week. I did not

118

know whether her tennis-playing ability had been affected by this railway activity or not, but in any case, it was quite apparent that what we were trying to do was quite different. I pointed out that our maximum train service would probably be two or three trains on Sunday afternoons in the summer only, but it was a complete waste of time. The army were the professionals and we were a lot of dangerous amateurs playing at things that we did not know anything about. I could see that her prejudice ran too deep. With great pleasure I left their company.

We had by now gained outline planning consent for our proposed steam shed and workshop on the exchange sidings at Liss. In spite of the vehement objections from Liss Forest, the planning authorities considered that our proposals would add some life to an 'otherwise meaningless place', as they themselves put it. However, the consent was only for a period of five years because yet another shadow now hung over our future. This was a proposal to divert the A3 trunk road right across the railway somewhere in the vicinity of where we were hoping to set up our steam centre.

Another figure now joined the battle. The local Conservative MP for Petersfield, in what I saw as a misguided and uninformed outburst, furiously attacked the county planners for what she described as the deplorable way the applications had been handled by the planning committee. She wrote to the local papers complaining that the 'objectors' had not been given the full facts of the proposed steam centre and had not been granted a fair hearing. This was totally untrue; they had been kept fully informed. Their problem was that they spent too much time writing abusive letters to the local papers. The County Planning Officer decided to call a meeting of all parties concerned on the site itself. I well remember that meeting. After it had taken place our MP friend wrote, once again, to the local paper. She complained, on behalf of the objectors (she had not been at the meeting herself), that they had been 'forced to walk beside the track putting their case "breathlessly".' It is true to say that the objectors never stopped talking. That's probably why they were breathless. It finally got to the point where one of the representatives from the authority told them to 'keep to the point'. The chairman of the parish council at Liss had the support of most of the villagers and the planning people couldn't understand why there was so much fuss from a few people up at the other end of the railway.

We realised that with only outline planning consent, and for such a short period, it would be most unwise to go ahead with raising funds and investing them in permanent buildings. For the next few months we were in constant contact with the planning authorities to try to ascertain what the situation was concerning the proposed road development but, as is so often the case with this sort of thing, there seemed little chance of any firm decisions in the foreseeable future.

The Longmoor Trust continued to hold its meetings at Waterloo station in the room set aside for it. Now, however, the first cracks began to appear in the unity which had sustained us in such a marvellous way. Some of the meetings became quite acrimonious as individual members began to express their strong doubts about the future at Liss. Proposals were put forward for alternative sites. One of these was the BR steam depot at Three Bridges in Sussex. After some lengthy discussion amongst ourselves and tentative negotiations with BR, we actualfy decided to inspect the site. It did have some advantages. The whole steam depot complex was still there, in an otherwise desolate wasteland. However it was an intensely built-up area and it seemed that there was a strong possibility that the site might be wanted for industrial development in the future. Moreover, road access and potential areas for car parking were almost non-existent. We turned the site down.

Further disillusionment crept in and we seriously began to doubt our future. The army had granted us a lease on the Liss site for six months only, and now the authorities made it perfectly clear that it would not be renewed unless we undertook to purchase the whole remaining part of the railway system. Further meetings were held and it was at this point that the Merchant Navy Society and the Bulleid Society both decided to pull out and go elsewhere. They could not be blamed. They both had heavy locomotives and naturally hoped to see them on a really worthwhile stretch of railway line, which we could not really offer them. The Merchant Navy Society took *Clan Line* to the steam centre which was being set up at Ashford in Kent. (After much further heartbreak for them, the preservation scheme there also folded and they moved on once again.) *Blackmore Vale* went to the Bluebell Railway. Subsequently the Transport Trust decided to pull out as well, and *Gordon* and the three blue saloons went to the Severn Valley Railway.

In spite of these massive set-backs, those who remained still believed in trying to retrieve something of the crumbling project. We carried on as best we could, steaming our various locomotives on odd occasions and giving great pleasure to our visitors; for that, after all, was surely the purpose of our activities in the first place, although one would scarcely have guessed it from the unending torrent of abuse still pouring forth from Liss Forest. The local newspapers continued to thrive! I was frequently invited by the papers to reply, putting my case, but I preferred to remain silent. I had no desire to give further ammunition to the opposition.

The BBC had by now completed the fifty-minute colour documentary about myself, *The Man Who Loves Giants.* It was to be shown in the BBC 2 series, 'The World About Us', and this was duly announced in the *Radio Times* with a full page of publicity. One of the leaders of the group at Liss Forest immediately wrote to the BBC stating that, 'As David

Shepherd is such a bad influence on people, the programme should be withdrawn'. I was extremely upset by this (being, as I have said, given to emotion). The BBC, on the other hand, were delighted—they said that at least they had a guaranteed audience of one!

The army authorities told us that, as it seemed that there was no chance of permanent planning permission being obtained, they had no option but to auction the land under our feet. The date was set for 28 July 1971. We still saw some hope, believe it or not, and in spite of the now almost insuperable obstacles, decided that we would try to buy the land outright. However, I did not forget the opposition, which was still as determined as ever, as we were soon to discover. Possibly one of the most hysterical outbursts of all came just before the auction. There was a small and little-used footpath which crossed the railway at Liss Forest; one of the residents contacted the army and the county council complaining that somebody had nearly been run down on the public footpath, by *Lord Fisher* hauling eight coaches over the crossing at 25 miles an hour. *Lord Fisher* was immensely flattered at the suggestion that she could achieve such an astonishing feat. The fact that we didn't possess eight coaches, and that *Lord Fisher* was nowhere near the crossing in question at that time, made no difference. The damage was done. All our activities were immediately curtailed by the army and the county council. A complete steam ban was imposed until after the date of the auction.

Our only washing facility was high above ground, in the water tank! This view clearly shows our heavily stocked compound with preserved locomotives and ex-army rolling stock filling both roads, the whole area surrounded by our security fence. On the right is the Liss BR goods yard and station (*Photo Dick Weisham*)

As our future now depended on our ability to purchase the line, I thought that it might be worth one more desperate effort to try and explain to the opposition that we were not a bunch of hysterical, irresponsible schoolboys who were going to kill people with our steam engines. We knew the group had expressed an interest in buying the line, but it seemed ridiculous that a handful of people were willing to spend a large amount of money buying a railway line simply to stop us having it. There must be room for some sort of a compromise. I suggested that the same representative whom I had met with his wife, on the previous occasion, should meet me in the local pub; he agreed. After some lengthy discussion, we did reach some sort of a compromise, although from my point of view it was very far from satisfactory. He agreed that he and the Liss Forest Association would not bid against us for the extreme southern end of the railway at Liss, provided that we in turn agreed to give up our interest in buying any of the area towards Liss Forest itself. This in effect meant that we would lose all our running line, which would halve the already depleted potential of the project. We shook hands on the deal and parted.

The day of the auction arrived. It was a lovely sunny afternoon when Barry and I went along to the auction rooms at Liphook. The first section to come under the hammer was the part of the railway that we were interested in. We were appalled to see that the Liss Forest representative was bidding against us. He went well up over the value of the land, reneging on everything that we had agreed and shaken hands on. They bought the land from underneath us, and he was quoted in the local press afterwards as wishing to defeat us 'at almost any price'. He achieved his aim. It was the end of our dream. We left the auction room deflated and sickened.

The steam ban was now lifted, and we had four months to prepare for our final departure. This move was a far greater challenge than the transfer from Longmoor down to Liss, as absolutely everything had to be dismantled. We had to steam almost every weekend, and we now cared very little about the reaction of the people at Liss Forest. I at last agreed to make a press statement. I did not, however, realise how funny my remarks would look when they were in print. I was asked by the reporter what the residents of Liss Forest proposed to do with all the railway line that they had just purchased: would the wife of their representative at the auction 'actually tear up the track with her own bare hands and sell it to the nearest scrap merchants'? I replied: 'I hope so, and I hope she gets a bloody hernia when she does it.'

Several months after we had left Liss, I received a letter asking us whether we would consider coming back to the area. Apparently the A3 re-routing was 'on the cards' and the people at Liss Forest had decided that they would rather have us!

8

'Young Winston', down to Eastleigh and the end of a dream

With just a few weeks to go before our final departure from Longmoor, Columbia Pictures Corporation came on the scene. They were looking for a suitable location to film a steam-engine sequence for their epic of the early life of Winston Churchill, *Young Winston*.

Richard Attenborough and his team came to inspect the section of railway line that still remained, most of which had of course now been purchased by the local people. Columbia were satisfied, and also wanted to use *Black Prince*, suitably disguised as a South African Railways steam locomotive of the Boer War period. The sequence in question was to show the young Winston Churchill, a war correspondent, escaping from captivity in South Africa over the border of Mozambique, Portuguese East Africa. Richard Attenborough duly arrived on the scene and asked me to walk up the line to show him the limits of the area in which he could film. We had to inform the Liss Forest Residents' Association of this as they were now the owners of the property. We made an appointment to meet them and, as Richard Attenborough and I walked towards Liss Forest, we saw the people who had led the protest campaign coming down the line to meet us. It was one of the funniest sights that I have ever seen: it was raining, and the four of them came towards us under their umbrellas, rather like a Panzer division in full charge.

Before I had a chance to introduce Richard Attenborough, their spokesman said: 'Oh, you must be these bloody film people.' Richard Attenborough was astonished. He took me to one side and asked me whether all the local people were like that. I told him that four of them certainly were. However, after this rather unfortunate start, a reasonable rapport was established between us and the group. I had suspected that even people like these would not object too strongly, bearing in mind that the film was to be about the early life of the greatest Englishman of this century. They would have got some shocking publicity if they had really tried to cause trouble and sabotage the film. In fact we had no further clashes with them except for one hilarious incident which I will describe later.

What remained of the Longmoor Military Railway was certainly making its exit in a blaze of glory. For a few hectic days, Columbia pictures worked with us to get everything ready. In true film-company tradition, a very realistic halt was erected in a matter of days at the road crossing at Liss Forest. With perhaps less success the whole area was then 'dressed' as Komartipoort station. This was the point on the border between South Africa and Mozambique where the young Winston Churchill leapt from the train in his escape to freedom. The appropriate flags erected on poles, and all the other details improvised as only a film company knows how, added up to a reasonably convincing African frontier post, amongst the Hampshire pine trees. To complete the illusion, sand-bagged gun emplacements with fibreglass machine guns were built on either side of the road.

Enormous numbers of technicians and extras, and dozens of people who, to me anyway, didn't seem to have anything particular to do, began to arrive from London. An assortment of large road vehicles descended on the scene, and tents sprang up everywhere to provide all the facilities required for a huge and expensive film unit. This was the first time that most of us at the railway had been closely involved with the making of a major film. We certainly saw and learned a great deal. A veritable army of very fierce-looking 'Portuguese' soldiers (most of whom, it seemed, came from Streatham and Fulham) were walking around aimlessly. Other people were lying around in the sun, and most of them spent most of the time complaining that they had much too much to do. If I remember correctly, some of them in fact went on strike the very first evening for 'danger money', 'boredom money' or some other obscure form of financial reward. It seemed to me that ten men were employed to do the job of one.

We struck up an excellent working relationship with many of the personnel, including Richard Attenborough and Simon Ward, who played the part of young Winston.

It had been arranged that *Black Prince* would be in steam for the best part of a week. We charged Columbia Pictures £250 a day for her use and, in fact, we made little profit. The coal had to be paid for, and there had to be some recompense for the volunteers who had taken time off from their work to service and drive her and to attend to the diverse other railway tasks when required. *Lord Fisher* was also in steam as a general-purpose locomotive, together with the USA tank 30064. So we were kept much busier than some of the people on the film.

I was somewhat amused at the attempts to disguise *Black Prince* as a South African locomotive. The letters 'SAR' were stuck on the side of her tender. Her smoke deflectors were removed, with considerable difficulty; this certainly altered her appearance dramatically. A grotesque fibreglass chimney was fastened on to her smoke box over her real one. She also had

The not entirely successful attempt to disguise *Black Prince* as a Boer War South African Railways steam locomotive. Note the not very subtle change of number *(Photo Philip Rowe)*

a particularly ugly imitation dome fixed on top of her boiler. Mr Riddles, who designed the Standard 9s, would have had 'fifty fits'. Columbia had managed to borrow a headlamp which had originally come from the famous Lickey Banker locomotive of London, Midland & Scottish fame, and this was fixed to her smoke-box door. Eventually the 'make-up' department were satisfied that they had a successful disguise. Just as she was about to appear in front of the cameras for the first time I pointed out that she was still carrying her original smoke-box number. I suggested that one or two people might realise that she was *Black Prince*. After urgent consultation, they solved the problem. The 9 and the 3 were covered over with black tape, which didn't convince anybody.

Eventually everyone was ready for the first run past the cameras; it was now suddenly realised that *Black Prince* was facing the wrong way! This meant that she had to be turned, and the only way that she could achieve this was to take her up to the triangle on the Longmoor Military Railway

Black Prince was facing the wrong way for Sir Richard Attenborough's filming, so we took her back on to the Longmoor Military Railway for turning on the old triangle. Her smoke deflectors have been removed prior to her being fully 'made up' for the film (*Photo Donald Eades*)

itself. We were of course delighted, because none of us had ever believed that the rest of the line would see steam again. With special permission from the military authorities, she was allowed to steam all the way up to Longmoor Downs station and then to the triangle, now almost totally overgrown. This was a most exciting event for us, and an added bonus was that the press came and did quite a substantial feature on it in the local newspapers. They recognised its significance as the very last steam-train movement of all on that part of the Longmoor Military Railway.

For her part in the film *Black Prince* was to storm down past the Panavision camera which was placed in a strategic position on top of one of the small hills beside the line. She was to pull a motley collection of railway wagons made up from some that we had purchased from the

126

military, plus a number which had been especially imported into the railway from BR by Columbia. In order to achieve this spectacle she had first to reverse up the line backwards with her train, well past the road crossing which was the limit of the railway owned by the Liss Forest residents, and almost as far as Longmoor Downs station on the other part of the military railway.

Because of her speed and the weight of the train behind her, *Black Prince* could hardly be expected to stop immediately she was out of camera range. Throughout the filming period we had a walkie-talkie apparatus on her footplate; this little gadget enabled Arthur, who was driving the Prince, to keep in contact with the film crew up on the hill, who had similar equipment. We kept getting rather strange messages from the crew as we stormed past them down the hill. 'Why on earth can't you stop sooner, darling?' they asked. 'You're wasting precious time and film.' (I have never been able to understand just why so many people in the film industry call each other 'darling'.) They seemed to expect us to stop on a sixpence once we were out of their view. This so exasperated Arthur at the end of one particularly fast and long run that he grabbed the intercom and, with a wink at me, shouted into it to the film crew: 'What the bloody hell do you think we've got, a f . . . ing wheel-barrow?' The whole Columbia crew was incapacitated by laughter for several minutes.

We set fire to the undergrowth beside the line several times and had to put out the fire ourselves from the footplate. I was all the time making a colour film record of the filming of the great epic, and a number of people who have seen my humble effort have said that mine is better than the film itself! It certainly includes some extremely funny episodes (a number of the volunteers involved were very colourful characters).

On one of our runs they decided to take some film from the train itself, with Simon Ward leaping from the wagon as the train was moving, and making his escape to freedom. This necessitated building a platform 2ft out from the side of the wagon on which they placed the multi-thousand-pound Panavision camera. On to this small projection crowded a quite astonishing number of people, all of whom were apparently required to operate the one camera. To our astonishment, and it wasn't our job to tell them, it had not occurred to anyone in the film unit to do a slow dummy run first to make sure that the projection would clear any telegraph poles or any other obstructions along the side of the line. The order was given to start, the train stormed down the hill and, sure enough, the whole platform hit an obstruction—hard. The camera, Richard Attenborough and attendant personnel were all sent flying in different directions into the undergrowth of Mozambique! Fortunately no one was hurt, but Richard Attenborough was clearly shaken.

The runs *Black Prince* did for the camera were certainly spectacular.

On one particular trip down the hill, one of the film crew was on her footplate, and he was as white as a sheet. If he had had an ejector seat, I am quite sure that he would have used it. On several of the runs it seemed that we were going so fast that we might well have gone through the gates at Liss onto the BR main line, and then on down to Portsmouth. What fun that would have been! To our great delight, all of us who were involved with the making of the film were allowed to make use of the facilities provided. Pantechnicons came down from London every day and parked alongside the large marquee which was erected as a cafeteria. Judging by the large number of strange faces which were seen in the queue every day, I feel quite sure that half of the local villagers caught on to the idea of free food. Smiff, who was never averse to acquiring things which belonged to other people if he thought that he could put these items to better use than they did, was helping himself right, left and centre to Columbia Pictures butter and other goods, which were duly stowed away in the footplate cupboards of *Black Prince*. We lived very well on the engine herself as well as in the cafeteria.

Although *Black Prince* was in full steam for the whole period during which she might be required, she was only actually used for less than a quarter of that time. We would be parked on the exchange sidings burning valuable coal and, when we voiced our frustration, a message would come through from the film crew to the footplate: 'We don't need you today, darling.' Half-way through the filming, disaster nearly struck. An enormous generator for the use of the film company had come in one of the BR wagons. The wagon was shunted up to Liss Forest by *Lord Fisher*, but it was then discovered, to the horror of the directors, that they had no means of lifting this heavy item on to the platform. With time costing thousands of pounds an hour, people started running all over the place waving their arms about as if the world was going to come to an end. We saved the situation. In the last few weeks of our occupation of the site, a friend of mine, Bill from Godalming, had been allowed to bring Bertha, his 1908 vintage vertical-boilered steam crane, to assist with the dismantling of all of our equipment. It so happened that Richard Attenborough had seen this marvellous vehicle in our station compound down at Liss, and he realised that this might be his only salvation. 'We simply must have that crane, now!' I pointed out that, apart from the fact that Bertha was not in steam and would probably protest if she was rushed, her owner was working.
'Who for?' Richard Attenborough asked urgently.

(*opposite*) The moment of glory for Bill's vertical-boilered steam crane, Bertha, as she triumphantly lifts the generator our of the wagon and saves the day for Columbia Pictures Corporation

128

Black Prince, disguised for the filming of *Young Winston*, poses with her crew and Sir Richard Attenborough

'He works as a porter for British Rail at Godalming', I replied.

'Then for heaven's sake go to British Rail and get him, now!'

'It may not be as simple as that; he may be on duty', I tried to point out.

'I don't care what you do, or what it costs, do anything—we have just got to get that generator out of the wagon.'

I had over the years got to know Bill pretty well and I did not expect him to be over-exerting himself in Godalming station. At the now almost desperate request of Richard Attenborough, I telephoned the station master at Godalming and explained the situation. 'No, Bill is not doing anything in particular at the moment', he said 'although he is supposed to be on duty; we'll put him on the first train to Liss.'

Bill eventually arrived, complete with bowler hat; if he was going to do something important, he always dressed for the occasion. A couple of hours later, with a full head of steam, Bertha, who was thrilled to bits at the opportunity to avert a major disaster, was ready to go. She steamed up the line at less than walking pace, with jib proudly held aloft and Bill, still in his bowler hat, at the controls. As he approached the high-voltage overhead cable which supplied electricity to most of Liss Forest, we wondered whether *Bertha* would repeat the little episode of a few weeks previously, when she succeeded in slicing through the cable and blacking out the whole area for a Saturday afternoon. However, this time the jib missed the cable by inches and we arrived at 'Komartipoort'. Bertha shunted herself into the appropriate position and, with almost no effort at all, lifted the generator out of the wagon. Columbia Pictures were saved, and it was a day of triumph for both Bertha and her owner. Neither of them have ever been the same since.

Even during the course of filming, we suffered opposition from one of the more colourful characters at Liss Forest, who was determined to disrupt everything at every available opportunity. On this particular occasion, *Black Prince* was marshalled into her train astride the small road which crossed the line at Liss Forest, at 'Komartipoort station'. The train was only there for a few minutes while the camera was being prepared for a slow run through the frontier post. This particular Liss Forest resident drove up to the crossing in her small car to find the road blocked by the massive 2-10-0 locomotive. She got out of her car and angrily approached Arthur Young who was on the cab. 'My man, if you don't move that thing, I shall ram it!' What a marvellous piece of film that would have made.

After three weeks of filming, the day finally came when Columbia Pictures considered that they had all the footage they needed. Normally, all the temporary structures that had been built for the film, including the station at 'Komartipoort', would have been burned, because this was apparently cheaper than dismantling it all. There was a veritable fortune in brand new timber there, and we were only too pleased to save the film

131

company the trouble of setting fire to everything. It took only a matter of days to dismantle the whole lot and everything was packed into our already overloaded wagons for future use; everything, that is, except some of the timber which was used to erect various garden sheds at the homes of a number of my railway enthusiast friends. These stand to this day as tangible reminders of the visit of a great film company to the Longmoor Military Railway in its final hours.

It now only remained for us to pick up the pieces and finally depart from Liss. We had no home to go to; our position was desperate. Barry and I went to see BR at Waterloo in the hope that we might find a siding somewhere to serve as a temporary home while we searched for somewhere permanent. They offered us a length of track alongside their diesel depot at Eastleigh, Southampton. We were told we would have to pay £20 a week, but at least there was room to accommodate all our stock. We had little choice but to take it.

One locomotive was to leave us altogether at this time. The society that owned the USA tank, 30064, decided to take her by road to the Bluebell Railway.

Everything around us at Liss was now looking more and more derelict. In the last few days we had to retrieve as much as we could; the site was no longer ours. We were shocked to be told that we could not have our chainlink fence. Apparently it was a question of whether it was a fixture or a fitting. We didn't care about that. We had paid for it and we believed that it was our fence. A few months previously I had purchased a Bedford 3 ton truck, and one suitably dark night a dozen of us piled into the lorry, drove to Liss and dismantled the fence. We also managed to retrieve most of the valuable signalling wire which we had installed, with such dedication and effort and so professionally, only a few months previously. We removed it by unceremoniously hacking down the telephone poles which carried it. There was no time for a more sophisticated method. We took as many of the poles as we could fit on to my truck. We also saved the attractive and intrinsically valuable London & South Western lattice signals which I had purchased from the Longmoor Military Railway some months before and which were still lying around in the undergrowth. These found temporary storage at a farm near Liphook. There were literally tons of equipment which had to be taken away, and a great deal of it was taken by lorry to my home in Surrey, where it was deposited at various points around the property.

Bill's steam crane was used on many occasions and, together with *Lord Fisher*, was absolutely invaluable in the last days. Many of us took away what we could carry, and an amazing variety of locomotive spare parts, bits of signalling equipment and heaven know's what else found temporary storage in various bedrooms and under beds. Our long-suffering mothers and wives never seemed to mind too much, thank goodness.

Lord Fisher was the very last locomotive to leave the Longmoor Military Railway, on 6 November 1971. Determined to go out in a blaze of glory, she steamed on to her low-loader and, still in steam, proceeded down Godalming High Street in the middle of the Saturday morning shopping crowds *en route* to her new home at Eastleigh (*Photo Dick Weisham*)

The time for our final departure from Liss arrived. We had been given some precise instructions from BR as to the exact order in which our locomotives, coaches and wagons should be made up into the train which would travel down to Eastleigh. On the day before we left, *Lord Fisher* had to perform the daunting task of doing all the shunting by herself; she had probably never worked so hard before or since. It was truly amazing to see her towing *Black Prince* with such apparent ease.

When the news spread of the motley train which would be travelling to Eastleigh, several people, including some who actually worked for BR, asked if the train would be steam hauled! After all, it contained two perfectly good locomotives which were more than capable of doing the job on their own. With tongue in cheek, I did actually suggest it to BR, pointing out that it would save them the trouble of providing one of their own diesels, and I was prepared to pay the going rate for the job as though they were providing the engine power. The idea was not very favourably received in high places!

So the day arrived—Sunday 24 October 1971. The Brush 47 was due to come in just after daybreak, and I was up early to film the event.

133

We had done absolutely everything that we had been asked to do in the most professional manner, and everything was prepared as per the BR instructions. The locomotive arrived on time, but when it came through the gates on to the army railway, BR suddenly realised that they had forgotten the 'second man'. There was a delay of some two hours while they sent a taxi all the way to Guildford to get him.

Just prior to our departure, I was handed the official BR consignment note. It was exactly the same sort of form that one receives when one sends a small parcel from one point to another; the difference was that, in this case, the parcel consisted of two steam locomotives, three railway coaches and an assortment of wagons.

A number of us had been given special permission to travel on our own train all the way down to Eastleigh and, as it was an event for us to be out on BR metals again, I had my film camera with me. We went through the gates to the sound of detonators on the track, and we didn't care very much whom we woke up. We stopped at various stations *en route*. At one, when we alighted on the platform, to my amazement and great delight, I suddenly saw smoke coming out of the chimney of *The Green Knight*. Had steam returned to the Southern Region? Somehow or other, Smiff, who was always up to some sort of mischief on an occasion such as this, had found an old pair of my trousers and, soaking them in paraffin and oil, had thrown them into the fire box and set them alight. I have little doubt that word of this soon got around, and questions were probably

The end of a dream (*Photo Dick Weisham*)

asked for many weeks afterwards at BR headquarters in London; we didn't care if they were, because it was all good, harmless fun.

The train finally arrived at its new home at Eastleigh and was accorded a 'royal' welcome by the personnel at the shed, who were delighted to see steam engines back once again on their home ground. The area traction engineer, Max Millard, was also there to greet the arrival of the cavalcade; over the next couple of years, he was going to become a true and valuable friend to us all.

Back at Liss, the final rites were performed. The steam locomotives had all departed, except for *Lord Fisher* who remained to perform his final duties, shunting the ancient wagons which we had had to leave behind. These were put on low-loaders and taken to Godalming to be deposited in a builder's yard until a permanent home could be found for them and the rest of our rolling stock. *Lord Fisher* had the distinction of being the very last steam loco ever to work on the Longmoor Military Railway. She was determined to leave in the most dramatic way possible. We lit her up, she steamed up on to her low-loader and left the railway for the last time in clouds of black smoke deliberately and, I suspect, slightly maliciously created for the occasion. Half an hour or so later I filmed her going triumphantly down Godalming High Street with a trail of traffic behind her. She was still in steam, belching healthy clouds of smoke and hardly any of the Saturday morning shopping crowds even seemed to notice! She was finally lowered on to a short length of track in the builder's yard. Her fire was dropped. It was all over.

9

Eastleigh
and a search for a home

Our instructions from BR were quite clear: 'You're not to go inside the shed with your locomotives.' As if we would—I cannot imagine why they thought that we would ever stray off our rusty siding out in the rain! In fact, of course, it was not very long before *Black Prince* was inside the diesel depot having the wheels of her tender turned and all sorts of other little mechanical things done to her, about which BR knew nothing, officially. Who were we to complain when we were encouraged by all the marvellous friends we were quickly making in the depot?

It was basically a happy time for all of us at Eastleigh. However, £20 a week is no small consideration. For most of the time our stock was out on the siding in all weathers. The few of us who had stayed together were allowed to work on the locomotives and coaches for essential maintenance purposes although, generally speaking, physical conditions were extremely difficult indeed. There was one redeeming feature about the place, however. We were secure. Being surrounded by electrified rail is the best deterrent to thieves and vandals.

It was now late 1971. If I had had stars in my eyes when I first bought *Black Prince* and *The Green Knight*, those stars had faded. I had become a realist through the disappointment and traumatic experiences of Longmoor and Liss, and I began to realise that the steam-locomotive preservation business was far more than just an enjoyable hobby. There is undeniably plenty of enjoyment in it, but it can also be a financial nightmare, and we were beginning to find this out the hard way. The £20 a week was dead money being poured down the drain for nothing except security. It was a time of continual worry. I know, and so do Barry and the rest of my friends who stuck with me all through those days. Without wishing a situation like we had gone through at Liss on anyone, I do nevertheless fervently hope that those enthusiasts who still have stars in their eyes even in the 1980s will pause to reflect a while and, perhaps, listen to those of us who have been through it right from the beginning.

Most of the societies that had been with us at Longmoor had now gone elsewhere. We nevertheless remained a very close-knit group; perhaps the times we had been through had brought us even closer together. We were

sometimes allowed to steam up our locomotives for essential maintenance. On one occasion, Southern television came down to do a
programme with Kenny Lynch and Harry Fowler and, as we were being
paid for the coal, it not only gave us a chance to steam up the locomotives,
which did them good, but we also had a lot of fun. Harry and Kenny both
drove *Black Prince* and *The Green Knight* and stormed up and down the
area of Eastleigh depot covering the surrounding countryside with
beautiful black smoke, which hadn't been seen since the end of steam four
years previously. We didn't get a single complaint from the local people
(Eastleigh is a railway town).

BR has an open day each year at the Eastleigh diesel depot, and all the
profit made goes to their orphanage at Woking. During the time that we
were in residence, two open days were held, and I knew perfectly well
from the beginning that the presence of our two steam engines would
boost the attendance enormously. The crowds would come in their
thousands to see steam back there once again. On the first occasion,

(*overleaf*) It was all quite unofficial but, somehow, within a few weeks *Black Prince* had
crept inside the depot (contrary to BR's express instructions!) to have some work done on
her. All the BR people at Eastleigh were super to us

(*below*) When we were allowed to steam at Eastleigh, we had to shovel up the coal the hard
way. It would have been even harder without the crane we managed to 'borrow'

On one occasion we were allowed to storm up and down the Eastleigh yard for Southern Television. The surrounding area hadn't seen smoke like this since the end of steam

therefore, I asked BR if we could steam *Black Prince* and move her up and down for the benefit of the public. Judging by their reaction to my request, one would have thought that we were asking to haul fifteen coaches up to Glasgow and back again on the main line. They gave me an extremely blunt 'no'. I emphasised that the extra attraction could only boost the money raised for their orphanage, but the answer was still the same. It seemed to me to be absolutely fatuous, particularly as it was their day and I was paying for the coal. Furthermore the whole event was being organised entirely by the staff of the diesel depot and they were as keen as I was to have steam back again. BR still said no until a matter of days before the event itself. Then, after a great deal of fuss, and a detailed inspection by the chief mechanical engineer which seemed only to stop short of a heavy major overhaul, the locomotive was pronounced fit (which I knew she was because the Eastleigh people had said so). We were allowed to light her up; as long as we did not move! This seemed to me to be the final indignity. I was very tempted indeed to have a showdown and tell the press, but I considered that it would not be worth it because we wanted to maintain our happy relations with the local BR people who thought that it was all as stupid as I did. The day finally arrived, and the crowds came in their thousands. The orphanage benefitted handsomely and a great many people asked me why *Black Prince* was not moving up and down with coaches behind her, which could have brought in even more money. I could only tell them the truth.

I am happy to say that relations gradually improved and common sense began to prevail, although slowly. When the second BR Eastleigh open day came, *The Green Knight* was given permission to steam with a train behind her, and she ran up and down the yard giving enormous pleasure to even greater numbers of people. Much more exciting even than this, however, was the fact that BR had told me that *Black Prince* would be allowed out on to the main line. The date was 13 May 1973. This would be the first time that steam had been seen on the Southern Region in the six years since the end of steam in 1967. The word had soon got around that the great event was going to take place. Eastleigh was gripped in a fever of excitement. There were incredible scenes as roads close to the works were jammed with cars, and crowds were still queueing a hundred yards along the main road at three o'clock in the afternoon only an hour

On the second of the Eastleigh open days held while *The Green Knight* and *Black Prince* were in residence at the depot, the latter was allowed to run down the BR line to Romsey and back, a concession which proved very popular with the public (*Photo Mike Pope*)

before the open day was due to close. The highlights for the huge crowd were undoubtedly the two trips that *Black Prince* made to Romsey and back, hauling nine coaches filled with enthusiasts. Crowds gathered on the embankment at the diesel depot and gave her a rousing send-off. On the second of the two runs, I had the general manager of the Southern Region on the footplate with me, and he was as enthusiastic as I was. The event was only slightly spoiled by a handful of stupid people, such as always seem to be around on such occasions. As *Black Prince* was steaming down the line to Romsey, I saw these people standing between the rails playing 'chicken' as the locomotive bore down on them, taking their photographs and jumping out of the way at the last moment. I nearly had heart failure. A fatality could so easily have occurred, and that would have been the end of steam on BR. Happily, the whole event was an enormous success, 15,000 people came, and a great deal of money was made for the railway orphanage at Woking. BR even wrote up the event in their own newspaper, admitting that steam had 'stolen' the day.

A team from the BBC Nationwide programme was there. They approached a long queue of children and adults waiting to look into the cabs of my two steam engines, and selected a few children at random out of the crowd. One small boy, who could not have been much more than seven years old, was asked why he was getting so excited by the steam engines because, surely, he belonged to the age of diesel. He gave the television crew a delightful answer: 'It's just like the old days isn't it mister!'

While we were at Eastleigh, another locomotive joined us. On several occasions in the past I had been to the Montagu Motor Museum at Beaulieu, in Hampshire. The Schools-class locomotive, *Stowe*, was a static exhibit, with three Pullman coaches. The locomotive had been purchased from BR by the Montagu family in the early 1960s. I don't know particularly whether it was because I was at the school of the same name but I wondered whether Lord Montagu might be persuaded to part with the locomotive. We had by this time at last found a home for our engines at Cranmore (as I describe in Chapter 11) and I managed to convince Lord Montagu that we could give the locomotive a good home on the East Somerset Railway, with the prospect of eventual restoration to running order. He agreed to me having joint ownership of the engine on these conditions, provided that I took her away. Through the various painting commissions that I had done for the army over the years, I had come to know quite a number of officers at various army depots in the south. The nearest rail connection to Eastleigh where *Stowe* might be off-loaded happened to be the army military port at Marchwood, near Southampton, and I knew one of the officers stationed there. It was arranged that if I could organise the road-transport side of things, he would do the rest. Then, it was hoped, BR could come into Marchwood with one of their diesels and tow *Stowe* the short journey across to Eastleigh to join *Black Prince* and *The Green Knight.*

I telephoned Wynn's, the heavy-transport people.

'I have a very large locomotive. Can you transport it by road from Beaulieu to Marchwood, please?'

'Yes, of course, that's no problem; how much does it weigh?' asked the girl on the other end of the telephone.

'Well, it really is a big one.'

'Yes, OK, but how much does it weigh?'

'It's not a model; it's the real thing. Are you sure you can do it?' I asked.

'Yes, of course we can, we're used to this sort of thing. How much does it weigh, please?'

'Well, I don't know, it's huge; I suppose about a hundred tons, or more. Are you sure that you can lift a locomotive that size?'

'Yes. That's why we kept asking you the weight; but you've got the wrong office here. You want our light-load division in South Wales. We only handle loads of over 150 tons in this office!'

Never question the specialists.

It was arranged that Wynn's would go down to Beaulieu with their low-loaders on 30 November 1973. They told me that they would be there at about ten in the morning. I decided to be there at roughly the same time to see the great event. I was extremely concerned because Lord Montagu had given me strict instructions to make sure that as little damage as possible was down to his grass edges, and his geranium beds. I need not have worried. I arrived twenty minutes late, and there was no sign of *Stowe*. She'd already left! Furthermore, no damage had been done to the grass edges. Leave it to the professionals.

I drove 'like the clappers' and caught up with the cavalcade on the main road to Marchwood. The whole job had been done with the utmost ease. When the low-loaders arrived, they simply positioned the vehicle at the end of the railway line, took the back wheels off, lowered *Stowe* gently down with a winch on to the railway line and the job was done. They then drove one low-loader up on to the other one, and went back to South Wales. It was as simple as that. The axle boxes of the locomotive were inspected. Everything was in order. A few days later, a BR diesel came into Marchwood and took *Stowe* to Eastleigh. A magnificent Southern Railway locomotive had joined our collection. She had returned to Eastleigh where she had been built thirty-nine years before.

It was soon after the return to steam on BR (at the Eastleigh open day), for which we had all fought so hard, that I received a letter from the Wirral Railway Circle. I knew that this group specialised in steam-hauled excursion trains on BR for their members. They were proposing to run a special called 'The Royal Giants' from Oxford, through Worcester, to the

143

Bulmers cider centre at Hereford. A number of engines had been classed as fit for main-line running and *Black Prince* was one of them. We were still at Eastleigh and had little opportunity for main-line running, so the invitation was manna from heaven.

A few years previously Bulmers Cider had become the custodians of *King George V*. This famous locomotive had had an uncertain career after withdrawal from BR service but she had now been restored to full running order. Indeed, she had blazed the trail by becoming the first main-line steam locomotive to return to BR after the end of steam. Bulmers had created a railway centre at their factory, which was open to the public on certain days of the year. It was, of course, rail connected, and on occasions the centre was visited by guest engines from other preserved railways. It was proposed that 'The Royal Giants' rail tour would coincide with the Bulmers Cider Festival. It was the first time that such an extravaganza had been organised by the company and many thousands of people were expected over the ten-day festival, primarily to drink Bulmers produce, but also to enjoy and see the steam engines, if they were capable of doing so after the cider!

All the organisation was done by the Wirral Circle; the run would take place on Saturday 19 May 1973. It was arranged that *Black Prince* would be fully prepared by our own volunteers, at Eastleigh. To serve the purpose of a mess and maintenance van (and doss-house), BR loaned us a coach for the journey to Hereford, the period of the festival itself and the return to Eastleigh two weeks or so later. We left Eastleigh a few days before the great event, to go to Didcot, near Reading. The Great Western Society had its headquarters here and it was arranged that *Black Prince* would have the final preparations made at the Society's depot prior to going to Oxford to pick up the special train.

At Didcot we were given a warm welcome by all the lads there. They were splendid hosts, although there were some ribald comments from a few of the 'dyed-in-the-wool' Great Western people about having a Standard locomotive, 'one of those new things', on Great Western territory; but it was all meant in good fun. Apart from her short run to Romsey from the Eastleigh open day, this was the first time that *Black Prince* had been out on the main line hauling a BR train since I had purchased her, and there was considerable press interest when we arrived. On the Saturday morning we left for Oxford, to meet the thirteen-coach diesel-hauled special train arriving from London. Both *Black Prince* and I have many happy memories of this whole event. When we arrived at Oxford there were several greetings telegrams waiting, not for me, but for *Black Prince*. They were addressed to her 'care of Oxford station', and included two from other locomotives privately owned elsewhere in the country. One read 'Congratulations and all the best for your return to steam; see you at Hereford, *King George V*'. Another one was from our friends up at Dinting Railway Centre from their locomotive, *Bahamas*.

The special duly arrived from London, with the diesel locomotive and carrying a 'Royal Giants' headboard. The diesel was taken off and *Black Prince* and her coach proudly backed on to the train. Unfortunately our own people were not allowed to crew the locomotive; we had to have a BR crew. This is where the first problem arose, if it can be called a problem. In fact it was part of the extra enjoyment as far as I was concerned. We had prepared *Black Prince* with 100 per cent efficiency. She was raring to go, with the needle right on the red line at 250lb per square inch boiler pressure. The BR crew climbed aboard. We left on time, but within minutes the needle started sliding downwards. What was to follow illustrates vividly, to my mind, how 'human' steam engines can be. They are like horses. If a horse knows that you cannot ride it, it plays up and acts accordingly. It's exactly the same with a steam engine; the fireman seemed to have the idea that you just threw the coal into the fire box and left it at that. I cannot think why he was picked for the job; there must have been a long queue of BR firemen who would willingly have done the job for nothing. *Black Prince* at once realised that she could play up and she did exactly that. The needle dropped further, the engine slowed down and the fireman worked harder than ever. He wasted more and more valuable coal, with absolutely no result. He sweated profusely and his language grew progressively worse, as he cursed me, the coal and 'bloody steam engines'. We lost more and more time, so that when we arrived at Worcester we were twenty minutes late.

I enjoyed every second of it. The only people who were slightly unhappy were those railway enthusiasts on the train whose sole object was to time the journey down to the nearest second with stop watches, by counting the telegraph poles flashing past the window. I do not really understand these people. They take a lot of trouble to go on a steam-hauled special, and all they see are telegraph poles and their stop watches. They probably thought that *Black Prince* was a 'rotten' engine, but it wasn't her fault. We arrived at Worcester, our only stop. There were enormous crowds waiting to see us arrive. Not another person could have squeezed on to the platform. The press were there in force, and *Black Prince* was accorded a real 'Royal Giants' welcome. The poor old fireman had to be almost carried from the footplate, still swearing his head off. I hope he never did another steam run. Still on the footplate, I welcomed the new BR crew. 'What's the matter with this bloody old bitch?' asked the new fireman as he saw where the needle had plunged to on the gauge. 'Come on, you old cow, we'll soon have you shipshape; you're not going

(overleaf) The start of it all—my very first view, at Wrexham, of 75029, later to become *The Green Knight*

to fool about with me.' *Black Prince* knew that she had to behave herself.

People were waving and cheering all along the line-side to Hereford. It was especially exciting taking the long, steep haul up through the Malvern Hills. Going through the long Ledbury tunnel was a very exhilarating experience, and a very dirty one. I remember particularly that the cab was filled with choking fumes and smoke as there was, I believe, just 9in clearance between the engine and the tunnel wall. We made a fine run into Hereford, making up all the time that we had lost on the first part of the journey. We steamed proudly into the station with our thirteen-coach train to another great welcome from a huge crowd waiting to see us arrive. *King George V* was in steam in the station and joined in the welcome with her whistle. *Black Prince* then came off the train and steamed into the Bulmers locomotive depot.

The cider festival was quite unlike anything I have ever experienced. The festivities took place in a building which seemed to be the size of a large aeroplane hangar. The various cider bars were set up in this building, with tables and chairs covering the floor. The festival was basically a promotional exercise for Bulmers and was quite clearly a great success. A special railway platform had been built for access to the building in which the drinking activities were taking place. Bulmers had acquired a number of Pullman coaches from BR which were used as a special train to take the visitors from the cider factory down to the festival itself, a distance of approximately 1 mile.

I have a number of very happy memories of the whole event and one or two particularly funny ones. One of these concerned the special platform that had been erected. Early in the morning of the first day of the festival, *Black Prince* had to run 'light engine' down to the new station to make sure that she was not going to meet any obstructions. She arrived at the platform with our coach and we all hopped out. Smiff, who seems to have a nose for anything either comic or out of the ordinary, was up at the far end of the platform. All of a sudden we saw him frantically beckoning us to join him. 'Just look underneath the platform', he whispered. We looked. Amongst the cement bags, bits of timber, old tin cans and all the other rubbish that had been dumped under the newly completed platform, a couple were indulging in sexual intercourse. It must have been extremely uncomfortable!

The festivities in the evening went on, I seem to remember, into the early hours each day. People were dancing and singing on the tables with cider flowing in extremely generous quantities. By the end of ten days, many gallons of cider had been consumed.

Some of the lads had managed to take their annual holidays to coincide with the cider event and, over most of that period, there were at least half a dozen of us dossing down in our coach. The vehicle suffered accordingly, as it was gradually transformed into a four-star hotel. As

148

We arrive at Worcester (as part of the 'Royal Giants' rail tour) to a huge welcome

At Hereford, the final destination of the 'Royal Giants' tour, *Black Prince* is privileged to stand alongside *King George V* (*Photo Rex Coffin*)

only he knew how, Smiff had come to some dubious arrangement with the local dairy and milk was being delivered to the coach every morning. Far from 'putting a note out for the milkman', Smiff was actually writing, on the outside of the vehicle, the number of pints required. She still had his orders marked up on her when she went back into BR service many weeks later. I don't suppose anyone noticed, and she is probably in the same condition serving BR today.

The day finally came for our departure from Hereford. It was a sad occasion because Bulmers and the *King George V* people had made us so welcome; and we left with a major problem on our hands. While we were at Hereford, a message had come through that BR were not prepared to allow *Black Prince* to run all the way back to Eastleigh in steam, the way she had come. For some reason better known to itself, bureaucracy had dictated that she would only run in steam as far as Didcot. There, at—no doubt—considerable expense to us, all the rods would have to be taken off, so that *Black Prince* could then be towed 'dead' to Eastleigh. Heaven knows who thought up that fatuous idea! It seemed totally illogical, as they had not insisted on such an arrangement on the outward journey. It cast a shadow over the whole proceedings which, until then, had been so marvellously well organised by all parties, including BR.

Uncertain as to what the immediate future had in store for us, we left Hereford with our coach, and ran up through the Malverns. When we arrived at Evesham, which was not a scheduled stop, we saw that the signal on the line was against us. We wondered what on earth was happening when, after a short while, the signalman came up to the cab of *Black Prince* and gave us a message. It was, he said, from Richard Marsh himself, who was then chairman of BR. The message told us that we would not after all have to have the rods off at Didcot! I am quite certain that Richard Marsh had better things to do than to worry about *Black Prince*'s rods. We never found out where the message had really originated, and we didn't care; common sense had once again prevailed.

We were back on our way, and all was well; or so we thought. For the rest of the journey to Didcot we had a riotous time. With the BR inspector on board, plus a number of other BR people who seemed to be coming along just for the ride, we spent the time playing with model trains on the floor of the coach as she lurched behind *Black Prince* on her journey home. Several crates of cider had somehow appeared from somewhere and these helped us on our way.

We arrived at Didcot, and yet another problem now presented itself. The BR crew who had been rostered for *Black Prince*'s return journey decided that they were not going any further. Apparently this was the end of their turn. For at least an hour, we were on the telephone trying to sort the mess out. Here we were, at a major railway junction, with our own steam locomotive in steam, and no one seemed to have a clue what was happening. It was very tempting to steam all the way up on our own into Paddington! Probably no one would have noticed if we had. After an hour, the BR inspector arrived, from Basingstoke, with a driver. It turned out that this particular man didn't know the 'road' down to Eastleigh. It happened that Smiff did know it, so he was allowed to fire *Black Prince* and show the driver the way. We finally arrived back at Eastleigh and all was well. Several weeks went by before BR realised that we still had their coach and asked for it back.

We were still paying £20 a week to BR and things were now getting desperate—we had to find a permanent site for our stock as soon as possible. I was offered a home at Tyseley, Birmingham. Another offer came from Steamtown, Carnforth. My two steam engines, in good mechanical order, would no doubt have been added attractions at both those places. However, the problem was distance. Driving to one's hobby for six hours in each direction would have been no fun.

I drew a circle on a map of the south of England. The centre was my home, and the radius was two hours' driving time. I decided that wherever I took my two locomotives would have to be in that circle. Two hours' driving each way would be quite enough. Inside that circle both Barry and I and some of our friends looked at no less than thirty-one different sites. We became very familiar with the railway map of southern England. It was heart-breaking. We trudged up seemingly endless lengths of disused and abandoned railway lines. We looked at some places which raised our hopes to fever pitch, only to have them dashed when we explored the situation in greater depth. Some of the problems were genuine, but it was very easy now for me to get a chip on my shoulder. It seemed that in some cases the local authorities simply did not want to know. Maybe they had been influenced by all the nonsense that had been said about us at Longmoor.

Templecombe

We got quite excited when we found Highclere and Burghclere. I had never heard of either of these two little places, but we discovered them in the depths of the countryside between Basingstoke and Newbury. I seem to remember that Highclere station was in the village of Burghclere, and Burghclere station was in the village of Highclere. It all seemed peculiarly British, and a relic from the days in the last century when a rash of railways appeared on the map of Great Britain almost overnight. At the first place, Highclere (or I think it was Highclere!), we found the most idyllic little railway station that we had seen so far. The ivy-clad station buildings were still there, the platforms were complete, and there was a beautiful little stone goods shed, with creepers growing all over it. The whole place was like a dream. The track had been lifted, but we could put it all back again. All the other original railway structures of this once quaint and beautiful branch line were still there.

At the second of these two places the scene was very different. Not only had the track been lifted but the track-bed itself had been severed and a considerable amount of it had been bulldozed away. Any ideas that we might have had of setting up a permanent, preserved steam railway for our locomotives at this place were finally dashed when we went to the county council at Winchester to talk to the planning people. We were told that there were plans for a road to go along the track bed. I have not been back since, but I am sure that the place must be much the same as it was in 1971—except that it is probably now a rubbish dump.

The place that we saw that must really take first prize for being the most depressing was Ludgershall. I had read somewhere that this place, just off the A303 road near Andover, had something to do with the army. When we got there, it was perfectly obvious that it had. We seemed to be right in the middle of one of the largest army camps that I had ever seen. The place had obviously seen better days. Now the whole site seemed to be derelict. Deserted platforms were covered with rubbish and rubble, and the lamps and platform canopies, if there had ever been any, had long since gone. The utter desolation gave us the shivers.

We heard that there was a rather obscure length of railway line that ran somewhere between Lavant and Chichester, into the Sussex countryside. Barry and I walked the whole length of this. To begin with, the track ran through some beautiful country, but we became more depressed every minute as we finally ended up in a disused quarry.

We looked at the Meon Valley Line in Hampshire. I can't remember how many possibles we had looked at when we came to this one, but we again got very excited when we saw what glorious countryside this little branch line used to run through. The track was still there. One of the most attractive sections of the line was being leased from BR at the time by a rather eccentric gentleman who had apparently invented some sort of new railcar. I never discovered what happened to his idea, but we were not accorded a very warm welcome in any case, and so that was the end of that one.

We moved on yet again. Although it was probably just outside my two-hour circle (depending on the traffic jams), we went to Templecombe, in Somerset. In its heyday, this had been quite a substantial railway centre, a relic of the Somerset & Dorset Joint Railway. Barry and I were elated when we found the place, which seemed to have quite an exciting amount of potential. The steam shed, which was modern, was still there, complete, and with a beautiful little stone cottage alongside it. We could almost hear the steam engines which had departed not so long before. We had with us a book with a photograph of the place, and it seemed to us that all we would have to do was to put the track back again. There were acres of land around the shed, and we were getting more and more hopeful when, wandering around the site, we saw somebody coming towards us. We thought he was just walking his dog. We stopped to pass the time of day. He asked us what we were doing. We told him, and he told us who he was—a property developer who had just bought most of the site!

We went to Maiden Newton, in the depths of the lovely county of Dorset. At the time of our visit, this beautiful little branch line, which ran through to Bridport, was still operating, although it was no doubt losing a small fortune every time one of the infrequent trains ran. We knew that it was due for closure about twelve months after our visit and, once again, our spirits rose. It seemed to have everything. We drove down to Bridport, where we found the familiar scene. One track had gone altogether, and the place was a shadow of its former self but it was still a beautiful little station.

A diesel multiple unit was standing at the buffer stops. It was an idyllic scene. The sun was shining and one could have imagined oneself fifty years back in time if there had been a steam engine on the train instead of the diesel. No one was around and the whole place seemed to be fast asleep. I didn't know the local train timetable, but I had the very firm impression that the train had been standing in the station for quite a long time. Perhaps it had arrived early in the morning and was sitting there all day until it was due to go back to Maiden Newton in the evening. Perhaps it was the weekly train and had been there all week. The thing that did surprise me was that the engine of the diesel was running as though it were about to depart. I turned to Barry: 'Why on earth don't they switch the engine off if the train isn't doing anything?' 'Because, probably, if they switch it off, they'll never get it started again. The batteries are probably flat. Let's go and have a look.'

We looked into the cab. The 'second man' was fast asleep and the driver had his feet up on the panel and was reading the newspaper. We knocked on the cab door. We were greeted by a welcoming smile and invited to hop up. I asked the driver why the engine was running. 'Ah,

153

I'll show you why.' So saying, he got up sleepily from his driver's seat and walked to the back of the cab where, somewhere in the mechanical bowels of the locomotive, he opened a sort of box, up on the wall. There were a couple of onions inside. 'If I switch the engine off, my onions won't get cooked.'

I found the whole place quite delightful—a sleepy branch-line railway from the past. It was a relic from the days when a train would stop at a wayside cottage and deliver eggs to Mrs Bloggs, and further on down the line would stop again to deliver a bottle of milk or the post for someone else. No one would bother too much about anything—it was all wonderfully rural and hopelessly uneconomical, and it was very sad to know that this line would go the way of so many others like it.

Once again, on doing some investigation, we realised that the problems involved were insurmountable. The whole project would be far too large for us to handle.

While we were searching, we continued our expensive residence at Eastleigh. We were still having a fair amount of maintenance done to the engine and coaches, with BR help, quite unofficially. We continued to steam up on rare occasions. Meanwhile the search for a home went on.

Radstock, near Bath, was one of the places that interested us very much. The Somerset & Dorset supporters were making valiant efforts to save this vestige of that once much-loved line. The beautiful stone locomotive shed was still there and they had put a tremendous effort into restoring it to almost its original condition. Similarly, the pretty little station was once again looking proud and smart in its new coat of paint. Up the line a short way, near the colliery, was an enormous and empty wagon repair shop which could possibly have been refurbished to provide ample accommodation for our locomotives, not to mention workshop facilities. Even the colliery itself was due for closure and, given enough support, we might even have saved that as well and turned it into a working museum (and it might well have provided us with an endless source of coal!) It was not to be; it was the same old story all over again. We heard that property developers were after the site. Now the shed and the station, restored with such loving care by volunteers, have been bulldozed aside. The whole area is a desert.

Over on the other side of Radstock we walked up the mile or so of track to a desolate place, called Mells Road, on top of a hill. One look at that place was enough.

We knew that the marvellous little Terrier tank engines had been running their 'puffing Billy' trains across the old trestle bridge to Hayling Island, in Hampshire, until almost the end of steam. We looked at that place too, but we knew that the line was doomed. Moreover it would have cost a vast fortune simply to keep the bridge in good order.

In the early days of preservation, when I had been buying *The Green*

Knight, I met the people who were trying to save just a small part of the once extensive network of Victorian steam railways on the Isle of Wight. They were trying to raise funds to buy one of the 02 tank engines, *Calbourne*. This was the beginning of the steam centre at Haven Street which is now a well-run and established preserved steam railway. I am proud that I have been president of the Isle of Wight loco society since its beginnings. Now we were looking at the prospects of taking our own stock over there, but the idea of humping *Black Prince* across the Solent on a ferry was too daunting for words!

We went to Corfe Castle, once again in Dorset. Corfe Castle is of course one of the prettiest villages that one could find anywhere, and the station was built in the same lovely mellow stone as the cottages. When we saw the place, in 1971, all the infrastructure was still there, including the track. However, yet again, when we began to investigate the situation, we discovered that there were proposals for building a bypass along some of the track-bed. There were many other problems too and, once again, we were to be disappointed. It is interesting to reflect that now, after so many years, with the track removed, there is a railway society trying valiantly to resurrect something out of the wreckage. They are still threatened by the bypass which has not yet been built. All I can say is, good luck to them. They have started at the Swanage end and they deserve to succeed because they are fighting against even greater odds than those which we would have come up against.

For a short time we became excited at the possibility of saving Bath Green Park station. The Midland Railway branch that ran into the station had disappeared several years ago and the track had gone. The beautiful terminal station, built with the lovely warm stone that is so typical of that part of Somerset, was still there, and was a 'listed' building. Presumably, therefore, it could not be bull-dozed flat, and we thought that BR might be only too pleased to get rid of the obligation of maintaining it. The building was slowly but surely decaying, at least superficially. The beautiful arched roof was still intact. The many and varied rooms around the concourse of the station, with their magnificent lofty ceilings, were empty. The rubble and the refuse of years of neglect were everywhere. The only sign of life was the fluttering of countless pigeons high up in the roof of the deserted station. The place seemed haunted by ghosts. The great train shed was now suffering, surely, the final indignity—the area where the steam trains had waited for their passengers was now a car park; and it had been the motor car that had killed the railway in the first place.

As soon as we expressed interest in Bath Green Park, we were given wholehearted support by the then mayor of Bath and many of her colleagues. They understood our aims, for they had seen much of their beautiful city destroyed by uncaring and hasty property development. They saw that we might create a new and significant tourist attraction for the city. Although the railway bridge carrying the lines out of the station had been demolished, thereby destroying any possibility of a proper running line, there were many compensations offered by this beautiful building, but, sadly, we got cold feet. It was just too vast a project. However, at least the building has now been fully restored to its former glory, albeit for a use very far removed from that for which it was originally intended—a supermarket development.

A few miles up the track-bed from Bath Green Park station is a sleepy little place called Bitton. This was the thirty-first site that we looked at. I was beginning to wonder whether we would find anywhere suitable, and we were still paying £20 a week for our Eastleigh siding. Bitton had great possibilities. Here was a very attractive Midland Railway station building with its attendant goods shed. All that was missing was the track. Unfortunately there was talk of a considerable part of the area of redundant railway land being used for industrial development. I walked down the track towards Bath and came across an enormous bridge over the river Avon. With thoughts of having to maintain that and fighting property developers also, I immediately lost interest. It is again interesting to see that, in spite of these apparent problems, there is today a group of enthusiasts who have partially restored the place and are fighting to make something out of very little. Perhaps the property developers who were hovering around when I was there have gone away. I hope so.

By this time Barry and I had spent a very great deal of time and worn out a great deal of shoe leather looking at so many sites, many of which were obviously totally unsuitable at first glance. We had been excited by others, only to have our hopes dashed. Then one day the telephone rang at my home in Surrey. On the line was a friend called Mike: 'David I know that you are bloody desperate. I don't know if the place is of any use, but there is a place near here which might do as a home for your locomotives. It is at a place called Cranmore.'

The consequences of this 'phone call were considerable—see chapter 11!

10

The Zambezi Sawmills Railway and the rescue of two relics from Africa

The client from Texas was hot on the trail of 'his' lion. He had paid the usual not-inconsiderable sum for his game licence and was now on the safari of a lifetime with his professional hunter. He had 'bagged' everything else that he was allowed and he now only had to get the magnificent black-maned lion dreamt of for so long.

The two men were alone, many miles from even the nearest Land Rover track, in one of the most remote parts of 'Mwumbwa One', the Zambia Safari Company's hunting concession area where only the professional hunter, with that uncanny sense of bush craft coming from years of experience, could avoid getting lost in a matter of minutes in those vast tracts of featureless African bush.

The excitement was mounting by the minute. The two men moved together, silently, through the trees, ever nearer to the unsuspecting lion, which was always enticingly just ahead of them. The trees were thinner now, and suddenly they came into a clearing, and there it was. The American's heart was thumping and the adrenalin was flowing. Picture the scene in all its remoteness, an area seemingly untrodden by man; the bush clearing, and, all by itself, an old steam engine. Shafts of sunlight filtered through the tree tops and caught the burnished copper and whisps of steam from an 1896 vintage, 4-8-0 ex-South African Railways, ex-Rhodesia Railways, steam locomotive. It was gently simmering away in the heat of an African afternoon, and not a living soul was to be seen.

Our American friend was speechless with amazement at the incongruity of the scene. Yet the old steam engine seemed to fit into this timeless picture and become part of it. The lion was at once forgotten and for the rest of the day our friend clambered all over the engine taking photographs. The old locomotive was one of many which were ending their long working lives in Africa, being operated by the Zambezi Sawmills Railway in the forests of Zambia.

I first went to Zambia in 1964. I was invited to paint twelve wildlife paintings for the new government. It was on that visit that I first met the president, Dr Kenneth Kaunda, and he invited me to paint the independence celebrations for him. I made many new friends on that first visit and we didn't just talk about wildlife. It seemed that they all knew about my other passion in life. They said that I must get myself down, as soon as possible, to Livingstone, where I would find the terminal of a most remarkable, antiquated, railway system, a great part of which apparently dated from the early part of the century. It was called the Zambezi Sawmills Railway.

Three years later, on my second visit to the country, I decided to make the journey. On the border where Zambia meets Zimbabwe, on the great Zambezi River, at the majestic and awe-inspiring Victoria Falls, I found elephants and steam engines in profusion, and in fact everything that I could wish for. Livingstone still retains the atmosphere of a lovely, old, unspoilt, colonial town. Down either side of the spacious main street are single-storeyed porticoed buildings, some of which date from the early days of the colonial era. For most of the year, the town basks in the scorching sun of the Zambezi Valley.

A few miles away, I could see great clouds of white spray towering into the sky from Victoria Falls. As I drove down to the Falls I also saw clouds of gorgeous black smoke coming up from behind a large mound beside the road. I knew that this smoke came from the steam locomotive shed of Zambia Railways.

My wife and I were in a hired car. I was determined to have a look at the steam shed. After all, what railway enthusiast just out from England, where steam was in its death throes, could resist such a temptation? Standing on the roof of the car, and stretching up as high as I could on tiptoe, I could just see the roof of the massive locomotive depot. 'I'll only be twenty minutes, but I must go and have a look' I said. 'I've heard that before.' I left her in the car and, walking over the bridge, which spanned a large number of railway tracks, came face to face with a sight which reminded me strongly of Nine Elms (except, of course, that the weather was very different).

Here once again was an enormous steam shed where everything was black and filthy, with smoke everywhere. A great number of steam engines of different classes, some of them strange to me, were in steam. I wandered into the shed. 'Have you got a permit?' I was asked bluntly and, it seemed, rather impatiently, by a man who seemed to be the shed master. He was obviously on his way home and didn't want people walking through the shed. I got the distinct impression that he had been bothered a great many times by people like me. 'No, I haven't, I'm sorry, but would it be possible to have a quick look around?' 'No, you can't come in here without a permit.'

The shed master then took a long hard look at me. It seemed that some sort of recognition was slowly dawning. 'Aren't you Mr Shepherd;

158

Zambia Railway's locomotive sheds at Livingstone. A few minutes after wandering into the yard without permission I was driving one of the shed master's Garratts up and down the yard

haven't you got a couple of steam engines back home?' His whole attitude changed immediately. A few minutes later I was driving one of his Class 20 Garratts up and down his shed. One of the nicest things about owning steam engines is that it is rather like a passport.

The magic of steam knows no boundaries. We were immediately engaged in animated conversation. He knew all about my buying *Black Prince* and *The Green Knight* from BR. (It had only just happened, and it turned out that he was an ex-Southern man himself!) When I returned to the car over two hours later, my wife, understandably, was fast asleep.

It was now the turn of the Zambezi Sawmills. I knew that their terminal was around somewhere. I was longing to find out for myself whether all the stories, most of them hilarious, and some dramatic, concerning this quaint and ancient railway were true. I soon found out that they were.

As we were driving away from Victoria Falls and back up into town, I noticed a railway track crossing the road at right angles and disappearing into the distance to the left. Running alongside the line, which, to put it mildly, looked as though someone had dropped it from a great height, was a dirt road. I drove up it. I soon came to a group of ancient, dusty wooden buildings on the right-hand side of the road; the headquarters of the Zambezi Sawmills Railway. Several rather battered Land Rovers were

159

The date of this scene is not around the turn of the century, but 1967. This was my first view of the Livingstone depot of the Zambezi Sawmills Railway, with Class 7 No 69 outside the shed

parked under the shade of some jacaranda trees. I went in. I felt at once as though I had stepped back into the last century. I was immediately impressed by all the beautiful woodwork. Everything was wood and the lovely smell of frequently polished tables and floors pervaded everything. Various rather musty maps hung on the walls, together with ancient, slightly faded photographs, in wide, heavily varnished wooden frames, of very dignified old gentlemen. I was rather surprised at the absence, on the wall, of Queen Victoria herself. I was shown into the manager's office, and we immediately started talking about steam engines and the activities of the logging company.

I then started to explore the place. This, the Livingstone end of the line, seemed to be a complete living railway museum. The steam locomotive shed was something beyond my wildest imaginings and looked as though it had stepped straight out of a book on Victorian colonial railways in Africa. The shed was built of massive timber supports and beams, with a tin roof. Behind it stood a tall and shady palm tree. A beautiful jacaranda tree was in full flower just behind the wreck of an ancient steam engine, standing up on piles of wooden blocks with all its wheels missing. There were a number of assorted ramshackle huts, and the corrugated-iron water tower was covered in Bougainvillaea in full flower. Inside the two-road shed, there was even an inspection pit and a wheel drop, although it was full of water, and frogs. An incredibly ancient engine, in steam for no apparent reason, simmered gently in the sunshine in front of the shed. No 70, I recognised it as a Class 7. I was told afterwards that she had been purchased by the Zambezi Sawmills Railway in 1925 and was still in working order.

A couple of old, extremely bent wagons, and an old passenger caboose, which had obviously seen better days like the rest of the railway, were in another ramshackle building. No one was about; the whole place seemed deserted. Time, in this fascinating place of railway memories, had stood still; yet this was a full operational railway.

Locomotive bogies, wheels and axles were everywhere, all disappearing gradually in the long, dusty, golden grass of an African dry season. The sun caught the maze of cobwebs which were enveloping these various pieces of ancient railway equipment, strewn in total disorder wherever I looked. Other cannibalised engines in various states of decay were lying around. I saw an old wooden clerestory coach, which still had its beautiful and ornate balustrade ends. I was told that it had been used by Cecil Rhodes himself and that it had been the very first coach ever to go over the Victoria Falls railway bridge. The local people were taking bits off this beautiful museum piece, for firewood.

The Livingstone depot was littered with old wheels and other railway 'junk'

Mulobezi, and the final resting place for one of
the old Ford plate-layer's trolleys.

The most amazing sight of all was the Livingstone graveyard, the 'scrap line'. In front of me lay two lines of old locomotives dating from the last century, some leaning over at precarious angles and looking as though they would topple over at any moment. They were resting on a track that had long since disappeared under the vegetation and sand. Most were separated from their tenders and were mixed up in total confusion. All were festooned with the tinder-dry vegetation of tropical Africa. Some had sizeable trees growing through their cabs or from the gaping cavities where driving wheels once turned. The searing hot sun of the many African summers had burned the sides of the tenders and, under the peeling and faded paintwork, the lettering of past owners was revealed.

I kept a watchful eye out for snakes. I had been told that the old locomotives and coaches provided a cool and shady resting place for many a cobra wanting to escape the hot African sun. Honey bees were nesting in one of the holes from which the plugs had long since been removed. Nature was rapidly taking over. I fought my way through the cobwebbed undergrowth and climbed up on to the cab of one of the ancient engines. Here was the greatest surprise of all. The engine was complete, with almost all her cab gauges and fittings. Most of the locomotives still sported their whistles and, on their buffer beams, the heavy, beautiful solid cast-brass number-plates. Obviously these items didn't have the

162

intrinsic value they would have had in England—back home, everything would have been stolen months before.

Being an inveterate collector of such items, I went back to the main offices of the company. I asked the general manager whether it might be possible to have some of the number plates off the 'old engines in the scrap line'. His answer amazed me: 'Yes, I'll get someone to take some of them off for you, but I would like to point out that the engines are not in a scrap line. When we get around to it, we will tow them up to Mulobezi, and give them an overhaul.' Then, with an absolutely straight face, he went on to say: 'But you know, the problem is, it's awfully difficult to get the spare parts.' Considering that the locomotives dated from 1896, I wasn't in the least surprised!

I then sat for a couple of happy hours with the general manager as he told me some of the dramatic and hilarious stories of the early days of the Zambezi Sawmills Railway, while a smartly dressed African brought in endless cups of tea and placed them on the beautifully polished table in front of us.

Exploitation of the vast 'Mukusi' (Rhodesian teak) forests of the southern and western provinces of what was then Northern Rhodesia began before World War I. At the beginning, the timber was cut, around the area of Livingstone, and then hauled out of the forest by oxen, in 10

The 'scrap line' at Livingstone, with the ancient locomotives rapidly disappearing into the undergrowth. (In fact, several of these engines were towed away later to be repaired for further service!)

ton logging trucks on wooden rails. These were laid 2ft apart directly on to the Kalahari sand. As the operations developed, this method became far too slow. A traction engine was purchased which hauled the wagons with its front wheels on the railway line and its back ones in the dirt on either side of the road. The African staff complained that this was far less efficient—they had to push the whole apparatus up hills, something they had never had to do with oxen!

Timber extraction expanded rapidly as the demand for products grew, in particular that for railway sleepers from Rhodesia Railways. By 1924, the Zambezi Sawmills Railway was relaying with steel rail, 3ft 6in gauge. Some of these ancient railway lines were second or even third hand and had been in use in other African countries during the last century. Some had been made in 1877 and were originally used on the old Cape Government Railway. Some of this rail is still giving good service today.

As operations expanded further, so the line stretched its tentacles further north-west into the forest. The line which, until a few years ago, was legally classed as a tramway, quickly became highly efficient and well run although, because of the incredibly ancient and decrepit atmosphere of the railway, it is very easy to treat it frivolously.

In 1934, the railway line reached Mulobezi, 101 miles from Livingstone as the crow flies. If you lived in Mulobezi you called the railway the Mulobezi—Livingstone line. If you lived in Livingstone, you called it the Livingstone—Mulobezi line.

Mulobezi must be one of the most fascinating places that I have ever been to. It is a sawmill township built in the middle of the bush. In the early days, its only contact with the outside world was the railway. It's not

Very much 'as the crow flies'—the railway line from Livingstone to Mulobezi

1902 on one side, and 1903 on the other !
the old Mulobezi wheel lathe, by Craven's of Sheffield.

much better today. In the 1960s, when I first discovered the place, if you wanted to get up to Mulobezi by road you just drove your Land Rover through the bush.

Around the sawmill, so many miles from the nearest town, a close-knit, cosmopolitan community had grown up over the years. Europeans of several nationalities lived cheek by jowl with Asians and Africans. A number of timber houses with overhanging iron roofs were dotted around, along the sawdust roads. In the centre was an incredibly ancient sawmill, with various old machines powered by other old machines, all steam-driven and of great antiquity. One of the first treasures that I discovered in the workshops was a splendid wheel lathe made by Craven's of Sheffield. This had the manufacturers' plate showing 1902 on one side and 1903 on the other. I was told that it took a year to get it to Mulobezi and build it!

In the workshops, complete locomotive rebuilds could be carried out. There were plenty of locomotives always lying around ready to be cannibalised for parts; some of these old engines may well have been written off in one of the variety of highly colourful accidents that were so typical of the railway over many years. Brand-new parts were often manufactured from scrap metal. It was always a question of make and mend, doing the best you could with second-hand material. In spite of the fact that everything at Mulobezi seemed to belong to the last century, the workshops soon established a fine reputation for improvisation. They were even making spares for Zambian Railways, because, I was told, they were more efficient than their customer. I watched as brand-new brass

165

spare parts were manufactured by the time-proven method of pouring molten brass by hand into sand moulds.

A freshly overhauled locomotive was standing outside the workshops in a sparkling new coat of paint, its shining silver wheels picked out in red. Apparently the colour schemes for the locomotives varied according to who was in charge of the painting job at the time. The loco shed foreman and the railway manager took it in turns to decide. Alongside the road going past the workshop was a line of locos of various shapes and sizes, but these were like those in the line at Livingstone, rapidly disappearing into the smothering jungle of creepers. Some of these locomotives were waiting for an overhaul. No doubt one complete new engine would emerge from several of them, after a variety of major transplants. I was told that in some cases, virtually all that remained of the original locomotive was its frames. There was one locomotive in the workshop which bore a plate on one side stating that it had been built in 1900, while on the other was the date 1910. No one seemed to know the correct date of her birth. The workshop staff were more concerned with getting the locomotive back into working order.

Built originally as a logging railway, the system gradually extended outwards in several different directions from the sawmills at Mulobezi. The forest spurs would sometimes stretch for up to 20 miles. A bulldozer

In the Mulobezi workshops, 100 miles from anywhere, they even made new brass spare parts, for Zambia Railways as well as for themselves. The method was the time-proven one of pouring molten brass into sand moulds

It was primitive but it worked—spacing sticks being used when laying track, to make sure that the sleepers are (more or less) the same distance apart

would push the trees over and then, within a matter of minutes, a railway line would follow it, along a line of poles stuck straight into the ground. The steel sleepers would be taken off the last flat wagon and, humped on the shoulders of singing Africans, would be dropped into the sand. Then, with a spacing stick to make sure that each sleeper was more or less the same distance from its neighbour, the rail would be clanked down into the grips of the individual sleepers. The method was primitive but it worked. The record for laying track, I believe, was 7 miles in a day.

After a new spur had been laid, the 'forest' locomotive, usually a Class 7, would take the train of timber wagons down the spur and wait until the trees had been felled, cut into lengths, and loaded on to the protesting ancient wagons. Many wagons were so bent that they had notices painted on the sides advising that they were 'not to be loaded', but nobody took any notice of that. The train would haul its load out of the forest to the junction with the main line, where a larger steam locomotive would take over. This was usually a Class 10, which would haul the train up to the line to the sawmills.

After a certain area of forest had been carefully and selectively felled,

The old Mulobezi sawmill, now swept away and rebuilt with horrible concrete

An ancient Class 7 working on one of the forest spurs

the rail spur would be lifted and relaid in another direction and the process would be repeated all over again. The ancient railway line for the spurs would therefore be used over and over again. There were occasional breakages but that didn't matter; there was an almost endless supply of railway line lying around.

The railway started carrying passengers in the late 1920s when it seemed obvious that it should provide a social amenity for people up country. Passengers originally travelled on flat open wagons; the ZSR did not obtain its first ancient coaches until the 1960s.

Inevitably the railway became associated with dramatic and amusing adventures and anecdotes and stories relating to it are legion. The locomotive drivers and firemen who lived up at Mulobezi were great characters. There was very little entertainment in such a place, and you had to make friends quickly, if you were not to be very lonely indeed. Hunting, shooting and fishing were the main occupations. If you did not participate in any of these activities, drinking was the only alternative. Alcohol was almost an essential part of life if you travelled on the Mulobezi line. Because the track was so bad, the average speed of the main-line trains was usually some 12mph and so the journey took anything up to 10 or more hours. Drink was therefore imperative, as the train lurched and jolted on its journey.

Loading timber into the ancient wagons. Like almost everything else on the Zambezi
Sawmills Railway, they had seen better days

Lifting and relaying track for a new spur into the forest

Derailments, some fairly spectacular, were frequent on the sawmills railway—early photographs, probably taken in the 1930s

The track was so bad in places that derailments at the rate of three a day were quite common at one time, often with disastrous results. One driver dragged three trucks on the end of his train for no less than 12 miles before he realised that they had derailed. The engines had no need for rocking grates in the fire box; the track had the same effect! Apart from derailments, head-on collisions were not unknown. On Simonga bank the safe speed was considered to be not more than 15mph, but because their brakes had failed, trains were known to hit the tight curve at the bottom at over 60 miles an hour. The result was inevitable; the engine tipped over and derailed. In the early days, trains had virtually no brakes at all. Loaded trains often had to stop completely at the top of a hill. The crew and native staff would then leap out and, as the train gathered momentum down the hill, stand on the wooden brake blocks of the wagons to retard the progress. At the bottom of the hill the whole train would be exuding smoke and would appear to be on fire.

Fires were common on the railway. All the locomotives were wood-burning and always left a long trail of burning embers on the track as they went on their way. On one occasion a loaded petrol tanker was coupled up to the engine of a train, for passage to Mulobezi. The engine set alight its own train and the story goes that the driver did not notice that he had a blazing tanker wagon until he had gone a further 6 miles.

A Rhodesia Railways Class 10, No 159, was involved in a major head-on collision and was derailed, some time during the 1940s. It lay in the bush for several weeks before it was possible to heave it back on to the track again. During this time, the track was bent around the engine to ensure that the railway was able to keep on operating. The engine was then taken back to Mulobezi. By the simple method of stretching a length of piano wire from one end of the engine to the other, it was established that the frames of the locomotives were badly bent and twisted. However, it was decided to give her a rebuild and she saw many more years of service on the Zambezi Sawmills, although her frames were never quite the same again; such things did not matter as long as the engine worked.

There were several bridges along the line. One was built from parts of an old turntable. Apparently, when a new bridge was required for the railway, you simply sat around a camp fire in the evening, with a couple of beers, and scratched out the general design in the sand. The bridge would then be built with whatever scrap girders and other pieces of steel framework happened to be lying around. Awful problems were created, because most of the bits of steel used were of different lengths, but, somehow, the bridge always seemed to get built in the end.

The most impressive bridge spanned the 400ft wide Ngwezi river. For most of the year this river was just dry sand. In the rains, however, if they came, the river was prone to sudden flash floods. The worst of these occurred in 1950. In a matter of hours the water had risen to 1ft over the

173

trestle bridge, 20ft above the river bed. The bridge had only recently been rebuilt after a previous flood, with wooden trestles bolted to concrete feet on the sand, and an island half way across. The force of the water not only demolished the island but on one side forced the bridge off its concrete foundations and tilted the whole structure over. It was decided that the simplest way of pushing the bridge back flat on to its foundations again was slowly to drive a Class 10 engine across. The experiment worked. However, the problems were not yet over. The river continued to rise after further heavy rain, and the story goes that the engineer was so angry at the possibility of his labour coming to nothing that, after a few drinks to fortify himself, he walked, in the pitch dark, on to the bridge. With the water lapping around his knees, he very carefully stepped from one sleeper to the next under the water, protesting most loudly at the forces of nature and waving his fist at the clouds as they scudded across the moon. He somehow managed to reach the centre of the bridge and shouted that if the bridge went, then he would go with it. The waters started going down, and the bridge was saved.

Further up the line towards Mulobezi is another bridge at a place called Bombwe. This was one of the few places where the locomotives could take water in the otherwise dry bush. There is an amusing story concerning this bridge, although the incident could have ended in disaster. Until this particular occasion, a train would stop on the bridge and the engine would replenish its tanks from the water tower. On this occasion, two members of the staff, one German and one Indian, had decided to take the train from Livingstone up to Mulobezi. They were each on their own, in adjoining passenger coaches. On departure from Livingstone, they had loaded several crates of beer on board to pass the time on the journey and to ensure that every time the train went over a bump, the jolt would be softened by the state of semi-oblivion into which they had drunk themselves. The train duly arrived on Bombwe bridge and stopped. The Indian in one coach shouted across the gangway to his German friend in the next coach, telling him that he had run out of beer. There was no means of passing from one coach to the other without getting out, walking along the track, and climbing up into the next coach. Our German friend decided to replenish his friend's beer supply. Filling a glass with beer to sustain himself during the long journey to the next coach, he stepped down, holding his beer in one hand, with a couple of further bottles in the other and, without realising that he was on the bridge, promptly fell through the sleepers into the water below. The story goes that, half drunk, he successfully swam to the bank, climbed up on to dry land, then walked back across the bridge, carefully hopping from one sleeper to the next, and climbed into the other coach, all without spilling a single drop! After this, the trains were left further up the line whilst the engine alone went on to the bridge.

174

The main line ran for most of its way across Kalahari sand which, in flat areas, was very prone to flooding. In the rains, considerable areas became swampy and because of the lack of ballast below the railway line the track frequently disappeared under water. One of the particularly colourful engine drivers was driving his Class 9 when he saw the track ahead of him gradually disappear in a flooded area. He thought that he had better stop his train and get out to inspect the situation. He was walking slowly along the line when, to his astonishment, he suddenly saw the track rising into the air out of the water ahead of him. As if that were not enough, he then heard a sound behind him and, on looking around, saw his engine coming slowly and inexorably towards him. Ever so slowly it began to slide over on its side and slither down the embankment. It took two months to get this engine back up on to the rails. When it arrived in the workshop at Mulobezi for repair, a puff adder slithered out of one of the boiler tubes.

Another of the characters who drove on the line for many years was a very keen fisherman and also liked the bottle. He would frequently take the main-line train from Mulobezi down to Livingstone and, because he had spent his rest days doing a lot of hard drinking at Mulobezi, he used to frequently go to sleep on the footplate. On the long journey down to Livingstone the line went over several hills. While the driver snoozed, the engine would slow down as it went up a hill and then race down the other side until it hit the many bad bits of track. There would be a massive thud, and this would wake the driver up; he would slam the regulator shut with his foot and then go back to sleep again until the train again almost stopped, climbing up the next hill. The slackening speed would then again wake the driver once more and he would kick the regulator open again.

Some 10 miles out of Livingstone on the line up to Mulobezi is a place called Simonga. This place is typical of so many small African communities dotted around the bush. The village consists of a number of thatched and tin-roofed rondavels and huts, a primitive village school, a couple of corrugated-iron shops and a Catholic mission. However, Simonga must be unique among such villages; it has two railway stations. The railway line comes down a fairly steep incline from both sides, into the village. A halt was built two-thirds of the way down each side, both platforms being for the village, according to which way the train was going. By this method, the train was able to leave the platform and get enough run down the remainder of the slope to get up the other side again!

Between Mulobezi and Livingstone communications were established by the simple method of a single strand of telephone wire supported on stumps of trees or poles. At every gangers' hut, usually a little round thatched structure, there would be an ancient telephone. To operate this the handle would be cranked and, if you were lucky, you would hear something from the other end. There was only one problem; elephants

Since the 1930s, a motley collection of old cars, usually ancient Fords, have been used as platelayers' trolleys to get around the sawmills railway. If a train was approaching from the opposite direction the car was simply lifted off to allow the train to pass

used to play with the poles and walk through the telephone lines. One story concerns a particularly playful elephant. He was on his way down to Livingstone and, as he progressed, he pulled up every telephone pole. Half a mile behind the elephant, following him as he went on his way, was a gang of Africans putting them all back again.

As previously mentioned, until the 1960s, if you went from Livingstone to Mulobezi by train, you slept on flat open wagons. The only way to get some sleep was to ensure that you had large quantities of beer with you. A European also took an African servant whose task was to sit up all night beside him and beat out the sparks from the engine threatening to set fire to his clothes. Perhaps things were not much better when the coaches and cabooses came in. One story tells of the accountant for the company journeying from Livingstone to Mulobezi during the rains. He had lulled himself to sleep in a state of intoxication. He dreamt that he was swimming. He woke up to find that he was! The water was up around his bed inside his caboose as it canted over at an angle of 45°. Then the vehicle slowly went over on to its side.

The Zambezi Sawmills Railway used to use a variety of plate-layers' trolleys to get around the system quickly. These were road vehicles

176

adapted in a most precarious manner to run on the railway line. A variety of cars were used. On my first visit to the railway they were using a Land Rover. It was hair-raising to sit in the cab and drive in the normal way, except that the steering wheel was tied to the floor to prevent you using it. On one occasion, the vehicle broke down. A Class 10 had to come down the line to tow me in, and it seemed most strange to sit in a Land Rover, on a railway, being towed with a rope hitched on to 100 tons of steam engine in front of you.

The most popular cars throughout the 1940s and later were a fleet of ancient Ford Anglias. These gave marvellous service to the railway for very many years. The record for the journey in one of these from Livingstone to Mulobezi was 2½ hours, at an average speed of 50mph. On the crazy track, laid straight on to the sand, this must have been quite an experience. If you were in your car and you saw a train coming in the other direction, you simply stopped and, with the help of the many locals who used to sit up on top of the tenders of the engines for the ride, you lifted the car off the rails to let the train go by. You then replaced the car on the railway line and went on your way. If you saw elephants and lions on the track it was a different matter; prayer was probably more appropriate.

In 1970 I returned once more to the Zambezi Sawmills Railway. This time, the BBC were with me and we were making *The Man Who Loves Giants.* They wanted to include a shot of me driving one of the ancient

When I visited the sawmills railway, they were using a Land Rover which frequently broke down—but there was always a passing locomotive to give a helping hand and a tow back to base. There was always plenty of surplus labour around to see the fun, too!

Class 7s up and down the yard at Livingstone. It was on this visit that I met Graham Roberts for the first time. Graham and I at once became firm friends. He was virtually in charge of his own railway empire. Crewe-trained in the best traditions of Britain's railways, he was responsible for the day-to-day operating and maintenance of the large fleet of ancient locomotives in his care.

The year 1973 included a strange 'first' for me. I don't much like package tours. Over the last twenty years, my wife and I have been privileged, and spoilt, because we have almost always been able to go out game viewing with the wardens in their Land Rovers. Imagine how surprised my friends were, therefore, when they learned that I was actually going to lead a wildlife package tour to Zambia.

I first met the twenty people who were coming with me at the check-in desk at Heathrow, and they were equally amazed: 'Why on earth are *you* doing this sort of thing, David?' I knew immediately that they were nice people. I told them that I would try anything once (and that my air fare was paid for me). I had brought with me a copy of the film *The Man Who Loves Giants.* On several occasions, because they kept on asking for it, I showed the film at the various safari lodges and camps where we were staying.

The tour ended with two free days in Livingstone. By this time my group had not only gathered (can't think how!) that I was a steam railway freak but also knew all about the Zambezi Sawmills Railway. We were sitting in the hotel near Victoria Falls one morning when one of the ladies said: 'Go on, David. I know you are bursting to go and play trains on the Zambezi· Sawmills Railway. You've had enough of us; off you go and enjoy yourself.' 'Would any of you like to see the Zambezi Sawmills Railway, if I can arrange something?' I asked them. Twenty pairs of hands shot up enthusiastically.

An hour later I was back in the hotel. 'Come on, they've laid on a train especially for us, and we are going up the line.' We all piled into a bus and arrived at the railway. No 69, an ancient Class 7, was in steam with a coach attached. We drove sedately and slowly up the line for a few miles. The train then stopped, and we all got out. Some friends of mine had a beautiful home within sight of the Zambezi river. We walked a few yards along a bush track from the train to the house, and were at once given a wonderfully warm welcome. For the next couple of hours we sat drinking tea and coffee in the shade of a large tree in their garden, while 'our' train stood on the railway line, awaiting our return.

On the return journey, backwards, to Livingstone, the engine driver asked whether anyone would like to drive. Everyone volunteered excitedly and, with frequent stops, most of them had the opportunity to do so.

On saying farewell to the group at Heathrow, I asked: 'What has been your most memorable moment? Was it the elephants swimming in the lagoon? Or was it that evening when we saw the lions on the kill?' The answer, from more than one in the party, was: 'Driving that marvellous old steam engine'!

While we had been filming the short sequence at Livingstone for *The Man Who Loves Giants*, the BBC had become quite captivated by everything they saw on the Zambezi Sawmills Railway. They decided that it would be worth coming back to Zambia with me, to tell the whole story. The result was a half-hour television documentary, *Last Train to Mulobezi.* By the time we arrived to make the film, in 1973, the logging operation with steam trains had in fact ceased. Moreover, it had been decided that the sawmills at Mulobezi would be completely rebuilt and modernised, so the old mill had also closed. When the company heard that we were coming to film their operations, they actually started the operations up again especially for us. A complete train was laid on, with the attendant railway gangs to cut and fell trees as and when we required.

The film crew obtained some marvellous footage in the graveyard at Mulobezi and we even managed to retrieve there the remains of one of the ancient Fords. By some miracle of improvisation, the workshops got the old car going once more for the film. One particularly amusing sequence shows me sitting in the car, while it once again breaks down. An ancient Class 7 comes up behind me, steam escaping from everywhere that it shouldn't and pushes me all the way back to Mulobezi. Reaching its destination the car finally died once and for all.

A year or so after we had completed the film, I was back in Mulobezi once again. I had a copy of the film with me and I suggested that it might be screened for all the locals who had taken part. It was an evening that I shall remember for a very long time.

When we heard how many people from the surrounding villages were coming to see the film (some walking 20 miles through the bush!) we realised that we must show the film in the open air. Power for the projector was supplied by a portable generator and the audience of several hundred Africans sat on the ground in front of a white sheet hung from a scaffolding frame. From the first moment that the film was on the screen, the noise was so great that we decided to turn the sound right off and run the film silent. As soon as the show was over, the audience clamoured for a second showing. This time I suggested that I should tell them a little bit about the film and how the engines and coach were taken away from Mulobezi to start their long journey across the sea to England (for that is what happened, as I explain later in this chapter). I stood in the arena lit by the headlights of a Land Rover. They listened in rapt silence as I told the story. We then put the film on for the second time with the sound and you could have heard a pin drop. It amused me to notice the audience's reaction, which was so completely different to that in England. When the scene showing me sitting in the car being pushed by the Class 7 comes on the screen in this country, it often arouses gales of laughter. At Mulobezi there was silence; after all they had seen that sort of thing every day of the week. When a particular friend of theirs, for instance the driver of the Class 10 who was well known to all of them for his eccentric behaviour, appeared, they erupted with laughter and cat calls. That's audience participation! I know that whenever I go back to Mulobezi I shall always receive a tremendous welcome from all the many marvellous Africans that I met while we were making this film which is a unique record of an almost 'Victorian' railway built by the British in the heart of Africa. When we had finished filming *Last Train to Mulobezi*, most of the locomotives and coaches were dumped in the bush graveyard at Mulobezi.

Mulobezi has now been rebuilt with horrible modern concrete and, after several disastrous attempts, Zambia Railways have now taken over the Livingstone–Mulobezi line and are running it with diesels. These, I am told, derail even more often than the old steam engines used to and they take even longer to reach their destination; so, one day, perhaps, steam may return. I would not be in the least surprised.

By the beginning of the 1970s, through the auction of several of my wildlife paintings in America, I had managed to raise, with the help of a lot of other people, enough money to purchase a Bell Jet Ranger

When we had finished filming *Last Train to Mulobezi*, the old sawmills closed down and the locomotives were dumped in the graveyard. I asked to have one of them and, with the personal approval of HE the President of Zambia, Dr Kenneth Kaunda, No. 993—the Class 7 in the best working order—became mine. Before joining the Zambezi Sawmills Railway to end her African working days (seventy-eight years of them!) there, No. 993 had been the last Class 7 in South African Railways service. Here she poses in Johannesburg alongside one of the SAR's new electric locomotives

helicopter to catch poachers in Zambia. I had arranged for the helicopter to be taken out to Zambia, where I subsequently presented it to the president. I don't know whether this had any bearing on what was to follow, but I would like to think that it did. Seeing all those marvellous old engines being dumped in the bush had been too much for me. I had become very fond of No 993, the marvellous old Class 7 and the best of her class still in working order. She had performed so well as the forest engine throughout the TV film. I asked if I could have her. They said yes!

No 993 had in fact only recently joined the Zambezi Sawmills Railway. She had been built by Sharpe Stewart in Glasgow, in 1896, and she began life in South West Africa for the Cape Government Railways. After working most of her life in that part of the continent, she was then taken into the South African Railways' stock. She ended her days there as a shed pilot in Johannesburg station. She was in fact their last Class 7 in

No 993 had started life on the Cape Government Railway in South Africa in 1896—this photograph, taken in that year, shows one of her sisters No 15

working order and photographs were taken at the time of her withdrawal showing her posing beside one of their new electric locomotives. Graham Roberts had been to South Africa to buy the last batch of steam engines for the Zambezi Sawmills Railway, and 993 was included in that package.

Not content with this one locomotive, which had been given to me as a gift, I asked if I could have the ex-Rhodesia Railways Class 10 No 156, as well. This engine, which had been given the name *Princess of Mulobezi*, was the main-line locomotive in the film. She was in full working order and they sold her to me for £100. I can only assume that as there was very little demand for scrap in Zambia, they thought that they were probably getting the best of the deal.

While we were filming, we had been given the use of a beautiful ex-

Rhodesia Railways first/second class composite sleeping car and I had now set my covetous eyes on this. What was the use of having two engines without a coach to go with them? No 1808, built in Birmingham in 1927, was still in its original condition. All the mahogany woodwork was as polished as when she was originally fitted out. It was complete with its green leather bunks and beautiful brass fittings on which, in the colonial days, you hung your solar topee. District commissioners travelled around the country in the luxury of such vehicles. In the lavatory at the end of the corridor was a notice which advised the traveller that he must not expectorate, that he must not spend more than 10 minutes in the lavatory and that hot and cold baths could be obtained at Bulawayo station.

My request for the coach was not too favourably received. The Zambezi Sawmills Railway people said that, because of its excellent condition, it would probably be taken into the stock of Zambia Railways for further use. I suggested that, surely, another coach, not in such good condition, would do just as well for them. It worked. They agreed, and No 1808 was mine, for nothing! As if I had not landed myself with enough problems with preservation in England, here I now was, the totally bewildered owner of a complete railway train, sitting in landlocked Zambia, without any money to get the thing home. Nevertheless, I was determined to do so, somehow.

To start with, I disregarded the financial problems. I know that this is easy to say, but, as I will describe later, for the first time in my life these were being looked after by someone else. I started exploring how I could get two locomotives and a coach back from Africa. I assumed that because of the apparent political problems in that part of Africa between 'black' Zambia and 'white' Rhodesia, there would be only one way to go and that would be northwards. I assumed that it would be quite out of the question to cross from Zambia to Rhodesia on the Victoria Falls railway bridge over the Zambezi river. This border was 'closed'; or so we were told by the politicians. Moreover, we were perpetually being informed by the media that the two countries were firing bazookas and rockets at each other across the river.

Looking at the map, I realised that I would have to go either northwards through Tanzania to the port of Dar es Salaam, or, turning left, through Zaire and along the Banguela Railway to the port of Lobito in Angola. I was at once filled with misgivings, which were immediately confirmed by everything that I was told in London. This was at the time when there was considerable political upheaval in Angola. Indeed, there was a full-scale war going on and I didn't feel particularly keen to get involved in it. Very few ships went to Lobito and in any case the Benguela Railway had been blown up in several places. As if that was not enough, I was told that it would be a complete waste of time to go through Zaire to get to Angola anyway; everything removable on the locomotive and coach would probably be stolen, and I myself would quite possibly never be seen again!

The alternative was the Tanzam Railway, only recently completed by the Chinese, linking Zambia with Dar es Salaam. This railway, to put it extremely mildly indeed, was having teething problems. Furthermore, the docks at Dar es Salaam were apparently choked with a backlog of several years' cargoes and the whole place had almost come to a grinding halt. It seemed to be the end of the whole idea. I should have known that things are never as bad as they are painted, and I had not taken account of my friends in Zambia.

It was in 1973, after the railway train had been sitting in Zambia for over three years, that I was once again in Livingstone with Graham Roberts. More for fun than for any other reason, we decided to go into the customs post on the Zambian side of the border, within sight of the Victoria Falls railway bridge. At this time, as I have said, the border was officially closed. Apparently no one in Zambia was talking to anyone in

Rhodesia, and vice versa. In fact, I knew that the situation was very different. Zambia had to export her copper southwards to Rhodesia because she needed the income. Rhodesia similarly had to export her coal to Zambia for the same economic reasons. This meant that several times a day there were train movements in each direction over the bridge. While no one, supposedly, was looking, a Zambia Railways steam locomotive would push a copper train of twenty or more loaded wagons on to the bridge. The end wagon would then be very carefully stopped on the white painted line, exactly half way across the bridge. That was the border. The Zambian engine would be uncoupled and would scuttle back into Zambia. The loaded wagons would be left standing on the bridge for several hours. This caused much concern to those who were looking after the bridge because, when it was built at the turn of the century, it was certainly not designed to have loaded copper trains sitting on it for any length of time. After an interval, a Rhodesia Railways steam locomotive would surreptitiously venture on to the bridge, carefully couple up to the copper train on the white line, and haul it across into Rhodesia.

When a coal train was going in the opposite direction, the whole procedure was repeated in reverse. I was told that on one occasion a Zambia Railways engine driver accidentally pushed his train a couple of feet over the white line by mistake and the African guard was promptly arrested by the Rhodesian authorities. He was accorded every hospitality by Rhodesia Railways, given lots of cups of tea and was then allowed to go back into Zambia. Unfortunately a happy story like that never seems to get into the press.

It was with the full knowledge of this rather crazy situation that Graham and I decided to go into the customs post. We were greeted with a beaming smile from an African customs officer sitting behind his desk in an immaculate white uniform. 'What can I do for you, gentlemen?' he asked. I decided to come straight to the point. 'I've got two steam locomotives and a railway coach, and I want to take them over the bridge into Rhodesia, please.' I fully expected him to say that the customs had better things to do than to waste time with cranks. He didn't say that. His reply was quite astonishing: 'That's all right, there's no problem, you can call them your personal effects!' I was stunned. The customs officer could see that I was. I am not sure that I was any the wiser when he tried to explain the situation. Apparently, it was something to do with the law that, providing your luggage was originally from England and you were returning it from whence it came, it did not really matter whether it was a suitcase full of books, or two steam locomotives and a railway coach. However, I suspected that in reality things could not be as simple as that, and these fears were confirmed by my friends in Lusaka. It was obvious that the president himself was the only man who could really help, and actually get my rolling stock into Rhodesia.

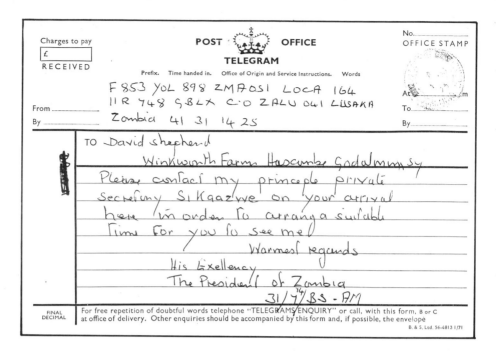

F 853 YOL 898 ZMAOSI LOCA 164
11 R 748 GBLX C.O ZALU 041 LUSAKA
Zombia 41 31 1425

TO David shepherd
Winkworth Farm Hascumbe Godalmmy sy
Please contact my principle private
Secretary Sikaazwe on your arrival
here in order to arrange a suitable
Time for you to see me
Warmest regards
His Excellency
The President of Zambia
31/7/83 - AM

As I explained earlier, I had first met Dr Kaunda on my first visit at the time of the gaining of independence by Zambia in 1964. From our first meeting, he and I had a common bond—a great love of, and passion for the conservation of, the country's natural heritage, its wildlife. That had drawn us together immediately, and we had at once become firm friends.

Now I had to talk to him about my railway train. I managed to arrange a meeting with him. I felt pretty awful about the timing, because it was during one of his very rare holidays. When he does manage to take a break, he goes into his beloved Luangwa National Park. We both regard this as one of the most wonderful places on earth. My wife and I have been privileged to go out game viewing with him on several occasions, and we know what the place means to him. However, even there, he is inevitably surrounded by the affairs of state, and now I was going to talk trains with him. I hoped that he wouldn't mind. He didn't.

I flew out to Zambia and went to his private lodge on the edge of one of the beautiful lagoons which are such a special feature of the park. He was quite relaxed and alone. We sat talking in the shade of a tree, watching elephants bathing in the water just a few yards away. For several hours we discussed the world's problems, crime, unemployment, racial problems and many other things. We got around to wildlife, inevitably, and talked about the problems of poaching and conservation with which he had so closely and personally associated himself. Finally, it was Dr Kaunda who brought up the subject. He knew why I had come. 'David, I believe that you have a problem with the old engine we have given you. Is there anything that I can do to help?' He had been well briefed.

I came straight to the point. He likes things that way. 'Yes, I do have a problem. Would you allow me to take my two locomotives and the coach over the bridge into Rhodesia please?' He pondered for just a few seconds, and then gave me his answer: 'Yes, that's all right. I can arrange it for you.' He rang a bell, and one of his personal staff came out of the lodge. 'Could you take this down for Mr Shepherd, please, on my state house notepaper, and I want a copy for members of my cabinet.' I then listened while he dictated what was, to me anyway, a remarkable document; in fact, it must be unique, and I am privileged to have been given the original copy to keep.

President Kaunda works long hours every day, and well into the night, with all the enormous and complex problems of an emerging African nation on his shoulders. Nevertheless, I began to think, as I listened to him dictating, that he had nothing else on his mind except my own problem of getting a railway train back to England. He stopped half way through, and turned to me: 'David, what were the numbers of the engines and coach?' (He knew about the coach and the second engine!) He wanted to get everything correct.

It was as simple as that. With the valuable document in my pocket, I went up to Lusaka. In less than a day I was through all the essential red tape and possible problems that it might have taken months to solve in more normal circumstances. With the necessary paperwork to ensure the safe passage for my train southwards, I went to the exchange control authorities, the bank, the customs and excise, and when they saw the document signed by the president an 'authorise' stamp appeared immediately on every bit of paper, with no questions asked. I could not believe it. I was walking on air.

A few days later I returned to Livingstone. By this time the locomotives and coach had come down from Mulobezi and had been 'prepared' for their long journey home. They were together in the Zambia Railways steam shed. Graham Roberts was there to meet me. 'Everything is OK and ready to go' he assured me.

A few hours later the two engines and the coach were marshalled into one of the copper trains for passage over the bridge. I looked somewhat alarmed at the mining cable which had been twisted around the coupling between the tender of 993 and the first wagon. Graham could see that I was worried: 'Oh, that'll be OK for the whole journey. It will be quite safe.' It didn't look very safe to me; what might have been satisfactory for the Zambezi Sawmills Railway would surely be a different matter for Rhodesia Railways. However, it was too late to do much about it, because they were going over the next day.

187

IMMEDIATE ACTION

Minute by His Excellency

HON. A.J. SOKO, M.P.,
MINISTER OF POWER, TRANSPORT AND WORKS.

       This is to let you know that I endorse the decision taken to sell one of the locomotives that belong to the Zambezi Sawmills to Mr. David Shepherd. The Government has also decided to give him one free of charge. The two locomotives concerned are Nos. 993 and 156.

2.   This minute also serves to allow him to take these engines through Livingstone. I have given this authority because this action will not break sanctions in any way at all.

10th August, 1974.   PRESIDENT

cc.   His Honour the Secretary-General
        Rt. Hon. Prime Minister
        Hon. Minister of Foreign Affairs
        Hon. Minister of Planning and Finance
        Hon. Minister of Home Affairs
        Hon. Minister of Mines and Industry
        Mr. David Shepherd.

The following morning, I went into the headquarters of Zambia Railways to see how arrangements would be made for the reception of my train on the other side of the bridge. It was all so simple that I could hardly believe it. The officials of Zambia Railways rang up Rhodesia Railways on the other side of the border on a wonderful old mahogany-cased wind-up telephone (I wish I could have acquired it for the East Somerset Railway, but they were still using it). 'Can we send David Shepherd's engines and coach over tomorrow, please?' I heard the voice on the other end of the line: 'Yes, that'll be fine.'

The Zambia Railways police even gave me permission to film the great event. The whole area around Victoria Falls was a very tight security zone and no filming was ever allowed, but the granting of this very special facility was typical of the co-operation that I received from everyone on both sides of the border. With a Land Rover full of very friendly African police alongside me, I filmed and watched as the Zambia Railways Garratt slowly hauled the long train out of my sight down the line towards the bridge over the Zambezi. Then, with my friends, I walked to the hotel from where I would get a fine view.

We sat together on the terrace of the hotel and, in a very short time, we saw the end of the copper train slowly edging on to the bridge up to the white line. There, sure enough, and to my great joy, were my two steam engines and coach. I filmed the great and historic moment with my movie camera on full telephoto. It was a magnificent sight, with the unbelievably steep gorge and the Zambezi river thundering over the falls and under the bridge; the train itself looked like a tiny model.

The guard's caboose stopped on the white line. About half an hour later the Rhodesia Railways engine came on to the bridge and hauled the train into its own country. They were over. I finished filming and put my camera down on to the table. It was then that I noticed that I had not screwed the lid of the camera firmly down. The film was totally ruined, and I could not very well ask them to do the whole thing all over again.

I now had to get myself into Rhodesia. This was far more trouble than getting the engines and coach over. The footpath and road over the bridge had been closed when the political situation had become sensitive between the two countries. Now, if someone wanted to drive into Rhodesia, he had to go 90 miles up the river and 90 miles down the other side, instead of going just the few hundred yards over the bridge. This is what I had to do. I drove up parallel with the Zambezi to a point where the countries of Zambia, Botswana and Rhodesia all met. Here, an ancient hand-operated car ferry took me across to Botswana. I then had to drive a few miles before crossing another border into Rhodesia, and then another 90 miles back to Victoria Falls.

When I arrived, I walked into Victoria Falls station and there was my train. A reception committee was waiting for me. Trevor Wright, who was then the general manager of Rhodesia Railways, and his deputy, were both there. They had come up to the Falls for a conference and had decided to take a short break in the proceedings to walk into the station to see what had arrived from across the bridge. Trevor said: 'I am very sorry, but your train is not going any further.' It was really rather a shock to hear this. Had I come all this way only to come unstuck now?

We looked at No 993 and I could see the reason for Trevor's concern. The mining cable had frayed almost right through and the locomotive was about to part company with the wagon next to it. 'You see now, we really

189

can't allow that on our main line', Trevor explained. 'But, we'll fix you up.'

A few days later, a repair team came up all the way from Bulawayo. The end of 993 was lifted up into the air in the middle of the station. They did something, I am not sure what, to her front bogie wheels, and a new coupling was put on the rear of the engine. All this much-needed surgical work was done over a period of five days and it didn't cost me a single penny. I knew that I had made new friends over the border already.

I said earlier that I had counted on the financial side taking care of itself. It did. Over the years, I had struck up a firm friendship with Jack Hayward. Jack is a great Anglophile. I had discovered very quickly that he would support any worthy cause that was near to his heart, providing that it was British. (Jack lives most of the time in Freeport, Grand Bahama Island, but also has a beautiful estate in Sussex. As you go through the driveway there is a big notice saying: 'No foreign cars allowed on this property.')

Jack had told me that he was quite willing to pay the whole cost of bringing the engines and coach back to England, providing that it was not over a certain amount. That seemed fair enough. My agents in England assured me that the amount would be quite sufficient to cover the whole operation. Jack arranged for his son-in-law to fly out to Zambia. A friend of mine from the Zambezi Sawmills Railway, who had become greatly excited by and involved with the whole project, had also managed to take a week or so off from his work and came along for the ride too. My two chums accompanied the train on the first part of the journey down to Bulawayo. I decided to fly down, and welcome the train when it arrived.

With the remedial work complete, the two locomotives and coach were put into a Rhodesian Railways freight train and, a few days later, arrived in the fine old colonial station of Bulawayo. Trevor Wright and I were on the platform, and the press and a large crowd were with us to welcome the new arrivals. My two engines and coach were then shunted into a siding, to await developments. I had dinner with Trevor Wright and his wife that evening. Trevor said: 'You're OK now, David; just go down to see the South African Railways people in Johannesburg and it should be plain sailing right through South Africa down to Cape Town.'

I did just what Trevor said and, when I reached Johannesburg, I was most surprised by the welcome I received. I had made many friends in South African Railways over the years and this only made things more upsetting. It seemed that I had come up against a cold wall of bureaucracy.

(opposite above) Nature soon takes over—Stockbridge soon after closure. Nothing now remains, the entire station site having been swallowed up by a new roundabout; *(below)* Cashmore's yard, Newport; the end of a coach—seat cushions, curtains, mirrors and all

191

I had also been given an ex-Rhodesia Railways sleeping coach built in Birmingham in 1927. It is seen here in Victoria Falls station, together with my Class 10, *Princess of Mulobezi*, and my Class 7. My 'train' had just made its historic crossing from Zambia into Rhodesia, over the Victoria Falls railway bridge spanning the Zambezi river. The river is the border and it was officially closed at the time, but President Kaunda had personally given permission for the locomotives and coach to cross over

They quoted such an exorbitant charge for the tow down the line that it made the whole exercise futile. My hopes were finally dashed when South African Railways said: 'Even if we could get the engines down to Cape Town, we have no facilities to lift them on to the deck of a ship.' I could only make one reply: 'That seems a bit odd to me, because you managed to lift my engine off the deck of its ship in 1896 without any problems; now, in 1974, you're telling me you can't do it.' They didn't make any further comment. I returned to Bulawayo disillusioned. It seemed that the whole exciting project was falling apart around me.

Once again, I received a warm welcome from Trevor Wright: 'How did you get on? Presumably everything is OK down south.' 'Far from it; the whole idea is off.' I then began to have visions of having a railway train stuck indefinitely in Rhodesia. But Trevor had other ideas: 'Well, don't let's bother with the South African Railways. Let's see if we can turn left and go down through Mozambique, out through the Port of Beira and round the Cape.'

I was in close contact with Jack all this time and he now told me that he did not feel able to pay the cost of transporting both locomotives and the coach back home to England. He was being incredibly generous as it was and I could not really question that decision. No 156, the ex-Rhodesia Railways Class 10 would have to stay.

Rhodesia Railways were marvellously co-operative. They told me that they would be perfectly happy to look after the locomotive until I might be able to take her away. She was given a general clean up and de-rusted, and was at first put into the workshops in Bulawayo under cover. A few months later she was towed round to their splendid little railway museum on the outskirts of the town. To this day she has stood in front of the only other Rhodesia Railways Class 10 in the world. This one is now owned officially by Zimbabwe Railways. Last time I was in Bulawayo I went round to the museum for a quick look to see if *Princess of Mulobezi* was OK. I happened to remark that it seemed a shame that she was still in her original Zambezi Sawmills green paint which, by now, was looking just a little tatty. The supervisor of the museum said: 'OK, we'll give her a repaint for you.' Two days later she was out in the sunshine gleaming in a brand-new black paint scheme. It was all done, need I say, free of charge; nor have I been charged a single penny for storage of the locomotive since 1974.

We now had to arrange for 993 and the coach to be towed down to Beira. To start with everything seemed to go remarkably smoothly. The agents had found a ship—the *City of Singapore*. Things now started to go

Only two ex-Rhodesia Railways Class 10 locomotives are still in existence and, at the time of writing, one lies forgotten in the railway museum at Bulawayo, in Zimbabwe. *Princess of Mulobezi* has now returned to Zambia to take her place in the projected railway museum at Livingstone, political problems and lack of funds having made her return to England impossible

My sleeping car begins its long voyage home at the port of Beira, Mozambique

wrong. I was told that the *City of Singapore* had stuck on a sand-bank outside Lobito. This was right round the other side of the African continent! An alternative ship had to be found quickly—the *Clan McIntyre.* Something went wrong with this ship as well. I never discovered what.

The agents then found a third ship, the MV *Tactician* of Harrison Lines, of Liverpool. The ship was just about to start loading 993 and the coach aboard at Beira when I was told that, because of the delays with the first two ships, several thousand pounds would be added to the bill. This seemed strange, to say the least. It was not my fault if ships got stuck on sandbanks! I couldn't help it if they were held up for days outside ports which were (or seemed to be) in a state of semi-chaos waiting for huge backlogs of freight to be cleared. However, it seemed that there was little choice but to pay. I had to ring Jack in Grand Bahama Island in a semi-panic to ask if he was prepared to pay the extra; otherwise the coach would probably be shoved into the water from the dockside. When I finally managed to get through to Jack on the 'phone, I discovered that he was attending a very smart reception for Her Majesty the Queen on the royal yacht *Britannia.* I managed somehow to explain the crisis and, to my intense relief, he readily agreed to pay.

At long last the ship was on its way down the east coast of Africa. There were now further problems and delays. It seemed that the ship's bottom had not been cleaned, and the growth of weeds was slowing her down. Then, without any warning, the *Tactician* had unexpectedly to go to Dublin on its way to Manchester.

Finally, the ship arrived in Manchester docks. The BBC television team who had made *Last Train to Mulobezi* with me in Zambia were there to film the arrival. They had planned all along to finish the television documentary with this footage. It would have been a fitting end to the story. They had told me that if the ship arrived on time in Manchester, they could rush the footage of the arrival through just in time. It had been a nail-biting exercise as there was one delay after another. Still the BBC had hoped for success but the diversion of the ship to Dublin finally made it impossible; a substitute end had to be made for the film. Nevertheless, they still came to Manchester docks to film the unloading for the television news that evening.

Space was not (and is still not) yet available on the East Somerset Railway (see chapter 11) for the new arrivals from Africa, and I had managed to find a temporary home for them at Whipsnade Zoological Park in Bedfordshire. Steam trains of the 'Umfolozi light railway' take visitors through various animal enclosures at the zoo, and the company owning the railway offered me a small length of siding which was surplus to their requirements, on which the coach and engine could sit as static exhibits. The Royal Zoological Society of London were only too pleased to help as they realised that these exhibits would be an extra attraction for the visitors.

The ship arrived in Manchester docks on a Sunday evening. The following Friday was Good Friday. Four low-loaders were required for the job; one for the locomotive, one for the tender, one for the coach body, and one for the bogies of the coach. The zoo had perfectly reasonably told us that they did not want the cavalcade coming into the zoo over their busiest time of the year. This meant that we had from early Monday morning until Thursday night to unload in Manchester docks, to go down the M6 and the M1 into the zoo, unload and get away from Whipsnade. The low-loader people expressed considerable misgivings. In fact, they told me that the job could not be done in that time. I knew that if they could not complete the job by the Thursday evening, then it would cost poor Jack a lot more money to pay for the retention of the low-loaders over the Easter period, until they could complete the operation the following week. I persuaded the transport people to have a go.

We went down to the docks as soon as the labour force arrived for the day's work on the Monday. I was on board as I watched the ship's own heavy lift derricks begin to prepare to swing the locomotive over the side and on to the low-loader which was waiting on the quayside below. At that moment I saw a shop steward going around talking to a number of the dockers, who seemed to be doing nothing in particular. A few minutes later, they all downed tools. They had come out on strike for 24 hours. I knew that I was back in dear old England!

I was now told that it would be quite impossible to do the job in the time remaining before Easter. 'For Heaven's sake, let's at least try', I said in anguish. They agreed.

The following day we again went down to the docks early in the morning. Jack was now with me. The saga was very nearly repeated once again. I was on board and I saw the same shop steward going around talking to the dockers. He saw me and came over: 'It means a lot to you to get these things off the ship, doesn't it, guv?' 'Yes, actually it does; do you think that you could possibly consider working long enough to complete the unloading. After that, what you do is your own business.' 'OK mate, we'll work especially for you.' He then went on: 'You know, us dockers in Manchester aren't the bastards that you posh people in Surrey think we are. We raise a lot of money to buy kidney machines.' I was suitably impressed, until one of the dockers standing around and who had overheard the conversation came over to me and said: 'You don't

Having departed to Africa in the reign of Queen Victoria, my Class 7 comes home again—Manchester docks, 25 March 1975 (*Photo Elsam, Mann & Cooper*)

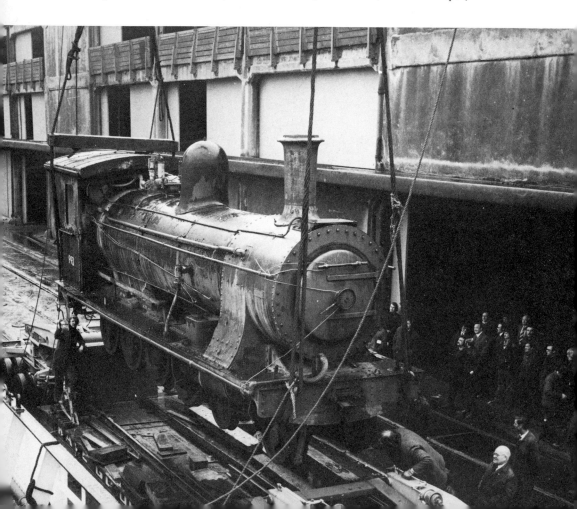

want to believe a bloody word that that bloke says, mate, we never do a f . . . ing thing for anybody.' I didn't believe that either. Most of them were actually jolly good blokes, but I had other things to think about apart from kidney machines at that moment.

Whether this gesture of working especially for me was genuine or not, I never found out. They decided to work and I stopped biting what remained of my finger nails. The coach came over the side, and disaster very nearly struck once more. Through what looked to me like sheer incompetence, the coach suddenly slipped and lurched sideways in its cradle as it was swinging out over the side of the ship. Its entire weight was now forced on to the edge of the roof. It was only saved by its substantial construction, otherwise it would have collapsed like an egg shell. One small and amusing thing happened to relieve the tension. As it tipped over sideways, many hundreds of gallons of Zambezi river poured out of its water tank on to the dock below.

With the coach safely on the low-loader and on its way, I then watched the engine being lowered on to its vehicle. Once again, more problems; the engine would not fit the flat bed and the coupling of the engine had to be cut off with oxy-acetylene. That was not the only damage done that morning. Because of the weight of the engine, there was very little clearance between the bottom of the vehicle and the road surface. As it turned out of the docks into the main road, it promptly scraped the 'cat's eyes' off the road.

We were on our way at last, down the M6. It had been arranged that the four low-loaders would spend the first night in one of the service areas. We received a tremendous welcome. *Last Train to Mulobezi* had just been screened on television and that, together with the coverage on BBC news in the Midlands a few hours before, had created enormous interest. A large number of people rushed out of the service area restaurant and crowded around the engine and coach. The driver of the low-loader with the coach on board was so concerned about any possible interference from members of the public that he decided to sleep in his cab that night. He told me later that, at very nearly midnight, he heard a car draw up alongside with a screech of brakes. He looked out and saw two people gazing at the coach in amazement. It seemed that they had seen the arrival of the ship on television and when they discovered that the cavalcade had stopped at the service area for the night they had decided to rush out and see the sight for themselves. The husband was obviously more of a railway enthusiast than his wife. He had not even given her time to dress. As he was examining the coach with great enthusiasm, she was left standing in the freezing cold in the service area, in her nightdress!

On the Wednesday, the vehicles left according to plan and proceeded on down the M6, on to the M1 and up into Whipsnade. The BBC were still with us, to film their arrival at the zoo, in case it was decided to repeat *Last*

197

My party proceeded down the M6 motorway and into Keele service station for a tea break. There wasn't much room for anyone else in the lorry park!

Train to Mulobezi on television, in which case the more appropriate ending could have been incorporated.

The arrival in the zoo went remarkably smoothly. The enormous vehicles managed to scrape through the trees without doing too much damage. Two cranes were waiting and the massive operation was accomplished by Wednesday evening. By the time darkness fell, the low-loaders had departed on their way, with a day to spare. It was a marvellous achievement.

The next day, I was telephoned by several newspapers. The reporter on one of the more sensational dailys seemed already to have written his story. He said excitedly: 'What an incredible story; you mean to say that you actually got over *that* bridge? How many people got shot?' He could obviously see a marvellous John-Wayne-type headline: 'David Shepherd blazes trail across bridge firing from the hip!' I tried to explain that, if that was his idea of Africa then so be it, but in fact things were not quite as sensational as that. I tried to explain that I had received nothing but the fullest co-operation from everybody on both sides of the border. No one was shot. He was quite disappointed: 'Well, that doesn't really make a story, then, does it.'

The great adventure eventually received almost no notice in the media.

What a nice story it would have made, in happy contrast to the blood and guts that we are now all accustomed to. I had hoped that this great story would show Africa in a different, happier and truer light. It seems, however, sadly, that only bad news is news. I must have been more naive than I thought.

After *Last Train to Mulobezi* had been screened, I received a tremendous response from many people. A number of letters referred to the star of the film, the little Ford Prefect, which had been shown trundling around the bush on the rickety railway lines. Many people asked me if I had brought the car back as well as the engine and coach. The answer was simple; no, I hadn't, because it literally fell apart in the bush after we had finished filming. However, it did make me realise that if I could find a similar car and put it in front of the engine at Whipsnade, it would be of great interest. I decided to ring up the publicity department of the Ford Motor Company at Dagenham. 'Did you see the film?' I asked. 'Yes we did, why?' I asked them whether they would like to try to find me a 1938 Ford Prefect, which perhaps they might like to give me, and then we could put it in front of the engine, providing that I could get it converted on to railway wheels.

The arrival at Whipsnade—at last (*Photo Philip Heley*)

A few weeks later I was telephoned by the publicity people. They had found a 1938 Ford Prefect, and they would be only too pleased to donate it to me, providing that I came up to Dagenham to collect it. I drove up there with my 3 ton Bedford truck and was slightly dismayed when I saw the car. It was in fact almost as decrepit as the one which we had left in Zambia. However, I certainly did not want to appear ungrateful, so I took the car away. It was a most generous gesture to find me a car at all.

It just happens that one of the senior executives of Mercedes Great Britain is a very close friend of ours. I asked him whether he might be able to arrange for the company to take the car away and 'do it up'. My suggestion was received with enthusiasm and, a month or so later, the little Ford returned to me in Surrey, in show-room condition.

There was one more problem to be solved. Somehow or other we had to convert the car so that it could sit on the railway line at Whipsnade. It happened that I was giving one of my talk shows for the benefit of the World Wildlife Fund and the East Somerset Railway in the lecture theatre at the Warminster army depot. I knew that I was speaking and showing my film just a few yards from one of the largest military vehicle

A 1938 Ford Prefect, standing in for the one left behind in Zambia, sits proudly in front of the Class 7 and coach at Whipsnade. The car was donated by Ford of Dagenham, restored by Mercedes and converted for railway use by the Royal Electrical and Mechanical Engineers. What it is to have friends!

workshops in the south of England, those of 27 Command railway work-shops, REME. I showed *Last Train to Mulobezi* that evening and, at the end, I asked if 'anybody happened to know a friendly garage where a little conversion job could be done, on the car'. The commanding officer came up to me and said: 'We will do it for you.'

A few weeks later, I drove down to the workshops with my car in the truck. Three weeks later they rang me up to tell me that the job had been successfully accomplished. I drove down once again and there she was outside the workshops: a little car with railway wheels on it. Apparently, the 3ft 6in gauge fitted the track of the Ford almost exactly. I asked them how they had achieved the conversion. 'Oh, we simply took the wheels off an army Bedford three-tonner and converted the hubs.' Somewhere in the Warminster area there must be an army lorry without any wheels on.

In 1976 we had a most delightful ceremony at Whipsnade. Sir Terence Beckett, who was then chairman of Ford, accepted my invitation to come to the zoo to hand the car over officially. We broke a bottle of champagne and a number of VIP guests also attended the celebrations. The Zambian high commissioner came from London and this, I felt, was particularly appropriate as President Kaunda had himself referred to this part of Whipsnade zoo as 'a little part of Zambia'. The little Ford now sits at Whipsnade in front of the engine and coach. The car is in running order and, from time to time, runs up and down its length of track in front of the engine, to the great amusement of the visitors.

Inside the coach I have mounted a comprehensive photographic exhibition telling the whole story of the Zambezi Sawmills Railway and the home-coming of the historic engine and coach. The engine is now in full working order. It has just been given a new boiler certificate, which is not bad for an engine that was sent out in the reign of Queen Victoria, to work for seventy-eight years in Africa and then to come home to England again.

The fate of *Princess of Mulobezi* is at the moment uncertain. There is no chance of towing the engine down through South Africa, and there is no money anyway. I am still looking for a friendly shipping company. I have applied for a grant to bring home this historic British-built and unique locomotive but, surprisingly, it has been turned down. Meanwhile, Zimbabwe Railways, who have been so marvellous about the whole project, are now, ever so gently and nicely, beginning to put the first pressures on me to move the engine. They tell me that they are gradually running out of space in their museum, and: 'Do you think, eventually, you could possibly consider moving it?' So it is anybody's guess what will happen now, but the engine will perhaps return to Zambia to form the nucleus of a railway museum to be set up at Livingstone, on the site of the old Zambezi Sawmills Railway headquarters. Perhaps this would be an appropriate final home for this fine old locomotive.

11

Cranmore and early days on the East Somerset

When Mike phoned me (as related at the end of chapter 9), I had never even heard of Cranmore. We were desperate to find a home for our locomotives. I looked at the map and found the village, about 17 miles south of Bristol, between Frome and Shepton Mallet. I estimated that it would take about two hours to get there from my home in Surrey.

It was November 1971 when I first went to Cranmore. It was rather a pretty little place; a bit deserted, but it was a weekday, and it was raining. I saw a railway line ahead of me and, turning to the right, drove up a lane full of potholes. There was a field on the left with a lot of corrugated-iron pig shelters in it. On the other side was a line of dirty black bitumen tankers spewing fumes and smoke into the air from over the hedge. The weather only made the whole scene more gloomy.

Through the struggling windscreen wipers I saw a small station at the end of the lane. On the derelict platform was a little stone building, looking cold and neglected, and a wooden hut; that was all, except for an ancient and rather marvellous cast-iron 'gents'. That seemed to be the only redeeming feature. There was precious little else to get excited about.

When the rain eased, I got out of the Land Rover, put on my survival kit, and set out to investigate. On the other side of the line, the platform had gone altogether. The signal box looked reasonably in one piece, although it had obviously been stripped of all its equipment.

Mike had told me a little about Cranmore. The place *was* linked to the main line. That must have been why the bitumen tankers were there. He also told me that somewhere up from the station was a parcel of land which, he thought, might possibly serve as a base on which we could establish our operations and build a shed. I now rapidly began to wonder if he was being over-optimistic. Perhaps the sun had been out when he had been there, but to me the place could not possibly have looked more depressing.

By now, the rain had stopped altogether, although there were scudding black clouds belting towards me from somewhere in the direction of Land's End. With my wellingtons on, and leaning against the howling wind, I walked up the line a few hundred yards. The land that Mike had

My very first view of Cranmore—an almost derelict station—on a wet November Sunday in 1971

mentioned was completely derelict. I struggled through the matted undergrowth and tripped over some rusty railway lines which were below the dank and tufted grass; they had certainly not seen daylight for many years but obviously there had been some sort of railway operation here at one time. The nettles and bushes were up to my waist as I finally reached what I was looking for. In front of me was an old tin shed. According to Mike, it had, in years gone by, been a wagon repair shop. Now it was derelict like everything else around it. Over the noise of the howling wind, I could hear sheets of corrugated iron clanking and banging as they hung from the ribs of the shed. Pulling one sheet of tin aside, I went in. Rain was dripping through the many gaping holes in the roof. The whole shed was creaking, threatening to collapse at any moment. The floor was made from old railway sleepers made slippery by the damp and lush covering of weeds and moss.

Outside again, I looked further up into the distance, over the hill. At least a railway line was still there although it had obviously not seen a train for years.

After an hour or so, by which time I was freezing cold and soaking wet, I decided to drive back home. All the way back, I was thinking hard. How on earth could we make a railway out of all that? On the other hand, we had very little choice; we were still paying £20 a week to stay at Eastleigh. At least Cranmore was linked to BR, obviously a very considerable advantage. Further on, the line was still there. Maybe one day it might see trains running on it again. There was a station. Maybe it was for sale.

203

There was a field, full of pigs. Maybe that was for sale, without the pigs. Then there were 2 acres of derelict ground, and an old tin shed, whatever that was worth. I noted the mileage; Cranmore was exactly 98 miles from home, and the journey took me two hours and ten minutes.

I found out the name of the line; it used to be called the East Somerset Railway. It was worth a try; and it was certainly better than some of the other places we had looked at.

My subsequent investigations told me that the original East Somerset Railway began life on 9 November 1858, when the first train ran from Witham, on the Weymouth branch of the Great Western, through Cranmore, to Shepton Mallet. In 1874, the line was absorbed by the Great Western Railway and was converted from its original broad-gauge to standard gauge. Of the several attractive stations built on the line in the local Mendip stone, Cranmore was the only one remaining in use as a station, albeit now just for the use of the bitumen tanker trains. Cranmore station was built in the 1850s and obviously was of some historic interest. Almost all the remaining buildings on the branch had been demolished.

From Cranmore to Shepton Mallet, the line rose over the hill at 1:70 in parts for over a mile, to the summit of the branch. It then descended at 1:56 through a deep cutting in the limestone and, from here, great blocks of stone were apparently brought by horse-tramway to the railway to provide materials for Cranmore station itself.

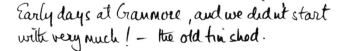

Early days at Cranmore, and we didn't start with very much! — the old tin shed.

Cranmore had been on the original East Somerset Railway, which had begun life as a broad-gauge line in 1858. Having become part of BR's Western Region, the line closed to passengers in 1963. It struggled on for a few more years with the occasional freight train, worked by grubby ex GWR pannier tanks (*Photo Ivo Peters*)

I also discovered that there used to be a narrow-gauge railway which brought stone from other nearby Mendip quarries to Cranmore. This explained the strange walls and remains of earthworks which I had noticed as I walked up to the shed on my first visit. I had found traces of the original exchange sidings, near the old tin shed. This traffic apparently mounted to 100 wagons a day at one time, but then gradually diminished. The quarry line closed shortly after World War II.

As with so many other picturesque branch lines throughout the UK, passenger traffic on what was now known as the Cheddar Valley Line, or locally, with affection, as the Strawberry Line, gradually fell away. At the end, with no Sunday service, just four trains a day were hauled by time-worn tank engines of Great Western or London Midlands origin. On 9 September 1963, the line finally closed to passenger traffic. Freight lingered on for just a few more years and then the line closed altogether in 1967.

When we discovered Cranmore, some 11 miles of line remained from Witham to beyond Cranmore, over the hill and into Shepton Mallet.

From the junction of the main line at Witham up to the Merehead stone quarries of Foster Yeoman, the track remains to this day for the very heavy stone traffic; indeed the quarry sidings have been considerably expanded over the years. From Merehead up to Cranmore, a distance of about half a mile, the line was still open, used by BR for the operation of the bitumen tankers which I had first seen in the old goods yard at Cranmore. The remainder of the branch had been removed long since.

After much deliberation my friends and I decided that it was worth going ahead. We now had to sort out our priorities. We had to discover who owned the 2 acres of land and the old tin shed. BR presumably owned Cranmore station. There were other parcels of land between the station and the shed which also had to be investigated. Little did I know the problems that they were going to cause. Over the next month, I was to spend countless frustrating hours (when I should have been painting in my studio, earning my living) down at Cranmore, crawling around in the undergrowth trying to find out who owned what. I was usually there with representatives from BR and various people from the huge quarry organisation that seemed to own just about everything around Cranmore, including the 2 acres. (This company was not Foster Yeoman.) At times, the situation bordered on farce. First of all, BR did not seem to know what it owned. The BR gentleman from Bristol had a lovely old map with him. It was apparently the most up-to-date they could find, but it was the sort that usually ends up on lampshades. It was about 2ft long and in beautiful script at the top was written 'Great Western Railway'. We did establish that BR owned the station. At least that was something. The problems really started when we began to investigate the bits of land between the station and the 2 acres at the other end, a distance of just a hundred yards or so. If I could have had a pound for every valuable hour that I, BR and the quarry people spent crawling around with rulers and tape measures in the stinging nettles and weeds looking for boundaries that were not there, we could have almost built our locomotive shed and workshops with the money.

Negotiating with the quarry company over the purchase of the 2 acres was an experience that I never want to repeat. We badly needed those 2 acres, and the company knew it. They quoted such a fatuous price for the land that I decided to have it valued by an independent firm of estate agents. It had no road access whatever, possible planning permission only for railway use, and, at the lowest agricultural rate, the 2 acres were valued at £1,500. The quarry company wanted £10,000. It was a shattering blow, and I began to get the Liss feeling all over again. Were

(*opposite above*) Grandpa's Workshop. Young Andrew has dashed home from school, grabbed a packet of crisps, and is helping his grandpa to make a model of the old man's favourite engine, an LBSCR Atlantic. (*by courtesy of Solomon & Whitehead (Guild Prints) Ltd*); (*below*) Mulobezi graveyard

they going to be like that down here, too? What was the matter with everybody? Agonising weeks followed, with phone calls, meetings, and letters flying backwards and forwards. Many hours of valuable time were wasted; the company was completely intransigent. As it seemed quite immoral to ask that sort of price, I suggested that the managing director and I should meet in the pub at Cranmore next time he was in the area. I had been told that he was quite approachable. He probably didn't even know that this miserable piece of land in the middle of nowhere was part of his company's vast international empire. I thought that we could sort it all out amicably over a beer, as this is surely the best way. My suggestion was turned down bluntly. We had to pay. Even that wasn't enough. The company demanded to retain the mining rights! This, I believe, means that, to this day, it has the right to dig up uranium, diamonds, gold or whatever else it might find in that part of Somerset, underneath our new and magnificent Victorian locomotive shed; that would obviously be the end of the East Somerset Railway, but it would make interesting headlines in the newspapers!

I was now beginning to realise for the first time just how the borrowing from the bank would escalate over the next few years and would very nearly break me.

The purchase of Cranmore station went relatively smoothly. BR quoted us a reasonable price, the main asset being the old 'gents' loo! This marvellous old cast-iron structure, so beautifully decorated along its top with little animal heads and other features, had been built at about the same time as the station building, in 1857. I don't know whether it ever occurred to BR but I felt sure that they could have sold it to an American millionaire who would have taken it over to Los Angeles to install in his penthouse—our friends over there have bought stranger and certainly bigger things than that from 'Ye olde England'.

We now put our minds to the question of how we might adapt for use any part of the old tin shed, on our expensive 2 acres of land. The decision was made for us. While one of my friends was up on the roof taking off some of the corrugated-iron sheets, the whole structure began to sway dangerously. Most of it fell down a few days later, in a gale.

George Davies was, at this time, my bank manager, at Longsight, Manchester. George and I had first met when he was running the Dinting Railway Centre at Glossop in Derbyshire, and had become close friends. Having a bank manager who is not only a friend but also a railway enthusiast means that it is possibly much easier to get an overdraft out of the bank! This rather dangerous circumstance was, in fact, very nearly to be my undoing, but that was to come later. We had to build a workshop and a shed, and a lot of track would be needed to get into our new depot. We had to buy the station and, if possible, a field for a car park. We had decided, furthermore, to build a house on the platform, in the style of the

Our new locomotive shed in the process of construction

old station building, in which someone would live as a caretaker, sales officer, and probably lots of other things as well. The estimated total cost of all this came to a hair-raising amount.

During these formative months, George was of inestimable help to me, and I finally decided to ask him if he would leave the bank and come and work for the railway as its first general manager. The bank was about to offer him a senior post, but he turned this down in favour of the new challenge. He decided that he and his wife Audrey would leave Manchester and look for a place to live near Cranmore. With George joining us full time, most of the administrative load would be taken off my shoulders, enabling me to return to the studio where I belonged. I felt a little embarrassed about taking George away from the steam centre at Dinting, but we had established a marvellous friendship with the people up there and they took it in the spirit in which it was meant. They wished George good luck and, happily, we have maintained our very close links with that steam railway centre to this day.

We now began to consider our new locomotive shed. I was determined that we should build a depot which would be appropriate for the locomotives going into it; something more substantial than an agricultural-type building made of asbestos sheeting. I remembered the lovely old loco shed at Radstock particularly, and, although it was built in stone, we used it as a reference. The plans were drawn up with the planning officials. They were passed, and came back in what seemed like record time. Someone told me that the planning officer had his own model railway!

The design of the shed followed closely the traditions established by the great Victorian builders, down to the finest detail. The brick building, which must be the only one of its type to have been built in this country in the last 100 years, is 130ft long, with two roads and an inspection pit. Alongside is a workshop. The length of the shed was determined by measuring *The Green Knight* and *Black Prince* coupled close together and then adding a few feet at each end, so that our thinner members at least could get round! I knew that every extra foot in width, height or length, would add many more hundreds of pounds to the cost.

The great day eventually came for the first sod cutting ceremony. It was 7 April 1973. I drove down to Cranmore with my wife, four daughters and two dogs. The weather was rather more kind than usual. The wind was only blowing a gentle Force five or six and it wasn't raining. I have the historic moment on film. Behind my wife, as she dug with the spade into the dank undergrowth and soil of Somerset, stood the gaunt skeleton of what was left of the old tin shed. Whenever I see that piece of film now, I wonder how on earth we ever managed to establish a successful steam railway from such a beginning.

First of all the site for the shed had to be cleared with a bulldozer in order to obtain some semblance of level ground. In the process the numerous lengths of rusty and very ancient railway lines appeared from underneath the deep undergrowth. Some of this track was reusable but most of it went for scrap. The foundation for the shed was dug, and the brickwork began to rise.

It is sad for me to reflect that, although these early days were exciting, there were also some very unhappy moments. A few people had joined us who were extremely headstrong and impetuous. When they saw the shed and station house springing up from nothing, they gained the impression that my finances were quite limitless. 'Can we have another 4ft on the height of the shed? It's not tall enough' was a typical request. That little extra alone would cost a few thousand pounds more, and the overdraft was in my name. On many occasions they came to my home in Surrey on a Sunday evening after spending all day on the railway, to complain bitterly that everything was wrong. I began to dread Sunday evenings; they thought that they knew it all.

There was one particular afternoon which I will never forget. I had an urgent 'phone call from the architect who was on the site. He told me that he and the builders were having problems with 'some of your people who are telling us how to do our job. Will you please come and sort it out at once?' I was trying to finish a painting for long-overdue delivery to a patient customer. I had to drop everything and drive down to Cranmore. I was having terrible car problems at that time and the car broke down half way. I had to hire a taxi to get me there and when I arrived, two hours late, the architect and the builders were standing on one side of the half-built shed, with three railway people on the other, all glaring at each other. The architect came up to me and said: 'David, if you don't tell these people to behave themselves, I am wiping my hands of the whole project.' I had to sort it out and try to keep the peace. Sometimes it was one hell of a job.

From my experience of other steam railways and from talking to those who had already set them up, I knew that almost the most important thing of all was adequate car-parking space for visitors. With bitter memories of Liss still fresh in my mind, I knew that establishing and keeping good relations with the local people was absolutely imperative. Not everyone living in the peace and tranquillity of the countryside wants a steam railway on his doorstep. If we became established, with visitors coming to see us in the summer, but were without an adequate car park, we could well create a situation where cars might be parked in the driveways of local people or congesting the village. This would be the quickest and surest way to create ill-feeling between ourselves and those who lived in the surrounding area. So one of the first things to do was obviously to find out if the field with the pig shelters in it was for sale. It was owned by a man in Cranmore village and George and I went round to see him one evening. We had done some homework and we calculated that, at the agricultural rate, the field was worth somewhere in the region of £2,500. He was willing to sell the field to us– for £20,000! At moments like this, I wondered why I ever became involved with steam locomotive preservation. We had only just recovered from the shock of dealing with the quarry people over the 2 acres of land which we needed for our shed and workshop. Now, it seemed, we were once again in the same sort of situation. Happily, however, after a great deal of hassle and delay, we finally managed to persuade him to be sensible and sell the field to us at its true value. This meant that at least one problem was solved. We would now have adequate space for our visitors to park their cars when they came to see us in the summer.

When an imposing new locomotive depot has been built, the number of people who write and ask if they can put their rusting wrecks from Barry scrapyard inside it is quite astonishing. Precisely this happened and, if we had said yes, the line of Bulleid Pacifics would have stretched half way up the hill! When we began to set up the East Somerset Railway, we were, however, united on one thing. We had decided quite firmly that every engine must be under cover and under lock and key. Moreover, it would have to earn its keep as soon as possible. (We were fortunate in that some of our locomotives were already in working order.) The shed had been designed to fit exactly the locomotives that we already had, and covered space was at a very costly premium. We did not want a long line of rusting engines awaiting restoration outside our shed, under tarpaulins. Sadly, some steam railways seem to have allowed just this situation to arise and they remind one horribly of Barry scrapyard. We were determined that Cranmore would never look like that.

If a place of entertainment is open to the public, whether it is a stately home, a safari park or a steam railway, it has to offer the best possible facilities to the public, because it is on these that the public will judge the place and decide whether to come back again. Among other things, this means good toilets. There was nothing at Cranmore when we arrived except the old 'gents' on the platform, so we had to start from the beginning. Our new loos cost £6,000 to build. This immediately raised a few howls of protest from some of my vociferous friends who could think no further than steam locomotives. They said: 'We could have bought another locomotive from Barry scrapyard with all that money.' I endeavoured to point out that a rusty hulk under a tarpaulin would not attract the public and draw them back again for a second visit. Good clean toilets probably would. Cranmore station, with all its immaculate facilities, is the first part of the East Somerset Railway that the public see. Judging by the number of compliments that are paid to us during the summer, I know I have been proved right.

By the end of 1973, our brand-new locomotive depot finally stood completed, on its own in a large open space. The architectural correspondent of *The Times* produced a most complimentary write-up on the building, with a photograph.

All this time, we were still on our very expensive siding at Eastleigh and it was imperative that we move to Cranmore with our stock as soon as possible. To get our locomotives into the shed, we had of course to have

laying track into our new shed

While we were still building the shed for them, the first locomotives had arrived at Cranmore by road. That was no easy journey! (*Photo Dick Weisham*)

track laid; and because we did not have the manpower or the time to lay it ourselves, we had to go to an outside contractor. The company came in and laid just enough line to give us adequate sidings on which to park our locomotives, carriages and wagons, and to get into our depot. The overdraft went up dramatically once again.

Meanwhile, various other items of infrastructure were going up on the site. We acquired from the Bristol Water Authority a second-hand water tank which we were advised was in sound condition and suitable for our needs. With the aid of a large and expensive crane, which we hired for the afternoon, the water tank was placed on top of a steel framework especially put up for the purpose. The water tank immediately started leaking and it has hardly stopped ever since.

Some of my friends had by this time purchased their own locomotives and, as the track was being laid by the contractors, the first of these began to arrive. The Crane tank and Austerity arrived by road and were placed on their own short length of line. *Lord Fisher* also arrived by road and was the very first locomotive in steam on the East Somerset Railway. She was also the first to steam into our brand-new shed. She stood in the doorway for some time (deliberately, I suspect), immediately blackening the lovely brickwork above the door. The shed was looking authentic already!

Lord Fisher was the first engine to steam into the shed and she deliberately stood in the doorway to blacken the beautiful new brickwork!

We were now making hectic preparations for our departure from Eastleigh. To our great pleasure and astonishment, BR told us that *Black Prince* and *The Green Knight* could both steam, independently of each other and hauling our stock, from Eastleigh, through Westbury and up the line into Cranmore. This gesture gave a tremendous boost to our morale.

Cranmore station was now beginning to look like its old self. We put up new 'old fashioned' style wooden fencing at the back of the platform, and planted flowers. We repaired the platform edges, which had been allowed to collapse. We had acquired from the City of Hereford a number of period street lamps, which were duly erected, with new lanterns, on the platform. Barge boards, in period style, were attached to the original station building and the new house to complete the period atmosphere of the country branch-line station.

Television became interested in our various activities and the site was filmed several times as it began to develop. One of the incidents recorded in this way was the removal of a rather special telephone box which I had noticed in Bristol city centre. It was one of the rare models with a stamp machine and a posting box. The GPO were most co-operative—they sold it to me for £10, on condition that I took it away. I drove to Bristol with the Bedford truck, and a crane was ready to commence lifting. The box was being used until the day before and, when it was being carefully hoisted into the air with the crane, several old pennies and an ancient ejc

British Railways Southern Region

Waterloo Station
London SE1
Telephone 01-928 5151 Extn: 2575

G. A. Weeden Chief Operating Manager

David Shepherd Esq.
The Studio
Winkworth Farm
Hascombe
Godalming
Surrey

y/r
o/r M.24

Date 13 November 1973

Dear Mr. Shepherd

I am now able to give you details for the movement of your Locomotives and Stock on the 17/18 November 1973.

TRAIN NO. 1 FORMED

CLASS 9	92203	(in steam)
CLASS V	30928	(dead)
P.M.V.	1137	(vacuum fitted head)
P.M.V.	1396	(vacuum fitted head)
TANK CAR	82620	
VAN	47760	
VAN	47774	
FLAT	6095	
G.B.V.	12424	

TRAIN NO. 2 FORMED

CLASS 4	75029	(in steam)
B.S.	43289	(vacuum braked)
B.S.	43231	(vacuum braked)
	3322	piped
	S1000S	vacuum braked
	E 1767	vacuum braked

	1	2
TRAIN NO.	8Z02	5Z40
Eastleigh Depot	17 55	19 25
Eastleigh	17/59	19/29
Romsey	18/20	19/44
Tunnel Jn.	19/15	20/10
Salisbury	19/20	20/15
Dilton Marsh	20/30	20/50
	WR	WR
Westbury	20 40	21 00
Cranmore (Sunday)	08 55	09 40

The 17 55 Eastleigh Depot has been timed at approximately 20 m.p.h and the 18 25 Eastleigh at 40 m.p.h.

Yours sincerely,

Woodbines cigarette packet dropped out. With the box carefully tipped over on to its side and loaded on to the lorry, I drove to Cranmore, where it was offloaded again on to the platform, in front of the TV cameras.

Our workshop also began to take shape. We were enormously encouraged as various essential machines began to arrive from different places, some of them donated free by generous people who were obviously impressed with what we were trying to do.

The time finally came when we were ready to leave Eastleigh for our new home and BR told us that they could slot our two steam-hauled trains into their schedules for the weekend of 17 and 18 November 1973. Inevitably the news spread fast that steam was returning to the main line from Southampton, via Salisbury, to Westbury. I at once began to receive 'phone calls at all hours asking for full details of the event, and a huge quantity of letters, most of them without stamped addressed envelopes.

It was arranged that *Black Prince* would haul *Stowe* and our ancient collection of wagons, including the ones that we had purchased from the army at Longmoor for £4 10s and which were now, remarkably, passed as fit to travel on BR. *The Green Knight* was to follow about an hour later hauling our coaching stock. A large crowd gathered to see us leave Eastleigh, where we had been for so long, and Southern TV were also there to record the great moment. I was on the footplate of *Black Prince* and went with her as far as Salisbury, where we made a brief stop. I alighted on the platform, and *Black Prince* went on her way to Westbury. An hour or so later, the station announcer said: 'David Shepherd's privately owned steam train, hauled by *The Green Knight*, is shortly to arrive at platform three.' I felt very proud at that moment, as my engines were the first to come through Salisbury on the main line since the end of steam in 1967. It was now quite dark and she made a magnificent spectacle as she steamed into the dimly lit station. The station master himself—with, it seemed, his entire staff—and a large crowd were on the platform. I hopped up on the cab of 75029 and we were once again on our way. *The Green Knight* was behaving herself impeccably, full of the joys of life as though she felt she was at last being given her head on a proper railway line after so many years of confinement on her short siding at Eastleigh. After a marvellous, and very fast, run down the main line, we arrived safely at Westbury and joined the other train, which had arrived just before us. We were given an area on which to park both trains for the night, tucked away in the large complex of Westbury sidings.

We had only been in the sidings for half an hour or so before we had electric lighting in the train. I remember vaguely that one of our more adventurous members shinned up the nearest pole and tapped the electricity supply by highly devious, surely illegal and probably very dangerous means. I had decided to bed down for the night in a compartment of our sleeping car, which we had recently purchased from a

The evening of 17 November 1973. BR had given permission for *The Green Knight* and *Black Prince* to haul our stock from Eastleigh to Cranmore. *The Green Knight* is seen preparing to leave, with our coaches (*Photo Dick Weisham*)

scrapyard and which, to a degree, we had managed to refurbish. A good friend of mine from Cornwall was with me. He had come up from that part of the world especially to take part in the proceedings. Unfortunately, I did not have a particularly comfortable night because Cedric snored his head off for most of the night! However, it was a small price to pay for the great weekend that we were having.

I was rudely awakened before dawn by the lads. The locomotives had to be prepared for the second stage of their journey into Cranmore. I was asked to help with breakfast. We had packed all the necessary plates, cups and various packs of food into a very large container. As we were not at a platform, a ladder had been placed against the side of the sleeping car for our use. Stupidly, I decided to walk, forwards, down this ladder, with no handrail, carrying the box, in the dark. The result was inevitable. I fell through the ladder. I dropped the box, and broke my ankle. In considerable pain, I had virtually to be carried across the many lines of track to the BR administration building alongside the diesel depot. Here I was given sympathetic treatment by a member of the staff of the nearby ambulance depot. My ankle, which blew up like a balloon, was strapped up, to an accompaniment of a few ribald and well-deserved comments from my chums. The ambulance people ordered me to rest my ankle as much as possible and in absolutely no circumstances to stand on it. It was no doubt good advice, but I had absolutely no intention of missing the event about to take place.

The Jinty had been stored for several weeks at Radstock after rescue from Barry scrapyard and now she had been towed to Westbury for attachment to the rear of *The Green Knight*'s train. An hour or so after daylight, the two trains were due to leave. *Black Prince*, polished as never before and shining like a piece of jewellery, stormed out of Westbury station. One of my friends was filming and she was certainly a spectacular sight in the cold air of the November morning. *The Green Knight* followed shortly afterwards and I was on her footplate. I was enjoying every moment of it, in spite of the agony of my broken ankle. The two trains came under the bridge, and they were into Cranmore. Television filmed me hopping about on one foot. The press were there and a large crowd was on the platform. The East Somerset Railway had come back to life.

Although our locomotives, coaches and wagons had now arrived, there was still a tremendous amount of work to be done before we could be open to the public. One of the first things we realised was that our two main-line locomotives, *Black Prince* and *The Green Knight*, and *Stowe* (assuming that she could be restored), were all facing the wrong way for future operations. We had no turntable at Cranmore, so we obviously had to think of some other means of turning them. Fortunately for us, there was a triangle at Foster Yeoman's Merehead stone quarry. Yeoman's were

The Green Knight steams into Cranmore, her new home

Main-line power—*Stowe, Black Prince* and *The Green Knight* shortly after their arrival at Cranmore. (*Stowe* had joined us at Eastleigh from Beaulieu; she was later to leave for the Bluebell Railway) (*Photo Rex Coffin*)

only too delighted to let us use that facility and permission was given for the three locomotives and *Lord Fisher* to go down to the quarry in April 1974. When it had all been arranged, it was suggested that *Black Prince*'s strength might be tested by hauling a heavy stone train out of the terminal. Who was I to say no to such an exciting idea? *Black Prince* duly backed onto the line of stone wagons which, collectively, probably comprised a load of some 1,800 tons. This was approximately the length and weight of train which was hauled out of the quarry by sometimes two main-line BR diesel locomotives. One or two diesel enthusiasts in the quarry were laying bets that *Black Prince* would be incapable of doing the job. When everyone was ready, she stormed out of the terminal, under the bridge which carried the main road. At this moment I noticed a motor coach full of passengers passing above and not one of the passengers took the slightest bit of notice. A motorist behind the coach, however, who was obviously a railway enthusiast, was driving over just as a cloud of black smoke thundered from almost underneath his car; he was so astonished that he nearly drove off the road, down the bank and into a field.

We now gained another item of rolling stock which once again brought together my interests in steam railway preservation and wildlife conservation. In 1973 the World Wildlife Fund launched Operation Tiger. This was their last-ditch attempt to save this magnificent animal from extinction. I painted a picture called 'Tiger Fire', and gave the painting to

219

When we arrived at Cranmore, our big engines were facing the wrong way. Here, *Stowe* is hauled dead by the Foster Yeoman diesel shunter, to be turned on the triangle at their Merehead stone quarry

While *Black Prince* was at Yeoman's, she was given a train of fully loaded hopper wagons to haul out of the terminal, to test her strength (*Photo Rex Coffin*)

the fund, together with a limited edition of 850 copies. When we embarked on the marketing of the prints, I approached the Esso petroleum company. Their 'tiger in your tank' publicity campaign had been a great success and I felt that it was not entirely inappropriate to suggest that they might consider buying some of the prints. They didn't, so I asked them if they would like to give me an Esso tanker wagon instead! They did not know what I was talking about, so I told them about the East Somerset Railway. Nothing happened for a few weeks, and then I received a letter saying that they had discovered a London Midland & Scottish 1939 vintage Esso tanker wagon which was surplus to their needs. They told me they would be only too pleased to have it completely refurbished and then send it, free of charge, by rail to Cranmore. A few weeks later we had a handing-over ceremony, followed by an enjoyable lunch at a nearby hotel.

We were also collecting other items of rolling stock. We badly needed five open plank wagons for general duties on the railway. BR was charging up to £150 each for redundant wagons. We didn't have the money to pay that sort of price. One of the lads said that he knew the foreman of a National Coal Board colliery that was closing. He went along to see him. As a result, we bought five wagons for £10 each, and the last one had 3 tons of coal in it which were thrown in for good measure.

Costs were now mounting at such a pace that we decided that we must open our doors to the public as soon as possible. In August 1974, therefore, we opened a couple of bottles of champagne up at the shed and, most appropriately, our very first visitor with ticket number 1 was from the Dinting Railway Centre at Glossop.

When we first arrived at Cranmore, the signal box was lying unused. One of the best decisions we ever made was to turn it into an art gallery. My success as a wildlife artist had enabled me to buy my two steam engines, which eventually led to the setting up of the East Somerset Railway. Now we realised that if we could sell prints of my elephant paintings and other subjects to our visitors, it would help to pay our coal bills. The negotiations with BR to make use of the signal box were complicated (to put it mildly). Because the station building had road access, we were able to purchase the freehold. The signal box was a different matter. The rules stated that because it was on the other side of an operational railway line, without road access, we could only lease it. All the difficulties that were now going to be thrown at us apparently hinged on the word 'operational'. Since we had opened, possibly no more than two or three BR trains had come into Cranmore station on a Sunday, usually for weed-killing or shunting purposes. It was generally at weekends that we expected to have our largest numbers of visitors. Nevertheless, one of the clauses in the lease that BR initially insisted on was that every time we had a client who wished to cross the line on a

Sunday to view my prints in the signal box, we had to telephone the BR Area Manager at Westbury to ask him for permission to cross, in case a train was coming. We have worked it out that, to date, we would probably have made something in the region of 700,000 telephone calls to the Area Manager! The GPO would certainly have been very happy about this. The Area Manager of that time happened to be a member of the East Somerset Railway. When I told him of this rather strange idea, his comments were quite unrepeatable. In any case, he was far more interested in getting on with the job that he was doing when I spoke to him; his feet were sticking out of the smoke-box door of *Black Prince* and he was covered in muck from head to foot, thoroughly enjoying himself.

By this time, we had formed a committee of management consisting of volunteers who would be responsible for the day-to-day running of the railway. Individual committee members would be responsible for the various aspects of the railway—operating, carriage and wagon, sales, workshop, publicity and our newsletter. We had by now gained charitable status and the directors of the East Somerset Railway would be responsible for the overall policy-making and finance.

Jack Stanaway, who had been a friend of George for many years up at Dinting, decided to accept our invitation to join us, and Jack and his wife took up residence in the new station house which we had built on the platform. He immediately became our sales officer, with many other duties thrown in as well!

We had not been open very long when a railway society approached us to ask if they could charter a train from BR for their members and run into Cranmore. This was most encouraging and meant that we were already getting known.

When they started the negotiations with BR they were told that it was impossible, as no trains ran into Cranmore any more. BR had presumably forgotten about the bitumen tankers! Moreover the request from the railway society, unknown to its members, had, it seemed, triggered off a problem which was far greater than anything any of us could envisage. It seemed that the sale of the station to us had been a bit hasty and BR had not realised the full implications of selling a station on an operational railway line to a private organisation. These were the early days and there seemed to be many grey areas in these matters. Three or four times a week, bitumen tanker trains would crawl into Cranmore station at about lunch-time. The diesel would then shunt them into the siding and go out again with a train of empty wagons. Apparently this meant that the line through Cranmore station was just as operational as, for instance, that from Euston to Crewe, on which Inter-City trains did 100mph every hour or so. It was now discovered that the regulations stated that if a redundant station was purchased on a line still used by BR, a 6ft high chain fence should be erected all the way along the edge of the platform. This would

222

have been fair enough if we had bought a station between Euston and Crewe; it would have been sensible anywhere where it would stop children falling off into the path of a passing Inter-City train. We were not, however, buying a station between Euston and Crewe; we were buying a sleepy little station in Somerset. However, it seemed that the same must apply. The situation was further complicated by the fact that we had already purchased our station from BR. Nevertheless, we received a letter from their property department telling us that we must immediately erect such a fence. This would make a complete nonsense of any train which might be chartered from BR (and which would in fact be of some benefit to them) to bring people into Cranmore station to see us. If they did come in by train, they would not be able to get out of it! Furthermore, our friends on BR who drove their diesel trains into Cranmore station with the bitumen tanker wagons during the week frequently used to hop out of their cabs and have a pee in the 'gents' on our platform, so that the ruling would now create frightful problems for them too!

A great many letters went backwards and forwards between my solicitors and those acting for BR but they still insisted on the fence. The situation rapidly reached a crisis, while the railway society who wanted to come into Cranmore patiently sat by and waited to see what would happen. A high-level meeting was called at Bristol by BR. My solicitor came down from London to represent me. The two of us arrived at the appointed place and were shown into the room. Five very formidable BR people, including one lady, sat round a rather large table. One of them opened the proceedings: 'We have come here to discuss the detailed arrangements of the erection of a 6ft chain-link fence along the edge of Mr Shepherd's station at Cranmore. I believe there are some objections to this proposal.'

My memory of what happened after that is that the proceedings were short and to the point. My solicitor said that there was not going to be a fence along the edge of the platform. It was too late. We had become the new owners of Cranmore station. Common sense once again prevailed. The tour came into Cranmore station and everybody was happy.

We were now well and truly open, but for our first few seasons we had to be content with running steam-hauled trains with a couple of brake vans up and down past the shed on just a few yards of track, on Sundays only. The 10p we were charging for each passenger ride barely covered the cost of the coal. Our operating season started, as today, just before Easter, and ended at roughly the beginning of autumn when the schoolchildren went back to school. It was in many ways frustrating to run trains on such a short distance, but we were feeling our way and it made sense to get established slowly. Nevertheless, we were beginning to look longingly at the branch line which stretched past the shed and up the hill into the distance, all the way into Shepton Mallet, a total of 3 miles. This line had not seen a train since 1967 when the branch had closed. Even the station in Shepton Mallet itself was still there. BR was obviously going to tear the track up eventually, and we began to wonder whether we could perhaps purchase the whole thing and run trains again into Shepton. Although it would inevitably cost a very great deal of money, it seemed a very exciting prospect for the future.

Meanwhile, through our mutual interest in wildlife conservation, His Royal Highness Prince Bernhard of the Netherlands and I had become good friends. We had met on many occasions in England and Africa, and it was at a World Wildlife Fund party in London in 1974 that he came up to me and said: 'David, how are your locomotives?' I had not even known that he knew I was interested in steam engines. It seems, however, that every time I go to a wildlife conservation party in England or America, everyone seems to know about *Black Prince*. On the way home that evening, I decided to write to His Royal Highness to invite him to come over to England to open the East Somerset Railway officially. We would give all the proceeds from the event to the World Wildlife Fund. As soon as Prince Bernhard received my letter, he sent me a cable saying that he would be delighted to come. The great day would be 20 June 1975.

Although no one could be more informal than Prince Bernhard, a great amount of work had nevertheless to be done to ensure the success of such a royal event. At the Prince's invitation, I flew over to Holland to have lunch with him and discuss the important matters of protocol, security and the countless other things that had to be remembered. Prince Bernhard showed me his private collection of over 400 elephants in all shapes and sizes, collected over the years. It was a most happy day.

I was now to realise just how nice BR can be on the one hand and how difficult on the other. When the local BR people knew that a royal event was going to take place at Cranmore, the Area Manager and his staff at Westbury most generously offered to cease the operations of the bitumen tanker trains into Cranmore for a week so that they would not get in the way of our preparations for the event. In view of this gesture, I wrote to the BR Board asking for special dispensation for *Black Prince* to come down the few yards of BR track which separated our shed from our station and on which we were not allowed to run. I felt sure that they would say yes, bearing in mind the circumstances. After arrival at Cranmore station, *Black Prince* would be able to pick up Prince Bernhard and myself and steam up to the shed for the opening ceremony. After, I gather, some lengthy deliberations, I received a blunt refusal. Their reasoning was, apparently that, 'if we let you, we will have to let everybody else', or something like that. I don't know how many other people had royal princes opening their railways, but it seemed a great pity that they could not say yes. It would have been good publicity for BR. It was very tempting to give the story to the Press, and it would have made an interesting

HRH Prince Bernhard of the Netherlands, in his capacity as the International President of the World Wildlife Fund, came over from Holland to open the East Somerset Railway officially. (We gave all the proceeds to help save elephants) (*Photo Rex Coffin*)

headline: 'British Railways slaps Royal Prince'. I kept quiet, however, because, as I have said many times, I will move heaven and earth to retain my excellent relationship with BR and, in particular, the local people who have always gone out of their way to help us.

Among the many preparations, we had to build a special dais along the length of the shed, outside, from which the speeches would be made. It was planned that *Black Prince* and *The Green Knight* would then steam slowly past the dais. *Black Prince* would pick up Prince Bernhard and myself, and *The Green Knight*, following, would take on her two guests, my wife and Sir Peter Scott. Everything had to be arranged with split-second timing, efficiency and safety, taking account of the large crowd, television and the Press, who would be coming.

The day finally arrived. Prince Bernhard flew into the Royal Naval Air Station at Yeovilton, in his executive jet. He was appropriately given a welcome with a Royal Navy guard of honour. The Flag Officer, Naval Air Command, the Ship's Captain and other senior officers and myself were there to meet him. At the end of the formal proceedings, Prince Bernhard and I climbed into a Bell Jet Ranger helicopter belonging to British Airways, which was waiting to take us to Cranmore.

It was just a few minutes' flying time from Yeovilton to Cranmore and we landed in a field alongside the station. The whole village was *en fête*. A Dutch lady who lives in Shepton Mallet, dressed in traditional costume, was first to welcome His Royal Highness as he stepped out of the helicopter. She presented him with a carnation and, after the informal introductions were over, we walked on to the platform, amongst a very large crowd. On the opposite side of the line we had three flagpoles 'borrowed' from BR. The Dutch national flag flew from the centre pole, and on either side flew the Union Jack and the flag of the World Wildlife Fund. After the two national anthems had been played, all of us, including His Royal Highness, walked up to the shed where there was another large crowd waiting to greet us. The Blue Eagles Helicopter Display Team from the Army Air Corps Centre at Middle Wallop had generously offered to participate and they flew over the shed in salute, streaming coloured smoke. Exactly at the right moment, after the Prince had declared the East Somerset Railway open and unveiled the stone commemorative plaque which had been set into the wall of the shed, my two locomotives steamed out alongside each other and, simultaneously, burst through a tape held across the track by two of my daughters. This procedure was not exactly railway practice but it worked, and made a magnificent spectacle for television.

I presented the Prince with a fluffy elephant to add to his collection and then we gave him a beautiful model of *Black Prince* in a display case, made especially for us, free of charge, by a friend of ours at Dinting Railway Centre. After he had talked to the Press about wildlife conservation (and

226

My two engines stormed out of the shed through tape held by two of my daughters, and we were well and truly open! (*Photo Rex Coffin*)

steam engines!), and a number of photographs had been taken, the Prince did an informal walk-about on the railway, meeting all our members and members of the public. We then walked back to the station, where further celebrations were held in a marquee in the field. A veteran car was waiting outside to take him to Cranmore village. We felt from the beginning that it was very important that the villagers of Cranmore should participate in such a great day. Flags were everywhere and the Prince walked round the village and into the church. It was certainly a great day for both the East Somerset Railway and Cranmore village. We heard afterwards that a few of the surrounding villages were rather green with envy!

After some five hours, we climbed back into the British Airways helicopter and flew back to Yeovilton. After informal goodbyes, Prince Bernhard flew away in his jet back to Holland. As I was on my way back to Cranmore once again in the helicopter, a radio message came direct from the pilot of Prince Bernhard's jet to the helicopter pilot: 'Would David Shepherd please ensure that Prince Bernhard's engine driver's hat is sent to Holland, because he left it on the railway!'

We never received the bill from British Airways for the helicopter. The hire of a Bell Jet Ranger is extremely expensive. Even in those days, it would probably have come to several hundred pounds an hour. I can only assume that within the accounts department of British Airways there are some steam-locomotive enthusiasts. Perhaps one of them said to another: 'We can't really charge those super people on the East Somerset Railway; they are all volunteers and it is a registered charity, and they are trying to save steam engines. We'll add the cost of their using the helicopter on to the charge to the next person who hires it.' That was OK by us.

On the day of the royal opening we raised several thousand pounds and we gave the whole amount to the World Wildlife Fund. A few days later, I received a letter of thanks from Sir Peter Scott. He is not one of those people who gets terribly excited about things, or, if he does, he does not show it like I do. Nevertheless, his letter was one of the most delightful that I have ever received and it encapsulates my whole life into just a few words. 'Dear David,' he wrote, 'it was a GREAT day. Where else but England would you get lovely sunny weather, eccentric people like you, royalty, lots of VIP's, lots of super people riding up and down on steam trains to help save elephants!' I liked the bit about England, because it is full of eccentrics, and I am extremely proud to be one of them. I don't know about the sunny weather. I can only suppose that I must subconsciously have asked my namesake, the Bishop of Liverpool, to give a little prayer for that. It was answered in any case. Furthermore, as I have said on countless occasions, there would be no East Somerset Railway if it were not for the success of my elephant paintings.

There are even steam enthusiasts in the Inland Revenue; and why not? Shortly after our royal opening we received our first tax demand. On the back of the brown envelope with a little window in the front, which we all know so well, someone had drawn a little steam engine with smoke coming out of the chimney, with, underneath, the words, 'Good luck'!

The last steam trains in BR service ran in the North West of England in 1968, and almost immediately railway enthusiasts began to clamour for the return of steam in the form of chartered 'specials'. At first, the door was firmly closed. Then, gradually, through gentle pressure from behind the scenes, BR showed a change of heart. It finally issued a list of privately owned steam locomotives which had been cleared to run on a limited number of lines during the summer. In 1975, *Black Prince* was still on that list, and we were approached by the organisers of the Eastleigh open day to see if 92203 would run from Cranmore to Eastleigh and back again, to raise money once again for the railway orphanage at Woking. The locomotive was normally virtually incarcerated on the East Somerset Railway with little chance to do any really significant running, so this was too good a chance to miss.

Black Prince was passed as mechanically fit for main-line running and the date was fixed. BR gave their blessing for her move down to Westbury with our Mk 1 brake coach, which we had just restored to London, Midland & Scottish livery. Everyone was full of enthusiasm for *Black Prince*'s return for another open day at Eastleigh, where she had so many friends.

There is one aspect of running privately owned steam engines on BR which is perhaps not appreciated by enough railway enthusiasts. In the days when *Black Prince* was allowed to run on the main line, the owner of the engine, or the private railway on which it was stabled, had to put a very large amount of money up front and pay BR in advance. This was to cover the cost of their supplying the coaches and getting them to the point where the steam engine could take over, routing the train into the schedules and all the other organisation that was required. Furthermore, not unreasonably, BR expected to make a profit out of the exercise.

The interest and excitement that our run down the main line to the Eastleigh open day was generating among the railway fraternity was quite astonishing. Nevertheless, George and I had to work very hard indeed to sell enough tickets to fill the train and cover our costs. I believe I know the reason and I may make myself unpopular by stating it. For every railway enthusiast who was prepared to buy a ticket, travel on the train and therefore support the owner of the engine in his very expensive venture, there would be hundreds of people who would get their cars out of their garages, drive to a lineside vantage point and park. Many of these would then walk across a farmer's field, climb over the fence on to a BR embankment, trespassing in the process, and take their photographs of the passing train. They would then go home again. Whilst it is enormously gratifying to know that one's engine can give so much pleasure to many people, I would suggest that those who gain most from these activities are those who sell the petrol and the camera films. How very appropriate it would be if just a little more was put back into the activity by those organisations and individuals who have gained so much from it.

When it became known that 92203 was running to Eastleigh, I once again received a number of letters from the (happily small) minority of railway enthusiasts who always seem to claim it as their right to be informed of the timings of the trains all down the line, together with every other possible detail. As usual, only a very small number of these letters included a stamped addressed envelope!

For the run to Eastleigh, all of us at Cranmore took a very great deal of extra trouble to ensure that *Black Prince* and our coach were in immaculate condition. We left Cranmore in the early morning, when the summer mists were still on the ground, and steamed our leisurely way down to Westbury. The crowds had already gathered on the platform for the great event. The special train duly arrived from Bristol with fifteen coaches, hauled by a Western class diesel hydraulic. That locomotive came off the train and *Black Prince*, with our maroon coach, backed on. A few minutes later we were away and, all the way to Eastleigh, excitement was at fever pitch. Many hundreds, possibly thousands, of people must have seen the train go by. From almost every window in the coaches of the train, tape recorders were hanging out and over the roofs catching the thrilling sound of *Black Prince* working on a main line. At last, the racehorse had been let out of her yard and was on a proper race track.

The return journey to Cranmore was just as exciting, and when we finally went up the branch in the evening with our coach, we were all very tired and happy. *Black Prince* had had a wonderful day out. Sadly it was to be her last. It would not be long before she was banned from running on BR, and I suspect that the railway orphanage at Woking no longer make quite so much from the open days at Eastleigh as a result. A number of people have since asked me why 92203 is no longer allowed to run on BR. The official reason is that, because of her flangeless centre driving wheels, BR fears her derailing. As I write, there is only one other Standard 9 in running order and that is *Evening Star.* She is part of the national collection, and is allowed out on special occasions on BR. To that, I can make no comment!

On one occasion, in 1975, *Black Prince* was allowed out from Cranmore by BR to run a special train from Westbury, down their main line to their open day at Eastleigh, and back again. Here she is seen early in the morning, specially polished for the event, about to leave for Westbury (*Photo R. J. Blenkinsop*)

Events such as *Black Prince*'s trip to Eastleigh caused an amazing amount of interest and excitement (*Photo R. J. Blenkinsop*)

I am also often asked whether, in the event of the ban being lifted, I would take *Black Prince* out again on to BR. The answer is probably no. We have our own East Somerset Railway and, within our own financial limitations, we can steam whenever we like without any of the hassle of having to sell the large number of tickets needed to cover the costs of main-line running.

It was shortly after our royal opening that we were invited to take part in the celebrations at Shildon, in County Durham, to mark the 150th anniversary of the first steam-hauled train from Stockton to Darlington. BR and the local authorities were organising the event and the list of steam engines which would be allowed to go up to County Durham to participate in the parade had been drawn up. *Black Prince* was not invited because *Evening Star*, the last steam engine to be built in this country and a sister engine of 92203, was the official representative of her class. That seemed fair enough, but we were delighted to be told that *The Green Knight* had been selected. Furthermore we were told that we would be allowed to take two of our coaches with us. One, No S1000, was the fibre-glass coach that we had purchased from BR. This unique vehicle was one of only two ever built, as an experiment in 1957, and we had purchased it for use on the East Somerset Railway.

We were determined to ensure that 75029 was in perfect mechanical order for her long journey, for she was possibly to travel for the occasion as far as any other privately owned locomotive in the country. It was approximately 200 miles from Cranmore to Shildon and we were going all the way in steam. Her route would take her from Bristol to Gloucester, on to Tyseley in Birmingham, and then via Derby, Sheffield and York, to Darlington for the beginning of the celebrations. However, as a result of points on the route.

Early in the morning of the day of her departure, I received a phone call from George Davies. *The Green Knight* had 'failed', at Bristol. She had only gone a few miles. The engine had been in fine fettle when she left Cranmore and we could not imagine what had gone wrong. Apparently she had run a hot axle box. She limped back to Bath Road diesel depot, where she was examined, and it was found that a spring on an axle pad had collapsed, causing her to run hot. Temporary repairs were carried out, and later that day she steamed to Gloucester for a full examination and, we hoped, a return to full running order.

The Green Knight was invited to take part in the celebrations at Shildon, in County Durham, in 1975, to commemorate the 150th anniversary of the Stockton to Darlington railway. Unfortunately she suffered a spot of bother on the journey north, but BR was marvellously co-operative: she was immediately rushed into the diesel depot at Gloucester, where they even removed a set of her driving wheels to make sure that all would be well (*Photo Graham F. Scott-Lowe*)

The Merchant Navy Pacific *Clan Line* was fortunately following behind us on her way to the celebrations and it was arranged for her to pick up our two coaches and take them on ahead to Darlington. Meanwhile, 75029 went into the diesel depot at Gloucester for immediate attention. She was in there for two weeks. When I went to see her, it seemed that she was receiving a heavy overhaul! I have a photograph of her standing in the depot, with a set of driving wheels missing, as a 4-4-0. All the BR depot staff at Gloucester were only too pleased to have a steam engine to look after once more, 'just like the old days'. They didn't want to see her leave. It was very much 'touch and go' whether she would be at Darlington for the beginning of the celebrations. However, as a result of the marvellous co-operation from BR at Gloucester we just made it in time, and we never received a bill for the repairs either.

Two of the members of the East Somerset Railway had already gone on ahead to set up a sales stand for us at Darlington station. Now 75029 herself arrived in the station and took her allotted place in the line of other privately owned steam engines which had already arrived, alongside one of the platforms.

The celebrations opened with a church service on the platform, conducted by the Bishop of Wakefield, the celebrated steam enthusiast and railway photographer the Rt Revd Eric Treacy. I had heard so many wonderful stories of this truly great man and now I was going to meet him for the first time. The church service was a very moving little ceremony, in spite of a Brush 47 diesel parked far too close, with its engine running! After it was over, Eric Treacy came up to me and said: 'It's so nice to meet you at last. Now, show me your loco.' We walked up the platform together along the line of engines. *The Green Knight* was parked next to *Sir Nigel Gresley* at the platform. The A4 Pacific had arrived some hours before and they had had time to clean her up. She was shining like a piece of jewellery. No 75029, on the other hand, had steamed straight up the line from Gloucester. There had been no time to clean her and she was travel-stained and grimy. Walking straight past *Sir Nigel Gresley*, Eric Treacy came enthusiastically up to my engine, and, turning to me, rubbing his hands with pleasure said, 'Ah, a real *working* engine.' It was a delightful moment.

The celebrations took place from 24 to 31 August at Shildon, a town steeped in railway history. Over forty steam locomotives and twenty other pieces of rolling stock were to be displayed to the public, in front of the BR engineering works. Over 300,000 people were expected to come to the great event. Many famous engines were there: *Flying Scotsman, Princess Elizabeth, Clan Line, Sir Nigel Gresley, Evening Star, Bahamas, Gordon,* the London, Midland & Scottish *Compound,* the *Stirling Single* and a great many others from various preserved lines and museums. Together they made up an unparalleled pageant of Britain's steam railway heritage,

The late, much loved Rt Revd Eric Treacy, renowned railway photographer and enthusiast (and bishop!), gave me a wonderful welcome when we at last arrived at Darlington station for the Rail 150 celebrations

and almost all of the locomotives were in steam.

On 25 August, Rail 150 was officially opened by the Rt Hon William Whitelaw and he named the full-scale working replica of Stevenson's *Locomotion*, which had been especially built for the occasion. She was appropriately going to lead the great cavalcade of steam which was to be the climax of the great celebration, on Sunday 31. A dozen of us had come up by road to Shildon. With all the members of the preserved railways and preservation societies in Great Britain whose locomotives were taking part in the proceedings, a very considerable number of enthusiasts had to be accommodated, and we were allocated the local college buildings. It was all rather like a boy scouts' summer camp, and was well organised and most enjoyable.

For the next two or three days, we were all engaged in the final preparation and cleaning of our engines. The whole place was a hive of

The never-to-be-forgotten display of steam locomotives in front of the engineering works at Shildon. *The Green Knight* is there—somewhere in the smoke to the top left of the picture!

activity. Meanwhile, inside the engineering works, a comprehensive exhibition had been mounted, and the East Somerset Railway had a display stand. During the first two days alone, I signed over 3,000 post cards and East Somerset Railway brochures. One of our sales items was a sponge, in a variety of different and rather gaudy colours, in the shape of a steam engine. These sold 'like hot cakes'; in one day alone we sold over 1,500 and it seemed as though every child in County Durham was walking around with an East Somerset Railway sponge. The county can never have been so full of clean children.

Grandstands had been erected alongside the line between Shildon and Darlington on the original Stockton to Darlington Railway. The great moment for the cavalcade finally arrived and, one by one, the locomotives slowly steamed out of the yard at their allotted times, on to the line. The crowds had taken their seats eagerly anticipating an event the likes of

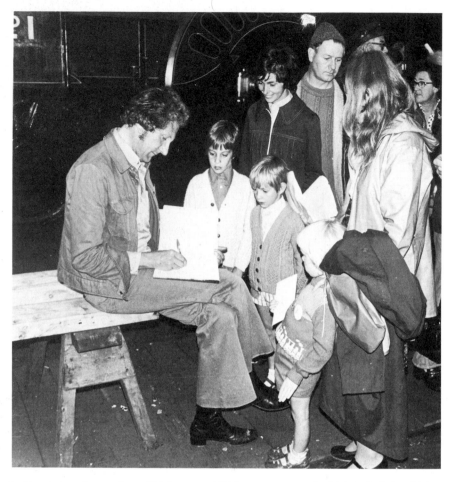

In the engineering works at Shildon an exhibition was mounted which included a display stand for the East Somerset Railway. I autographed postcards, East Somerset Railway brochures and copies of my book

which will probably never be seen again. *Locomotion* led the parade, and for several hours the engines steamed slowly past. I had been offered a vantage point from a private enclosure alongside the line, and I watched the cavalcade from there while George rode on the footplate of 75029. I was even offered a seat in a helicopter and, for a few minutes, I had an even finer view of the engines going slowly by below me.

By the early evening, we had all arrived in the marshalling yards at Darlington with our locomotives. From there, it had been arranged that they would all steam back to their respective homes throughout the country during the night. In some ways, this was perhaps the most enjoyable part of the whole event. Whilst the celebrations were exciting, it

The Green Knight playing her part in the Rail 150 cavalcade. Crowds lined the route from Shildon to Darlington. George rode on the footplate, while I watched from a line side vantage point

In the marshalling yard at Darlington, where the engines which had taken part in the parade gathered before dispersing home. For a few brief hours it was like a real working steam depot

was more 'real' now that we were back on BR with a job to do, to get home. No crowds were around. It was a cold dark night and the steam from many locomotives was curling into the cold night sky, illuminated by the tall lights of the yard. For just a few brief hours it was just like a real working steam depot and we could have been in Carlisle, Crewe or Nine Elms, in the great days of steam. For many of us these sights and sounds must remain almost as strongly in our memories as those of the parade itself.

It was during the early part of the evening that an alarming discovery was made. I suppose that in an event of this kind, when so much organisation has to be done, something is bound to go wrong. It was discovered that there was only one hose to water all the locomotives. It was obvious that it would be impossible for all of us to get away at our allotted times. As everybody rushed around trying to sort out the situation, the queue for water grew longer, and 75029 awaited her turn. *Princess Elizabeth* and *Clan Line* were in front of us in the queue. They were double heading their train down to the South, and for many people this must have been one of the highlights of the whole event, because it was possibly the first time that a Merchant Navy Pacific and a Princess had ever double-headed a train. Finally they got away, and it was our turn. We were due to depart at midnight, and it was one o'clock in the morning when we were finally given the green signal.

I had decided to bed down in one of the compartments of our fibre-glass coach but I was far too excited to sleep, and it was far too cold anyway. We were steaming down the main line through a sleeping England. This was our very own steam train and she was working on BR, with no crowds to see us. It was just like the old days.

It was a grey and early dawn as we rolled slowly into Sheffield. As we came into the station, we saw *Princess Elizabeth* and *Clan Line* storming up the hill away from us. We passed them shortly after this at Chesterfield, but they once more caught us up at Tyseley, in Birmingham, where we all had to stop and take coal and water.

There was one moment on the journey south which was particularly enjoyable for us. A main-line express was running behind us and we were ordered into a passing loop to allow it to pass. It was a lovely sunny day by now and, climbing up the embankment, I was able to take some very nice movie of a branch-line steam train, our very own, simmering gently in the loop while the express thundered by on the main line. While I was up on the embankment waiting for the main-line train I noticed an old firing iron in the undergrowth. Another steam train had been here before us! It was getting more like the old days every minute. Needless to say the iron was passed into *The Green Knight*'s cab for further use.

We were now on the Stratford to Cheltenham line. This line was due for closure and was by this time little used. We were able to slow down, taking a much more leisurely pace. As we steamed from one lovely station to another down this beautiful stretch of railway, we stopped at various stations and signal boxes where we would get out and have a cup of tea and a natter about steam engines, and then hop back in again. The sun was shining, the birds were singing and it was just as though the whole system belonged to us.

We steamed through Gloucester, and then we were once again on the Western Region main line. We came up the branch into Cranmore where we found, to our horror, that we only had an inch of water in our tender. To get from our station to the shed, we had to fill up. It was a close-run thing. All of us, including *The Green Knight* and the coaches, were travel-stained and weary, but very, very proud.

We now heard that BR intended to remove the track to Shepton. After giving the matter some very careful consideration we decided to go ahead and try to raise the money to save the line. The Chamber of Commerce in Shepton Mallet were delighted when they heard of our proposals. Shepton Mallet is a pleasant little country market town, and a magnificent new town centre had been built at enormous cost by the local drink company. Nevertheless there were a number of empty shops, and everybody seemed very excited and quite convinced that our scheme would be just what was needed to revitalise the town by bringing new trade and people into the place. Indeed, we were told by two people of some standing and influence in Shepton that we would almost certainly get considerable financial help. One trader immediately promised us £5,000 as a donation. It seemed a marvellous start.

There were several bridges on the line and the long-term maintenance of these alone would cost a great deal of money. There was also a small road that ran across the railway just before reaching the town itself which might be a problem. The station in Shepton had an ample area of sidings and was in an ideal situation. Beyond that, the line had long since been removed. The whole exercise was costed, and we estimated that we would need a minimum of £175,000.

After many hours of consultation with our legal advisers and others, we launched our appeal brochure. We sent it out to almost every potential source of financial support, throughout the country, that we could think of. On the night before the appeal was launched, Harlech TV gave us very good coverage and we sat back to await results. We fell flat on our faces, and the appeal was a flop. We soon discovered why.

The day after the launch of our appeal, a gentleman who had seen the publicity on the television rang me up: 'I've just seen the appeal that you are making on the TV for the railway. I see you are trying to raise a couple of hundred thousand pounds. Why don't you just paint six more elephant pictures and buy the line yourself?' His question had put our greatest problem in a nutshell. There is very little that one can say to a question like that. If people have the idea in their heads that you are a millionaire there is really nothing that you can do about it.

It was terribly disheartening after all the verbal encouragement that we had had from the town of Shepton Mallet. Now, it seemed, no one was prepared to back up their words with money. We didn't get a penny from the biggest employers in Shepton who previously had helped the place so much. We never saw any of the £5,000 which we were promised by our trader friend. It had been just words, and words do not buy track. The total amount we received from the entire town was £60. This came in the form of two donations. One, of £50, was from a man who had been a great friend of the railway since it opened and who had a small hotel right in the centre of the town. The other £10 came from an old lady who said that she would 'love to see steam engines running past her window again'.

We did not give up immediately. While we were still hoping that a 'sugar daddy' might turn up, we were continuing our negotiations with BR and other parties. We now began to realise that the obligations that we would be taking on were far greater than we at first realised. One concerned the small road over the railway near Shepton. George Davies and I met representatives from the council and BR at the level crossing. We were told that we must install modern automatic barriers with coloured flashing lights. (One would have thought that we were talking about the main line to London.) Our friend from BR supported us; he told the planning people that he considered the whole idea was quite stupid: 'Level crossing gates, hand-operated, have been perfectly OK for us since 1858, so why on earth won't they do for the East Somerset Railway when they will only be running a few trains on one day a week in the summer only?' It was a good point, but it fell on deaf ears. The barriers and lights would have cost us at least a further £20,000. It was the end of our plans to run into Shepton Mallet.

A few weeks after the failure of our scheme to save the line, one of the directors of the large company in Shepton Mallet whom we had approached for financial help but who had turned us down was presented with a watch on his retirement. Because he was a railway enthusiast, the company decided to make the presentation on Cranmore railway station. Fortunately, I was not there that afternoon; I only hope we charged him and his friends our full admission fee!

I believe that if in fact we had succeeded in raising the money required, it could well still have crippled us financially to a point, after a few years, where the East Somerset Railway might well have closed altogether. I have become more sure of this as the East Somerset Railway has developed, slowly but surely. The principles which we established right from the start have paid off. We are still seeing embryo railway schemes up and down the country trying to save 20 miles of track or more, usually with money they do not have. Others are running on large lengths of railway line which they do not own and which, in some cases, are subsidised by the local authorities. This, to our way of thinking, is no way to start. We have always believed in learning to walk before we run. The East Somerset Railway has never been big, but at least we have always paid for everything as we went along. The financial obligations of running efficiently even a small fully operational steam railway in this day and age are enormous and escalating all the time.

It was towards the end of 1976 that the contractors moved in and started lifting the track at the far end of the line, at Shepton Mallet. They moved slowly but ever nearer towards us. Several people who knew that we had tried previously to save the line questioned this apparently harsh action on the part of BR: 'Why can't they leave it a bit longer, and give you a chance to raise the money?' Some expressed their views in stronger terms and threatened to write rude letters to BR on our behalf. Poor old BR—in fact, they had given us ample time to raise the funds and we had failed. Some people tend to forget that BR is accountable to the taxpayer. Railway line is valuable either for reuse or as scrap and BR has an obligation to capitalise on any redundant assets.

Now we had to act fast. Was there any chance of saving just the first portion of the land and track from our locomotive depot, up the hill and down into the steep cutting? The railway certainly didn't have the money and neither did I. This is when a tiger once again came to the rescue! My painting 'Tiger Fire' had raised a huge sum to help save the animal from extinction and the East Somerset Railway had acquired a tanker wagon in the process. Now, my second painting of this lovely animal, 'Tiger in the Sun', was going to save at least some of the track that we thought we had lost. Like 'Tiger Fire', the new picture was published in a single limited edition of 850 copies, and by a generous arrangement with my publishers, we were allocated two-thirds of these copies to sell from the Signal Box Art Gallery and the talk shows that I put on during the winter months. Happily, the prints sold very fast indeed and we were thus able to purchase the line just in time. It would be some time yet before we could hope to run on it but at least it was ours. Meanwhile we had other problems to worry about.

During the summer of 1976 we suffered a major setback. No 75029, *The Green Knight*, was giving brake-van rides up and down past the shed when she blew a smoke tube. She was failed, on the spot. This was perhaps the moment when I truly began to realise the full obligations of owning a steam engine weighing over 100 tons. Sooner or later a locomotive has to be overhauled. It was all very easy for BR in the days of steam. They had enormous workshop facilities, and when the engine went in for a heavy overhaul, it probably came out again a few weeks later. It was very different for us. We had known that this moment was coming and now it had arrived.

241

The situation could have been worse. Our early decision to try to do things properly was already beginning to pay off. At least we had a reasonably well equipped workshop, although it was not exactly Swindon. However, at least we would not have to take 75029 to pieces out in the open. No 75029 went into Cranmore works in 1976, and she is still there in 1983. We decided to give her a major overhaul. Because there are, at best, only five or six volunteers working on her at any one time, and almost entirely at weekends, the job is inevitably taking a long time.

The loss of *The Green Knight* was certainly a setback for the railway, because it meant that one of our two 'glamour' engines was out of service, and it is undoubtedly the big engines that pull the crowds in. We were not desperately short of motive power as, at the time of 75029's failure, we had already rebuilt Barry's Jinty which he had rescued from South Wales. The Jinty was our first major exercise in locomotive restoration and the Austerity had followed her into our workshop. Nevertheless, the absence of 75029 created a major gap in our motive power. Furthermore, 75029 was not as hungry on coal as *Black Prince*, which eats the stuff like a monster.

The protracted overhaul of 75029 is, I believe, a magnificent example of what dedicated volunteers can achieve. I have shown many members of the public into our workshop to see for themselves, and they have agreed with my judgement. With no overhead crane and, sometimes, brute force where mechanical aids are really called for, an engine weighing over 100 tons has been taken slowly but methodically to pieces. We reached a point, in fact, when almost nothing else could have been taken off. The 6ft driving wheels were removed by slowly jacking up the massive frames of the engine on to sleepers until they were just high enough to slide the wheels out. (How much easier it would have been if we had had a wheel drop.) A part of her frame below the cab floor had wasted away completely and this had to be completely rebuilt. The tender body was removed from the chassis and shot-blasted, descaled and painted. The cab was partially rebuilt and received the same treatment.

The moment came for the removal of the boiler from 75029. This was a job which was beyond us as we did not have the heavy lift capabilities. We engaged a hire company who had a fleet of mobile cranes and their representative came to look at the job. It was his responsibility to decide the type of crane that was suitable. On the appointed day, the vehicle drove across the field and on to the railway. No 75029 was shunted on to the line alongside the crane. Everything went well to start with and I was filming as *The Green Knight*'s boiler was lifted off the frames, and the wheels were shunted away from underneath her. Knowing that the boiler would be on the ground for some considerable time we asked the crane driver to lift it again and move it a few feet to one side. What I now witnessed was a nightmare. I was still filming when, to my horror, I

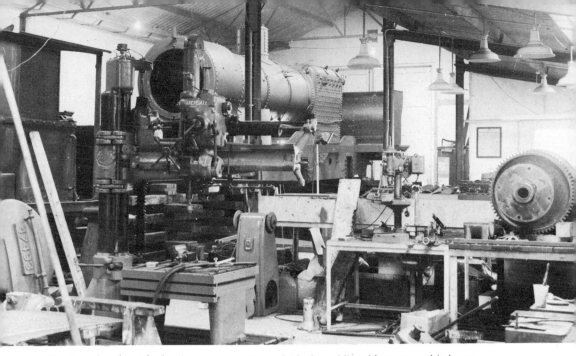

The 'blood and guts' of railway preservation, which the public seldom sees— this is our workshop at Cranmore, where the volunteers achieve miracles of restoration in their spare time (*Photo Rex Coffin*)

suddenly saw spurts of hydraulic fluid shooting into the air from the turntable base of the mobile crane. The bolts holding the jib to the turntable of the vehicle sheered and, very slowly, the jib crashed down on to the cab of the crane. With a rending of glass and metal, that side of the cab was completely flattened. Miraculously the driver escaped injury by a split second by swinging himself sideways in his seat. The jib now fell slowly in the other direction and flattened the rest of the cab. The driver leapt out of the wreck just in time. Then the jib fell on to the chimney of my locomotive smashing it down through the smoke box. The crane finally fell to the ground with a thud. It was all over in a matter of seconds. I was frozen to the spot; it didn't seem real.

Because we had set out right from the beginning to be safe and efficient at Cranmore, Barry had insisted that no one was near when the operation was going on. If we had not been so conscious of safety precautions, several people could have been killed. The driver of the crane came up to me and said: 'That's the third time that's happened to me.' I didn't really know what to say, except to suggest that he got a job with another crane company. The first thing that we did was to collect all the bolts from the crane and lock them away for subsequent metallurgical examination. When it discovered we had done this, the crane company insisted on their immediate return, accusing us of theft. We refused to give them back until they had been examined, and they were indeed proved to be faulty.

243

Would 75029 ever steam again? In fact, the damage could have been worse. If the jib had smashed down on to *The Green Knight*'s boiler, that would have been very different. I heard that the crane was back in service three weeks later. Of one thing I am certain; I will never refer to our volunteers as amateurs. Nor will we ever use that crane company again!

On a number of occasions over the years, the Press have come down to Cranmore to ask me if they can do a story about 'saving old locomotives'. I try to point out that the whole business of steam preservation is not necessarily a story of saving mechanical things. It is an intensely human story. I tell them the story about Jeff. Jeff walked on to the site as the builders were putting up our locomotive depot. Jeff is deaf and dumb. By sign language to the builders, he said that he hoped to become involved with the East Somerset Railway and would like to join us as a member. We deliberated for many hours over this matter. The hazards both for Jeff and for other people might well be considerable, particularly as he indicated to us that he hoped to work on the railway. Fortunately, we did not decide to try to discourage him from coming. He is now one of our key members in the workshop, and, ever since *The Green Knight* was failed, has been deeply and personally involved with her restoration. The BBC came down to Cranmore one summer and did a very nice little piece on Jeff, for one of their television programmes for the deaf. He talked for ten minutes to the interviewer in sign language, with *Black Prince* in the background, saying how satisfying it was for him to work on the East Somerset Railway. That gives all of us a marvellous feeling. There is far more to running a preserved steam railway than just lumps of machinery.

12

Further joys and sorrows on the East Somerset

The more the East Somerset Railway became established, the more some of our members who came regularly to Cranmore had to be restrained in their enthusiasm. On occasions, this was extremely difficult. It has always been a problem to convince people that not everything could be done at once. It was even harder for me personally to keep on reminding our volunteers that I was acting as guarantor for the enormous and ever increasing overdraft.

In the early days, George and I found that if things did not seem to be forging ahead fast enough, some of the lads would very soon become frustrated and start to lose heart. This was particularly so during the period when we were giving brake-van rides up and down past the shed and many of us were at the same time looking with frustration at the line, running up over the hill into the distance, which we had recently purchased, but which was by no means ready for running steam trains.

We had other problems too. There was one time when the spirit of enthusiasm reached what was perhaps an all-time low. It was disheartening to have *The Green Knight* in bits all over the workshop, and we were beginning to wonder if we would ever get her back in one piece again. A restoration job of this size can very easily break the spirit of the dedicated few who had started off with such enthusiasm for seeing her a new engine one day. Now we were to realise how desperately we needed our own road access to our shed. Up to this time, the coal for the railway could only be delivered to the end of the lane from the station towards the shed, and it then had to be manhandled in bags into railway wagons. It was back-breaking work. Nevertheless, something always seems to happen which makes everything seem worthwhile again. Norton Corp, the farmer who lives in Cranmore village and who owned the field, decided to come to our rescue. He agreed to the laying of a road right across the middle of the field, and this gave us our road access. There are not many farmers who would do that.

During the summer of 1978 George tragically and suddenly died. This was a very great personal loss for me. George's warm friendship and his support in everything that I did had given me great comfort in the early days. He had been with me before the railway was set up and had helped me lay its foundations. He had many unique qualities and the suddenness of his death was a tremendous shock. It created a void which has never been filled. I have realised over the years how much I owe to George's leadership at Cranmore during our formative years. When I first met him he had already had experience, at Dinting, of running a preserved steam railway. He had set Dinting up from nothing and turned it into a highly successful steam centre. He had a unique way of leading people. He could be tough but was gentle at the same time. These were the foundations on which we grew, and we are now reaping the benefit. Right from the very beginning George drummed it into all of us, as he had at Dinting, that at Cranmore there was only one thing that mattered and that was the East Somerset Railway. To co-ordinate a large number of headstrong, sometimes militant, always single-minded and individualistic railway enthusiasts into a working team with one aim is a very great exercise in human relations.

On some of the preserved lines, even to this day, it is perhaps doubtful if this lesson has been learned. At some of the steam centres, major problems still arise because the many people involved pull in different directions. If five or six entirely separate and individual railway societies are based on one railway and they each own an engine which they think is the only thing that matters, then, without good leadership, you have an almost guaranteed recipe for problems. The railway on which the different groups are based will finally suffer—George certainly taught me that right from the very beginning. Our success in this respect is illustrated by such incidents as one that took place one Sunday afternoon when George and I walked up to the shed. It was a very busy day and our car-park was nearly full. It was beginning to look as though people would start trying to leave their cars in the village and the surrounding lanes. We found one of our volunteer members happily working on an item of rolling stock of which he was a part owner. He was minding his own business and his time was his own. He didn't have to do anything that he was told. Nevertheless, he was needed down at the car park. 'Can you leave that now and go down to sort the cars out?' George asked. Our friend could easily have answered, 'Why should I? This is my coach; I can do what I like.' He didn't say that. He willingly left what he was doing and went down to the car park. The message had sunk in. The public get fed up if they cannot park their cars and, if annoyed by it, they will not come again. If they don't come back, there is no income for the railway, and the railway then closes. If it closes, then our friend would have nowhere to work on his coach and he would have to take it away.

As we were still running up and down past the shed with our brake vans, we continued to look towards the top of the hill, past our shed. We decided that the time had now come to start refurbishing the line and tackling the immense task of getting this length of track ready for the running of passenger trains. First of all, regulations demand that on a single-line working, an engine must pull the train in both directions. As the track was single, this meant that a loop would be required to enable the locomotive to run round from one end of the train to the other for the return trip. As it is illegal to have a run-round loop on a slope, this in fact meant that although the track was still *in situ*, we would not be able to run down into the cutting, the most scenically interesting part of the run. We would have to build a run-round loop at the top of the hill; this in itself would be a massive task, requiring, of course, two sets of points in order to double the track. Eventually, we decided to build a small station at the run-round loop. We had another problem to face. We would have to build another station near our locomotive shed because we were still unable to run into Cranmore station itself because of the bitumen tanker-train operation.

It seems that nothing daunts the really dedicated railway enthusiast. The lads at Cranmore had somehow heard that a redundant BR station was sitting all by itself in the middle of a farmer's field, not far from Cranmore. Presumably, in lifting the closed branch line, BR had forgotten all about the station. The farmer was tired of having it there, so he sold it to us, on condition that we took it away; so we did just that. It was, fortunately, the sort that was built in concrete sections. Nevertheless it was a colossal task, as we had almost no mechanical aids at our disposal. In just three weeks, during the winter months, with the volunteers working most of the time in pouring rain and up to their ankles in clinging mud, the job was done. We now had a new station near the locomotive depot, and we called it Cranmore West.

On Easter Saturday 1979, our very first train, with our members travelling in brake vans behind our Austerity tank locomotive, ran up the line. Then, with the run-round loop completed and ¾ mile of track from Cranmore West to the top of the hill completely relaid to the most professional standards, we at last opened the line to passenger traffic with our two coaches, on Good Friday 1980. Less than a mile may not be very much but it was a great deal more exhilarating than running brake vans up and down past the shed. It meant that the East Somerset Railway now had much more to offer the public. Moreover, our coal bills did not go up in proportion to our extra length of track.

During the summer of 1979 we suffered a major setback which had far more serious implications than simply the removal from service of another of our locomotives. In fact, it was at this time that my spirits sank to their lowest level and I was more deeply worried about my involvement with steam locomotive preservation than at any time since 1967 when I had made that telephone call to BR. The overdraft was reaching frightening proportions by this time and my personal life was becoming very deeply affected. The bank were really putting on the pressure and there was quite a real danger that I would have to sell my house in order to pay just a part of the overdraft back. As if this were not enough, we now realised that we would have to take *Black Prince* out of service. I had owned her for nearly ten years and her boiler tubes were coming up for replacement. The moment had come when both our glamour engines would be out of service at the same time.

The Green Knight was still in bits in our workshop and would remain that way for several years yet. When she was finally out-shopped, there would be so many urgent restoration jobs waiting to be done on our coaches and other engines that it could well have been ten years before we could even start on *Black Prince*. Her overhaul could possibly take that amount of time again. I was being quite realistic about it. The time was approaching when I wondered whether we could survive. Furthermore, I had little idea of the critical financial crisis into which I was about to sink, and it was all for *Black Prince*.

There was only one way to get *Black Prince* overhauled and back to Cranmore again quickly; that was to send her to outside contractors. The East Somerset Railway could not possibly afford to do this. The only hope was to get some sort of financial backing. It occurred to me that with the aid of a good press story this might be forthcoming. We sent out a press release inviting a story on the crisis that had befallen the engine and its owner. The story duly appeared as I had hoped and, a few days later, the telephone rang. It was a gentleman who had helped the railway on other occasions and my hopes soared. He asked me how much it would cost for *Black Prince* to go to Husband's shipyard in Southampton; he was a great friend of Phil Husband and was sure that I could get the job efficiently and properly done for as low a price as possible. First of all, I obtained a quotation from BR for the tow from Cranmore to Southampton by diesel, and back again. The price they asked was £1,100 each way. Already, therefore, we were talking about nearly £2,500, before the restoration job had even started. I then went to see Phil Husband and gave him a detailed description of what we considered had to be done to get the locomotive back into tip-top condition. The quotation from him was daunting, but not entirely unexpected. If it did nothing else, it made us realise how lucky we are at Cranmore not to have to pay labour charges! I telephoned my friend with the money, told him the figure and he agreed that, with the help of some of his friends, the money would be found. I was to go ahead. Greatly relieved, we went to have lunch with Phil Husband; it seemed that it was 'all systems go'.

Husband's shipyard was not rail-connected but the army military port at Marchwood was next to the yard and the army depot had a rail link with BR. I went to see the commandant and he readily agreed to help us. He told me that if we could get *Black Prince* to Marchwood, the army would build a cover for the engine of scaffolding and plastic sheeting, so that the men from Husband's yard could simply walk across the road and do the job on army property.

I telephoned BR, accepted their quotation for the tow and asked them to arrange it as soon as possible. One would have thought that it was a fairly simple job to come into Cranmore with a diesel, hitch on to *Black Prince*, and take her the 100 miles to Southampton. Then, when the job was completed, all they would have to do was to bring her back again. I immediately found that life was apparently not as simple as that and I could never have imagined the problems that were now to ensue. It took BR five months to organise the task. During that time I must have been on the verge of several nervous breakdowns. Months went by, and we were getting absolutely nowhere. First of all, Western Region readily agreed to do the job, but Southern Region refused to let the locomotive on to their territory in any circumstances. It reached the point where, it seemed to me anyway, Western and Southern Regions were not even speaking to each other. Meanwhile, I was waiting, and I was the fee-paying customer. When at last it seemed that we were getting somewhere, the Western Region decided that they wouldn't do the job after all. They had apparently now discovered that 92203 has a centre driving wheel without a flange on it, and this would be bound to cause a derailment. I learned

Black Prince had to leave Cranmore for an overhaul at Marchwood

that in a few places in the country a particular new design of pointwork had been installed after the end of steam and BR seemed to have an almost paranoid fear of a Standard 9 derailing at such a place. Apparently Westbury, or somewhere around there, was one of the places concerned. One of my friends in the Western region pointed out, however, that there was another way round which would avoid Westbury altogether. So I could not really see the problem, but the answer was still a very firm no.

After four months, there was a breakthrough. Western Region decided to do the tow after all, but Southern Region still refused to accept the locomotive. After a further month of incessant phone calls, while I was trying to paint pictures at my studio, BR at long last agreed to do the job. The freight manager and I had come to know each other on Christian-name terms by now, although we had never actually met. The last words that he said to me on the phone the day before the diesel came into Cranmore were: 'Do you know, David, this bloody job has cost us five times what you are paying us?' I could only point out that it wasn't my fault that the two regions wouldn't speak to each other. It wasn't my fault either that they had taken all that time to arrange such a simple job. At long last the diesel came into Cranmore. She looked as though she needed an overhaul far more urgently than *Black Prince.*

No 92203 arrived safely at Marchwood, went into her scaffolding and plastic shed, and Husband's men started taking her apart. Several weeks went by and I was just about to depart for Africa when the telephone rang. It was the manager of the shipyard. They wanted the first instalment of the charge, to cover the cost of the work done so far. This seemed perfectly reasonable, so I telephoned my friend to ask him if he could give me the first payment. There was a long silence. He had changed his mind! I think that 'phone call was one of the biggest shocks I have ever had in my life. My heart sank. Here I was, left high and dry with a half-built locomotive and the shipyard wanting payment.

I decided to go ahead and somehow retrieve the situation, although I should have halted the work there and then and sold *Black Prince* as she stood.

Husband's, meanwhile, could not possibly have been more helpful. They offered to finish the job for as low a sum as possible, knowing that we desperately needed *Black Prince* back at Cranmore to pull the crowds in. They also offered to defer payment for as long as they possibly could in the hope that it might make things a little easier for me. Meanwhile, I didn't dare tell my extremely tough solicitor all this. He was not remotely interested in steam railways and thinks that I am slightly crazy anyway. His only concern was, and is, to see that I don't rush headlong into complete financial ruin because of what he regards as my extravagant hobby. If I had told him about *Black Prince*, he would undoubtedly have washed his hands of my affairs altogether unless I sold her there and then.

Black Prince' in bits, inside her scaffolding and plastic cocoon, at Marchwood.

He was already telling me very bluntly that the time was rapidly approaching when I should very seriously consider getting out of the railway preservation business altogether. It was like a sponge, and it was soaking up money that I did not have. The rest of this story really has no place here. My reason for mentioning it at all is that I believe that it is relevant to the steam-railway scene today and perhaps others may learn from my own experience. I managed somehow to crawl up from this deep crisis at enormous personal cost, but I would never get into such a position again. I only hope that the people who, even today, still appear to be involving themselves with grandiose preservation schemes know what they are doing. In some cases, I doubt very much that they do. They may find out the hard way, as I have done. Steam locomotives can cause an immense amount of personal heartache and worry. I know. So does my wife, and she deserves a medal for standing by me.

With her restoration complete, *Black Prince* was ready to return to Cranmore. Now, very ironically, there were several people in the Southern Region of BR who assumed that she was going to be allowed to return to Cranmore in steam. One friend of mine in BR at Waterloo actually 'phoned me and said: 'Won't it be marvellous to see steam back on the Southern Region again?' There was obviously no question of such

251

a facility being granted, and she was towed back to Cranmore once again by diesel, fit for, we hoped, another ten to fifteen years of service.

We were still collecting items for the East Somerset Railway and we now started looking for a platform bookstall to provide an extra sales facility. We were contacted by a firm of stationers who told us that they had one which was redundant, on Salisbury station. We could have it if we took it away. We went to see it. I was delighted to find that it was just like the one that my father had had on his model railway all those years ago; all polished woodwork and roller blinds. Fortunately I still had my Bedford 3 ton truck and a number of us turned up at the station with all the necessary equipment to dismantle the bookstall. The station master and all his staff at Salisbury knew us well by now and gave us immeasurable help. The biggest problem was that the bookstall was on an island platform with the main line to and from London on either side, but the dismantling was not too difficult and everything went well. When we started taking it to pieces we found all sorts of goodies from the past; old coins, cigarette packets, bus tickets and artefacts from the thirties and forties were seeing the light of day for the first time for many years.

While we were at Salisbury, we asked the station master if he had anything else lying around which he did not need. With his approval, we raided the stores. We found various tables and other items of furniture which had been lying around for many years, and which would be very useful at Cranmore. We loaded them all on to the lorry. We also found some rather interesting old objects, including several shovels with rather strange metal guards at the bottom of their handles. Apparently these had been designed in the 1940s for the specific purpose of extinguishing incendiary bombs that landed on the station from the Luftwaffe above. I could not really see these being needed at Cranmore for this particular purpose, but I can never bear to see anything unusual or of intrinsic or historic value being thrown away, so these were loaded on to the lorry as well.

We also found a splendid old platform refreshment trolley among the cobwebs in the dungeons below Salisbury station. This hideous item was pure 1930s art nouveau and one day we shall restore that as well. Inside it were a large number of London, Midland & Scottish cups which had somehow strayed on to the Southern Region. The bookstall has now been rebuilt on the platform at Cranmore, freshly repainted and varnished and as good as new.

There is very little that escapes the notice of the British railway enthusiast. Because so much has been destroyed in the name of 'progress', he has been all the more anxious to save whatever he can of what remains. Often complete signal cabins have been moved to preserved lines, just in time. Signals, turn-tables and parts of (or even complete) stations have been saved from the demolition men. One Thursday evening, when I was for once actually at home, the 'phone rang. It was one of my friends: 'The bridge is coming out at midnight this Saturday.' 'What bridge?' I asked. 'The one across the Tonbridge–Guildford line at Chilworth. Shall we try and save it?'

I had enough problems as it was. I was trying unsuccessfully to keep up with an ever increasing backlog of work; wildlife conservation was taking over more and more of my life; and here I was being asked to save a footbridge. However, it did seem worth a try and rather exciting.

I only had Friday in which to act. I knew no one in the huge BR office complex at Croydon. However, apparently, they deal with people trying to buy footbridges there, apart from running a railway. I picked up the phone and said who I was. 'Ah, David Shepherd, the friend of British Railways. What can we do to help you?' I thought, 'How nice, I'm "in", they like me. I'm halfway to getting my footbridge.' 'I want to save the footbridge that you are demolishing tomorrow at midnight over the Guildford–Tonbridge railway line. Any chance? But I can't afford a fancy price.' There was few seconds' silence. Obviously BR was deep in thought.

'Well, if you take the bridge away, it means that we can cancel the demolition train. That will save us £800 or so. We will see what we can do. Hold on, and I will have a chat with my boss.' I waited a few minutes, and he came back to the phone. 'We will have to charge you something, Mr Shepherd, because it has to go through the books. If you take it away, will £10 do?' I accepted the deal at once!

I was now faced with a not inconsiderable task, but it was made a very great deal easier by BR telling me that it would retain the crane which was already laid on, together with their demolition team. In effect all that I had to do was to find the transport. It so happens that almost in sight of the bridge, at Shalford, is a large British Road Services depot. It also happens that, at that time, the manager was a member of the East Somerset Railway.

'John, I've got a problem. I've gone and bought that footbridge just up the line from here. I've got to take it away at midnight tomorrow, and I am desperate.' As I spoke, John must have noticed me looking longingly out of his office at a number of enormous British Road Services low-loaders doing nothing in particular, in his yard. 'OK, David, we will see what we can do for you.'

I arrived at the scene at 11pm the next night. BR had instructed its men to cut the bridge in as few places as possible. They were marvellous; I think that they were as pleased as I was to know that one day the bridge would see a new lease of life. At a few minutes to midnight, two low-loaders arrived and the bridge sections were carefully loaded aboard for transport the next morning to Godalming; to Charterhouse School, where, because one of the masters was an enthusiast, the bridge was given a temporary home on the edge of one of their playing fields. It was later taken down to the car park at Cranmore, for, we hoped, eventual re-erection, but that is another story.

As if a footbridge wasn't enough, I now became involved with buying a station; or, at least, great big pieces of one. We heard that the old London & South Western station at Ash Vale in Surrey was going to be demolished, to be replaced by one of the modern standard-type concrete and glass 'bus shelters'. The old station was substantially built, in brick and masses of timber which we knew would be burned on the site. We could find further use for it. There was also a very fine platform canopy with its glass roof supported on the customary cast-iron columns and supports.

We made contact with the demolition contractors and BR and they told us that, provided that we didn't get in their way, we could take whatever we wanted, free of charge. We would have to dismantle the canopy ourselves, of course, and remove it during the night, between the last train and the first one in the morning, when the electric current was switched off.

I still had my Bedford 3 tonner and we certainly made good use of it. Several of us participated in the exercise and very large quantities of valuable and reusable material were rescued. It all had to be transported back to my home near Godalming and this meant many journeys in the lorry back and forth while everybody else was asleep.

It happened that at this time the men suspected of perpetrating the Guildford public house bomb outrage were under very strict guard in Godalming police station. The town had never had IRA suspects in its midst before and the 'nick' was ringed by armed police round the clock in case, I suppose, of some sort of rescue attempt. This was the time when I chose to drive past the police station many times in my lorry, in the dead of night; it was the shortest route from Ash Vale to my home. It must have been on about the fourth or fifth journey at about 3.30am when, all of a sudden, a police car blocked my passage. Two policemen got out and came up to the cab of my lorry. 'Would you mind telling us who you are and what you are doing? We've noticed you driving backwards and forwards past us several times in the last few hours.' Then he paused, looked reflectively at me and said: 'Aren't you David Shepherd?' 'Yes, that's right. I wasn't speeding, was I?' 'Do you always spend your sleeping hours driving around Godalming in your lorry when you should be tucked up in bed? What have you got in the back of your truck, anyway?' 'Well, you won't believe this, but I've got a railway station.' Looking at me in total disbelief, he walked to the back of the lorry.

Satisfied that I was telling the truth, one of the officers then said: 'Sir, we've got a slightly touchy situation here at the moment with some rather nasty guys under lock and key. Do you think that you could choose a better time to go rescuing railway stations?'

254

Every year our volunteers at Cranmore organise what they call 'civil week'. As many as possible take their annual holiday at this time, and volunteers come in to help us from other railways (a marvellous example of the very necessary co-operation between different railways). During civil week they undertake a major civil engineering task. In 1980, they built a station. Where there had been brambles and a jungle of undergrowth there rose—in just a few days—a complete halt with platform, shelter, lamps and flowerbeds! Merryfield Lane was opened in 1981—we were beginning to look like a proper country branch line.

We had previously accepted the fact that we would never be able to buy any of the track-bed beyond the big bridge that carried the road to Evercreech over the railway, at the bottom of the cutting. All the track had been lifted from Shepton Mallet right up to the far side of the bridge. We had been told that the bridge was suspect, so a chain-link fence had been put across the line on our side of the bridge and this was the boundary of our property. Barry and I now decided to have the bridge professionally examined. Not being able to run through the cutting seemed a terrible waste and, if we could get under the bridge and buy the track-bed on the other side towards Shepton Mallet, up to a point where it levelled out, we could then build another run round and a terminal station, if or when we had the money. By achieving this then we could run through the cutting, having a further 1½ miles of beautiful line on which to run our passenger trains. We were lucky. We were told that the bridge was in far better condition than we were at first led to believe. Even more fortunate was the fact that BR had been unable to sell this last part of the track-bed from Shepton Mallet and this just happened to be the strip of land from the level up to 'our' bridge. We bought the 5 acres for £500. It seemed a good price, but it must be realised that no farmer can make much use of a very long, thin strip of land, covered in ballast, first on an embankment, and then in a cutting. BR was probably only too delighted to find a buyer.

At the time of writing, we are trying to raise the money to buy track, so that we can put it all back once more where it was only so recently torn up. We are going inch by inch towards our goal; it isn't easy, because the days are over when I can paint tigers for the railway!

In September 1982, Foster Yeoman had an open day for their staff. They invited *Black Prince* down once more to the stone terminal to test her strength. Two thousand people came, and they were certainly rewarded with a magnificent spectacle.

The average weight of a stone train that goes out of the Foster Yeoman terminal is probably somewhere in the region of 1,800 tons. On occasions, these stone trains are double headed by BR diesels. A train of this weight was prepared and *Black Prince* stormed out from under the bridge without the slightest effort. To the delight of the crowd watching

255

in the nearby field, another six wagons were added, which put the weight up to probably just under 2,000 tons. Again, she pulled this weight without undue effort up the gradient, to the end of the Foster Yeoman line, where it joins BR. The final run was even more spectacular. *Black Prince* hauled 2,178 imperial tons of stone out of the terminal. We are claiming it to be the record weight ever hauled in the United Kingdom by a single steam locomotive.

I was on the footplate of 92203 for the last of the three runs. It was one of the most spectacular experiences that I have ever had. Dave, who was driving, told me that as *Black Prince* was going under the bridge carrying the road, I must sit with my head between my knees, and cover myself with my coat. As *Black Prince* very slowly gathered speed from a dead start in the terminal, I understood why. There was probably less than 12in clearance between the top of *Black Prince*'s chimney, and the bottom of the concrete bridge. No words can adequately describe the sound and sensation of being on the footplate at that moment. I remember briefly looking up and seeing flames forcing themselves out round the edge of the closed box door and right up to the cab roof. She very slowly emerged from under the bridge and made it to the end of the run. It was like sitting on the top of a volcano.

Every time we have a donation of a few pounds, we can extend our line a little further, foot by foot (*Photo Rex Coffin*)

In September 1982 *Black Prince* hauled a record load at the Foster Yeoman quarry *(Photo Tudor Harwood)*

One railway enthusiast wrote to the railway press after the event complaining that it was quite wrong to treat an engine like this. All I can say is that, after all the heartbreak, financial worry and physical effort involved in keeping an engine such as *Black Prince* in working order for as long as I have done, aided by my dedicated band of volunteer helpers, it is hardly likely that any of us would do anything to the engine which would cause any damage. I have written of the several occasions during the years when I have been on the point of despair through all the worries attendant to the preservation of steam. All too infrequently there comes an occasion such as this when all the worry is forgotten and all the excitement returns. I don't know what the future holds for me personally. I would never say categorically that I would never sell *Black Prince*. It may come to that. What I do know is that during that afternoon at Foster Yeoman's, *Black Prince* meant a very great deal to me. It is quite astonishing how fond one can become of a steam locomotive.

13
What of the future?

What does the future hold for the steam railways of Great Britain? Who knows how many will be still running in twenty-five years' time. In an increasingly uncertain world it would surely be a foolish man indeed who would predict with certainty that the future is completely secure for any of us. Meanwhile we are still going through a period of proliferation which reminds me of the railway building mania of the last century. It is in the knowledge of what happened then that I have misgivings now. We are now living in a different world from that of the mid-sixties when the preservation mania began. The sources of finance which were there then have all but dried up. There are no more sugar daddies around. More and more railways are competing with each other to attract less and less available money. It is a sobering thought that if all the new and embryo schemes now trying to get established succeed in doing so, they will amount to an increase of over 70 per cent by 1988. This represents an increase in tourist lines in this country from nearly forty to nearly seventy, with a doubling of the route mileage; and every mile of track will have to be maintained to an ever higher standard at an ever greater cost. Will there be a corresponding increase in the numbers of people who, at increasing cost to themselves, will support this proliferation by coming to visit us? I very much doubt it. It certainly doesn't follow.

The number of steam locomotives already saved has reached the staggering figure of over 400. By no means are all of these in running order. Furthermore there are nearly 100 new projects to save other engines. The preservation movement as a whole is already responsible for the saving of and the consequent maintenance of over 670 coaches (and coaches probably take up more time and effort to keep in good order than locomotives). Moreover, coaches do not attract the same emotive response and consequent financial support for their maintenance as steam engines do; but you cannot carry passengers on steam engines!

Perhaps the most controversial subject in preservation now is that of Barry scrapyard. Should the duplication of locomotives to be saved continue until Woodham's yard is empty? Some people may consider that there are far too many steam engines in preservation already. A large number of these, purchased after so much hard work and dedication, are still waiting for money that is not there, to restore them to working order.

Portrait and subject . . . and the artist (*Photo R. J. Blenkinsop*)

They can be seen all over England sitting under tarpaulins looking just as scruffy as when they were in Barry scrapyard. I know you cannot stop people raising money for the cause they believe in. Nor can you stop people spending money how they wish. If someone tries to raise money for yet another steam engine from Barry scrapyard he will, I believe, raise the funds relatively easily, even today, for the glamour of saving engines from the cutter's torch will be with us until all the engines have finally gone. Try, on the other hand, to raise money for a carriage shed, and it is a very different story indeed. I know, because the East Somerset Railway is trying to do just that. There is no glamour in a carriage shed. Surely, however, covered accommodation is far more important than yet another steam engine or coach waiting for restoration out in the rain? It does not make much sense to buy a locomotive, restore it to working order, with enormous amounts of money and physical effort, only to see it then rapidly deteriorate because you have nowhere to put it under cover. We know, because we don't have a carriage shed, and there are few more demoralising situations than to sweat your guts out transforming a scrap-

259

yard coach into ex-works condition, only to see the weather sending you straight back to square one.

Many of us consider that there are ample steam railways in this country already for everyone to have one within relatively easy reach. Some may well go to the wall in the years ahead. Looking into the future, to keep these railways and locomotives and rolling stock on them in running order, we are now having to think not in terms of hundreds of thousands of pounds, but in millions. If this seems to be an exaggeration, one only has to consider the fact that the average cost of the full restoration of one single steam engine is somewhere in the region of £30,000 or more, and the engines on a railway are only the tip of the iceberg. Again, if all the embryo schemes which we have at the moment succeed, by 1988 the steam railways of Great Britain will be responsible for the maintenance of no less than 1,099 bridges. Any steam railway that has a bridge to run over or run under knows the awesome financial obligations with which it will be faced in order to maintain that structure into the long-term future.

All the steam railways in this country depend almost entirely on volunteers. Read any newsletter of any railway today and you will see the same heartfelt and sometimes desperate-sounding appeals for more help, and again more help. There was a time when some of us seemed to think that the volunteer had an obligation to help his nearest railway. We seemed to think we had a right to expect it of him. In fact the volunteer owes us nothing and can do what he pleases. The proliferation of steam-railway projects is far outpacing the proliferation of volunteers!

The East Somerset Railway has one problem which possibly makes it unique among steam railways. It is all too often referred to as 'David Shepherd's railway'. It is not. For most of its short life it has been owned entirely by the bank. Now all that I own at Cranmore is *Black Prince*, three coaches and a few wagons. From time to time the more sensational newspapers refer to me as a millionaire. I am not. Unfortunately too many people seem to believe what they read in the newspapers and it doesn't help. Although I was initially responsible for setting up the East Somerset Railway I am now possibly its greatest obstacle to the raising of badly needed funds. (I was standing in the ticket office at Cranmore one busy Sunday last year when a gentleman was buying tickets for his family. He did not see me and I overheard him say to his wife, 'That bloke Shepherd must be filthy rich to own all this.' I came out of the booking office and introduced myself to him. I told him the real story and suggested that he read another newspaper. He gave us a £5 donation!)

Matters are not made easier by the fact that I seem to be able to raise very large amounts of money for wildlife conservation. This naturally leads people to think that I can do exactly the same for the railway. I cannot. I must put wildlife conservation first. Apart from anything else, if it had not been for the success of my elephant paintings, the East

260

My long-suffering wife with me on *Black Prince*

Somerset Railway would not be in existence today. Furthermore, there are not enough days in the week to earn my living and paint for all the charities that are now asking me for free pictures. The man who rang me up after hearing of our appeal to save the line to Shepton Mallet could not have illustrated the problem more succinctly; he asked why I did not paint another six elephant paintings to pay for the line into Shepton Mallet. He put our problem in a nutshell.

The days of my own deep financial involvement with the East Somerset Railway are now finally over and they can never return. I have learned my lesson. However, I still subsidise the railway indirectly through the supply of prints of my paintings for the Signal Box Art Gallery. Moreover, during the winter months, the talk shows that I give (aided so tremendously by my team of helpers) for the benefit of the World Wildlife Fund and the East Somerset Railway, provide the railway with almost its only source of income during the winter months. The members of the railway, in return, now know only too well what is really involved in running a steam railway in the 1980s. It is much more than just running steam trains. They give countless hours of time in administrative work dealing with the Department of the Environment, insurance, legal matters, publicity and fund raising, and all the other tasks that are essential to ensure the smooth operation of an efficient, safe and professionally run steam railway, which is open to the public, and which has to sell itself.

The tasks are endless and diverse, and painting the Forth Bridge sometimes seems to pale into insignificance in comparison. Some of our members lay track in the depths of winter. They have to, because in the summer they are looking after the public. Some restore coaches out in the freezing cold. Some achieve miracles in our workshop, rebuilding 130 tons of steam engine, at weekends. Some members never even see a steam engine from the beginning of the day to the end because they are too busy cooking meals and washing dishes in the restaurant car. There are those who work in our Signal Box Art Gallery selling my elephant prints. They know, as I do, that these pay the coal bills. Without this facility, indeed, the railway might possibly close altogether. I only hope that no one on the East Somerset Railway ever has aspirations to turn the gallery back into a signal box!

Perhaps, above all, we have all now realised that we are in the entertainment business. For my part, whenever I go down to Cranmore, which is no longer very often, I spend almost all the time talking to our friends the public, who come to see us. After all, they have paid good money to come to Cranmore and the whole family reasonably expects to be entertained. I take them around the railway because this makes them feel welcome and then they are more likely to want to return to see us again. One can go to so many places in this country where you simply pay your money and no one takes any notice of you after that. Each and every one of our members now realises that it is the first impression that counts. We have a reputation that is second to none for being clean and tidy—you will scarcely ever see any litter on the East Somerset Railway. (In fact, our visitors hardly ever drop any and I am convinced that this is because they are impressed by the tidiness of the site.) Furthermore, we are friendly; this is what counts, and all our members know it.

The East Somerset Railway is not one of the major preserved lines in the country if length of running line is how we are judged. However, I have become quite convinced over the years that big is not necessarily beautiful. At least everything at Cranmore is paid for. I believe that the bigger the railway, the bigger the potential for problems. On one of the major lines recently, all the directors walked out at the same time because of the friction that had been building up between them, the paid staff and the volunteers. I hope that we never have problems like that. Running a steam railway is supposed to be fun and, if it isn't, then we shouldn't be doing it. As a result of all the hard work over the years, and because (we believe) we set up the East Somerset Railway on the proper footing in the first place, it seems to me that we now have one of the finest work teams of any preserved line in the country. Some members of our team work 40 hours in their spare time every week because they believe that what we are achieving is worthwhile. Whilst I do not seem to have much chance nowadays to ride on the footplate of *Black Prince*, nevertheless, whenever I leave Cranmore at the end of the day, I do so with an immense feeling of pride at having played a part in the setting up of our railway. All the members of our team at Cranmore believe fanatically in the survival of the East Somerset Railway—and so do I.

Memories? I have so many. All of us who love steam engines do. I love wallowing in the past, and perhaps my story has given just a small glimpse of the many happy moments and a few unhappy ones that I have had with steam engines. If I had to select just one place which reminds me of those wonderful days which are gone for ever, it must be Waterloo station. When I go to London by train and step on to the concourse of that great train shed, I shut my eyes for a few brief moments, and dream of the past. I can still see those scenes in the 1960s: standing at the buffer stops, in the gloom of the great station, the sound of escaping steam and the occasional whistle echoing up into the roof like a lament for steam which was so soon prematurely to die, I can see the great Bulleid Pacifics, anonymous under layers of grime, but still proud and most definitely not forgotten. As I said at the end of my first book, *The Man Who Loves Giants*, my unattained ambition is one day to ride into that great station on the footplate of my own *Black Prince*. Perhaps there is no harm in dreaming, just a little, sometimes.

Tired but happy?